REMEMBER ME TO MISS LOUISA

EARLY
AMERICAN
PLACES

Early American Places is a collaborative project of the
University of Georgia Press, New York University Press,
Northern Illinois University Press, and the University of
Nebraska Press. The series is supported by the Andrew
W. Mellon Foundation. For more information, please visit
www.earlyamericanplaces.org.

REMEMBER ME TO MISS LOUISA

Hidden Black-White Intimacies in Antebellum America

SHARONY GREEN

NIU Press
DEKALB

© 2015 by Northern Illinois University Press

Published by the Northern Illinois University Press
DeKalb, Illinois 60115

24 23 22 21 20 19 18 17 16 15   1 2 3 4 5

978-0-87580-723-2 (paper)
978-0-87580-491-0 (cloth)

Cover by Shaun Allshouse

Library of Congress Cataloging-in-Publication-Data

Green, Sharony Andrews.
  Remember me to Miss Louisa : hidden black-white intimacies in antebellum America /
Sharony Green.
     pages   cm. — (Early American places)
  Includes bibliographical references and index.
  ISBN 978-0-87580-723-2 (pbk. : alk. paper)
  ISBN 978-0-87580-491-0 (cloth : alk. paper)
  ISBN 978-1-60909-181-1 (ebook)
  1. United States—Race relations—History—19th century. 2. Man-woman relationships—
United States—History—19th century. 3. African Americans—Social conditions—19th
century. 4. United States—Social conditions—18th century. I. Title.
  E185.61.G7829 2015
  305.800973'09034—dc23

                                                          2015020485

For Louella Halbert

And also of the son of the bondswoman will I make a nation, because he is thy seed.

GENESIS 21:13

Silk stockings an purple dresses—course I don't believe what some folks been whisperin as to how y gets them things now. White folks always did do for niggers what they likes. An they jest cant help alikin you, Louisa.

JEAN TOOMER, CANE

Contents

Illustrations

ACKNOWLEDGMENTS

This book reflects the support of many people and institutions. I have been fortunate to have David Roediger as a doctoral adviser. He has taught me how to be a good scholar *and* a good human being. I have also been privileged to work with Augusto Espiritu, Clarence Lang, and Bruce Levine, members of my dissertation committee. My deepest thanks to them for support and guidance. I wish to also thank Erik McDuffie, Siobhan Somerville, Fred Hoxie, and Carol Symes for their insights.

Warm thanks to Linda Manning, this book's editor, and the entire staff at Northern Illinois University Press for backing this project. Thanks also to Tim Roberts, managing editor of the Early American Places series, and Sheila Berg, my copy editor, for their hard work in seeing this book to completion. I am especially grateful to my peer reviewers and to Nikki Taylor in particular for her much-needed wisdom at crucial moments. Thanks to Jennifer Hamer and Tiya Miles for their encouragement and tenacity. Special thanks also to the late John Hope Franklin for once whispering, "Never let them see you flinch."

My gratitude is also extended to the Center for Gender Studies at the University of Chicago for seeing the possibilities in this project via an Honorable Mention for the 2007 Ruth Murray Prize Best Graduate Student Essay award. Thanks also to the following departments, institutions, conferences, and workshops for their financial and intellectual support or research assistance: the University of Illinois Summer Pre-Doctoral Institute; the Graduate College and Department of History at the University of Illinois; the Newberry Seminar on Women and Gender; the Americanist workshops in the Department of History and the Department of English at the University of Alabama; the National Black Graduate Student Association (NBGSA); the Association for the Worldwide Study of the African Diaspora (ASWAD); the Atlantic World Literacies Network (AWRN) Conference; the Southeastern Women's Studies Association (SEWSA); Purdue American Studies Symposium; Remapping the Black Atlantic: Diaspora (Re)Writings of Race and Space conference at DePaul University; the 2013 Historians Against Slavery Conference in Cincinnati; the Cincinnati Historical Society; the Kentucky Department for Libraries & Archives; the Dolph Briscoe Center for American History, University of Texas; the Filson Historical Society Library; the North Carolina Office of Archives and History, Special Collections Department; the Albert and Shirley Small Library at the University of Virginia; Lexington, Kentucky, Public Library; the American Antiquarian Society; Manuscripts Department, University of North Carolina, Chapel Hill; David M. Rubenstein Rare Book & Manuscript Library at Duke University; the Department of History, University of Alabama; W. S. Hoole Special Collections Library and the Faculty Resource Center at the University of Alabama.

I also wish to thank B. J. Gooch, Special Collections Librarian and University Archivist, Transylvania University Library and Kathryn J. Lillethun of the Bainbridge, Georgia, Historical Society, for assistance during the beginning stages of my research. My gratitude is also extended to the archivists and researchers at Historic Georgetown, Inc., among them, Christine Bradley, Anne Marie Cannon, and Nancy Hale. Thanks also to Christopher Winters, bibliographer for Geography, Anthropology, and Maps, Regenstein Library, University of Chicago; and Craig Remington, Cartographic Lab, Department of Geography, University of Alabama. The visual images in this book are greatly owed to their good work. I wish to also thank Tim Barnes, manager of Geographic Information Systems, City of Huntsville, and Marie Bostick, Planning Services, Urban Development, City of Huntsville; Lynne Williams of the Weeden House Museum; and Linda Riley for their help as I learned more about Huntsville, Alabama.

Special thanks to Ola Gerald and Alexandria Gilbert for research assistance. Thank you, Virginia Cain, for proofing assistance.

Many others have offered lots of encouragement along the way. I would like to publicly thank my students in various courses who push my thinking, as well as my colleagues in the History department at the University of Alabama, among them, Heather Kopelson, Sarah Steinbock-Pratt, Teresa Cribelli, Kari Frederickson, and Lisa Dorr. I also wish to thank others, including Kimberly Snyder Manganelli, Lewis Porter, Trica Keaton, Ana Vazquez, Mary Vander Kinter, Keith Braynon, Camille and Michael Mendle, Kaye McKendrick, Lashieka Purvis Hunter, Cherise Fisher, Diana DaCosta, Amii McKendrick, Jill Campbell Trent, Rhonda Campbell Culver, Wanda Lewis-Williams, Denene Millner, Nick Chiles, Ken Jones, Tricia McElroy, Jessica Lacher-Feldman, Ann Powers, Anne Carson, Connie Biewald, Mimi Jennings, Valeria Bland Thomas, Courtney Cain, Veronica Mendez-Johnson, Kyle Mays, Tony Laing, Jeanine M. Mitchell, Darnese Williams Harris, Aniko Varga, Christa Vogelius, Francine and Bill Luckett, Melvin Van Peebles, Traci Parker, Tresa M. Saxton, Jacquetta Colyer, Trudier Harris, and "Jim, Buster and Bob" and others in the Friday afternoon Alcove crew. Heartfelt thanks to Celine Parreñas Shimizu, Lillie Mae Earvin, Duane Andrews, Brice Andrews, Bianca Harris, Kandice Hill, Tisha Andrews Pierre, Jean Pierre, Nick Beeler, Sue Circone, Hazel Beeler, Michael Kuric, Theodocia Cunningham, Alton Andrews, Iona Andrews and Estella Andrews Myers for love and support. To Garcia Dwight Andrews, Richard Earvin, Anne Boise Beeler, C. Donald Beall, Gloria "Gigi" Watson, Joan Cohl, the memory of you inspires. Thank you also to many more remembered but unnamed. Finally, my gratitude to John Beeler and the cutest little kitties in the world for love and sometimes humorous but always constant validation.

Remember Me to Miss Louisa

Introduction

On October 25, 1838, Avenia White, a young African American woman, sent her former master, Rice C. Ballard, a letter. In her letter White shared the difficulties she and another woman were having making ends meet. She was taking in sewing and laundry, and the other woman worked by the week as a live-in servant in Cincinnati. Their earnings, however, were not enough to feed themselves and their four children. They needed beds, she said. They also needed funds to buy fuel, as the nights were growing cooler. Money was so limited they had to borrow eight dollars from their landlord, an African American woman, who was sending a hello. White herself sent "love."[1]

What would make a former bondswoman utter this word to the man who had once owned and possibly raped her and, moreover, had probably done the same to another in close proximity to her? In considering possible answers to this question, this book offers one in particular: White and her former master had a level of intimacy that revealed itself in her use of the word love and in other ways, among them, that he had relocated her and the second woman and their children outside slave territory and had even sent financial support after they were freed.

Ballard did so on the eve of his marriage to a Natchez, Mississippi, woman. He and his wife would settle in Louisville, just 139 miles from Cincinnati.[2] Such appears to have been the level of concern he had for White, a woman one of his cronies once referred to as the "Old Lady," a euphemism since the sixteenth century for a man's female partner.[3] Ballard evidently planned to be able to visit two households with ease and anonymity, away from the meddling eyes of acquaintances in the lower South where he had acquired an interest in several plantations.

The frequency with which white men freed enslaved women and their children is now generally known to those familiar with American history.[4] Less is known about these men's financial and emotional investments in them, the sort that increasingly found prominent politicians like William Seward of New York and Stephen Douglas of Illinois consulted for advice on how to ensure the safety of such women and their children.

As sectional conflict continued, a white Southern man's pending marriage, aging body, or looming death often compelled him to free African American women and the children they produced with him. And as difficult as it may be for the modern mind to comprehend, some kind of connection, even if it was accompanied with a seemingly delusional utterance of love, existed between these individuals. Though they hardly stand excused for their ongoing claims to privilege, such men were hidden actors in freed women's and children's attempts to survive the rigors and challenges of life as African Americans in the years surrounding the Civil War.

Many such women and children, often of mixed race, were "fancy girls," a brand name for enslaved women who were sold for use as sex workers and sexual partners before the Civil War. These were the sort of women on whom white men spent considerable sums and whom they even cajoled to leave other white men. Faced with sadder alternatives, some such women, White included, seemed to have obliged them.[5]

The white men in question turned to women like White not only as sex partners, but as companions who were eventually freed with their children in one place: Cincinnati. Before the Civil War, this six-square-mile city, surrounded on three sides by hills and on the fourth by the Ohio River, was filled with individuals who straddled racial lines. Their presence in Cincinnati and other cities ultimately revealed the ways in which race mixing occurred and occurs in the United States regardless of attempts to separate people on the basis of race.[6] Indeed, by midcentury individuals who were young and female dominated the antebellum African American population in Cincinnati, which had the country's highest per capita proportion of people of mixed race outside the South.[7] By 1850, of the 3,172 African Americans residing there, 54 percent were of mixed race, a figure much higher than the North's regional average of 31 percent. Only the Deep South had a higher number of "mulattoes," 76 percent, among its free African American population.[8]

Previous research has largely taken for granted that the origins of most people of color in Cincinnati were two neighboring states, Kentucky and Virginia.[9] Certainly among the migrants to Cincinnati were some of the nation's most accomplished black leaders, including the Virginia-born lawyer and abolitionist John Mercer Langston and his brother Gideon, a fellow abolitionist who owned a livery stable business and a barber shop.[10] They were the sons of a white Richmond-based domestic slave trader and a free woman of mixed race who both died in 1834.[11] But numerous other people of color also arrived from the cotton-growing regions of western Georgia, Alabama, Mississippi, and eastern Louisiana.

Cincinnati was an attractive site for relocating African Americans for several reasons. It sat on a river that connected to the Mississippi, which stretched south into slave territory and thus offered easy access to the Deep South. It was also on the border of the upper South. In addition, it was a major port community in which free people of color could pursue the wage work less easily found in the South. It also helped that Cincinnati had an abolitionist presence, which generally assured African Americans of having local allies in a region where free people of color from the South could expect much if not more of the same racism they had experienced in slave territory, despite the presence of white antislavery supporters.[12] Racism led to the swelling migration of blacks outside slave territory as the century approached the halfway mark.[13] In 1855 a weekly newspaper of the American Anti-Slavery Society printed a letter from a black Cincinnatian who highlighted the advantages of living in Cincinnati in particular:

> From the window where I am seated, I see the slaves toiling on the Kentucky side of Mason and Dixon's line. . . . Situated in this lovely valley, with the murmuring Ohio running at the foot of the garden, I see the rafts and the flat-bottomed boats floating down the river, with the children playing.[14]

But location, potential allies, and a convenient river were not the only positive features of this region. Southern white fathers of mixed-race children and the children and women themselves were drawn to educational opportunities in the state. Ohio has long been known for having some of this country's first schools and institutions of higher learning for African Americans. Black migrants who could "pass" for white attended public and private grade schools throughout Ohio. Others populated schools that welcomed African Americans.[15] Oberlin College, about two hundred miles northeast of Cincinnati, opened in 1833, and Wilberforce, a prep school and later university, opened in Tawawa, a resort town sixty miles northeast of Cincinnati, in 1856.[16] Some of the earliest students of these educational institutions were the children of Southern white men and black women. "All our institutions are filled with gentlemen's children sent from the South," said Eliza Potter, a Cincinnati woman of mixed race who heard and saw much in her position as a hairdresser to elite whites. In Oberlin, she reported having seen "between three and four hundred children[,] . . . two-thirds of them being gentleman's children from the South."[17]

But when settling in Cincinnati, many such African Americans did so with considerable angst, as White's letter demonstrates. "Black laws" were enacted as early as 1804 to deter black settlement.[18] These rules prevented tax-paying blacks from serving on juries or testifying against whites. Black Cincinnatians were also barred from the militia and schools.[19] Local white antagonism, the most severe in the state, had to do with outright racism but also job competition, crowded living conditions, and other stresses of emergent urban life.[20] Cincinnati, a once-small settlement, initially comprised white men who in 1788 took advantage of federal land grants. By the 1820s it was a rapidly growing city with many attractions because of its place on a major river, which lured commercial traffic[21] that was furthered by its importance as a site for shipbuilding, pork processing, and whiskey production.[22]

As the century matured, determined black Cincinnatians, among them the Langstons and the intellectual and black activist Peter Clark, put pressure on local and state authorities to aid their efforts to improve their lives by, among other things, educating African American children in public schools.[23] Aided by abolitionists as well as working-class Germans, African Americans demanded more. By 1856 local blacks successfully lobbied to have control over their own school board.[24] Within ten years Cincinnati opened its first black high school.[25]

Given local white hostility, Cincinnati and Ohio were often mere way stations at which recently freed people assessed their options before moving elsewhere. Some of the African Americans in question scattered to places as different as Kansas, Colorado, Washington State, Canada, and Mexico. Others even returned to the lower South. Altogether, this sort of movement caused many whites grief as they realized that these favored ones were testing the waters of autonomy in ways that most African Americans would not do until the postbellum period.[26] As the often racially ambiguous children in particular drew on their white fathers' capital, many feared the world would be turned upside down.

Examination of correspondence, diaries, news reports, and other sources reveal that the contemporaries of these African American women and children were sometimes nonplussed by their inability to categorize them.[27] However, it is now possible to situate them in bigger stories that point to more than just their general oppression. Some of these stories concern what it means to be urban, what it means to be American, and what it means to be free.[28] For sure, Southern white men—whether they intended to do as much or not—participated in the "urbanization" of black women and children in this instance, particularly when these women and children had earlier lived primarily on farms or plantations. That such men did as much allows us to see the degree to which black women and children fit squarely into narratives concerning emerging urban life in America and rising industry. In the end, it appears their being freed was often no mere act of charity but an act unveiling the inconsistencies in human behavior.

Their proximity to white men had earlier permitted mixed-race children and their mothers to develop a certain kind of familiarity across the color line, disrupting prescribed scripts. Indeed, these women of color produced racially ambiguous children who bewildered those who could not distinguish their lineage or understand their access to white men's money and affection.[29] Attempts by observers to shape these children and their mothers as being "less than" were put to the test with each privilege they received.[30] Negative characterizations of African Americans, African American women especially, as unworthy and promiscuous were sometimes suspended although never discarded even by the men who extended favor.

Still, some such women and children seemed to adopt new personalities owing to their proximity to white men.[31] Though marginal actors, they tested the limits of laws intended to render marriage, wage work, and slavery in absolute ways in the years surrounding the Civil War.[32] While married white women faced legal and social restrictions on where they could go and what they could own, the unmarried African American women seemed to reap certain benefits. The latter emerged as extraordinary creatures in some circumstances while remaining victims in others.[33] Such women were ultimately part of a testing ground for human interaction.

With a thorough reading of the surviving evidence, the curtain on these women and their children can be parted, and we can finally make known long-hushed stories and unveil a world that was changed by their complicated interracial relationships.[34] We can do this by first moving the story of the fancy girl from New Orleans and other Southern port cities, where it is often situated, to a northern industrial city, Cincinnati.[35] Because the narrative is largely centered on a metropolitan area, it also allows us to see how African Americans plotted their futures alongside white Americans and Europeans in an increasingly urban and modern world. This foreshadowed later attempts of social Darwinists to designate them as racially inferior. The financial and educational investments white men made in these African Americans suggest that *some* such men believed in their abilities, no matter the obstacles that white men themselves created.

The extent of white men's generosity has earlier been hard to plot for an obvious reason: lack of evidence. Few antebellum Southerners left behind socially damaging information about their comings and goings, especially if it revealed their regard for black Americans, enslaved ones in particular. The lack of sources—especially from the point of view freed women and children of color—figures into how even the stories told in this book seem to emerge as case studies.[36] However, it is possible to infer from the evidence that black-white unions, coerced or consensual, were more widespread than has been documented.

Knowing more about the experiences of Rice Ballard, the man who freed White and five others, is possible because of the more than six thousand documents in existence at the time of his death. White's letter was one of thousands to him that he preserved, suggesting her importance in his life. When her letter and other documents are considered together, we can see how Southern white men made different kinds of investments in human capital. That they did so was not easily discussed in their lifetimes and remains polarizing today. Yet the growing contemporary interest in genealogy suggests that many people now want to learn more about African Americans who benefited from white men's assistance, no matter their ongoing persecution.[37]

White's persecution was ongoing. Ballard had not properly provided for her, the second freedwoman, and the children before his departure for the South, leaving room for us to ponder his true intentions. He had freed them, though with many tasks before him. He was spending most of his time in Natchez, where he had recently started investing in cotton plantations in the lower South after a brief but profitable career as a domestic slave trader in his native Virginia. There he had a long-distance partnership with Isaac Franklin, reputedly the most successful domestic slave trader in U.S. history.[38] By the mid-1830s, both men were preparing to leave trading behind to become planters. Ballard even bought clothes to look the part. He purchased a fine overcoat for $45, a pair of pants for $18, and a vest for $10, all from a New Orleans shop.[39] If he was lucky in the boom-or-bust economy typical of the early nineteenth century, he stood to do well.

Discretion was in order, however. He was not like the two men Levi Coffin, the well-known abolitionist, recalled once meeting. They arrived with two mixed-race women and announced their plans to settle in the area because they could not marry in Mississippi. Coffin told them Ohio's laws did not prevent such marriages and advised the men to marry their women. And they did.[40] Ballard's aims were more suspect.

It must not have been easy for White or the other freedwoman to know that both had slept with the same man. What they told the children about this arrangement we do not know. What we do know is that he freed them both along with their four children because some bond had been established. But freeing them did not mean he saw African Americans generally as deserving anything.[41]

His general care with money may help explain his not properly setting them up. Certainly in the early days of domestic slave trading, he once accused Franklin and his two nephews, who were also his business partners, of not reimbursing him in a timely fashion: "[You said] it was not worthwhile to send me funds when I lay in debt ever since last fall, eleven thousand dollars and now upwards of twenty. . . . I do not mean to complain on this subject any more. I know you will do what is right."[42]

While some black women, especially those who passed as white, arrived in Cincinnati with white men who enabled them to lead lavish lives, the ones Ballard freed were representative of the many others who arrived in more uncertain circumstances, with sometimes cranky men like Ballard by their sides. Still, arrive they did.

African American women and girls were positioned to apply leverage to men like Ballard. It is generally assumed that proximity to white men was dangerous for black women and girls. But in this instance Southern white men and the women and girls in question both wielded power, not necessarily because of their dependence on one another, but because they ultimately were addressing their own needs. Such needs included caring deeply for another human being while also tending to one's self in an age when ideas about individualism and self-determination were ubiquitous. White men's attachment and generosity made African Americans also act in independent, assertive, even defiant ways, emerging as rather individualistic too.

In the end, when numerous documents, many of them letters, are bundled together, a more unanticipated past that scholars are trying to understand reveals itself. White men invested emotionally and financially in black women and children during escalating sectional tensions over slavery and the South's slave-based economy.[43] A select group of individuals moved closer to the promise of freedom while being only one or two degrees of separation from influential people who debated some of the most critical issues of the day, simultaneously condemning blacks during such deliberations and being discreet about their aid to this very population with whom they were or others like them were intimate.

Given the all too evident horrors of slavery, it is imperative to clarify what is meant by the word intimacy. Put simply, the word intimate suggests emotional and physical closeness between two human beings, even unlikely ones. The word sheds light, too, on the wins and losses of such closeness when one party has more power than the other but both still find a way to reap some benefit. For more than a generation we have understood that oppressed blacks in and outside rural communities across time and space had and have influence on their own futures.[44] While the kind of intimacy presented here is often manifested as paternalism wherein slaveholders "purchased" slaves in an effort to "save" them, it points to another dynamic: the two-way exchange between white men and the people they freed and often supported.[45] In order to uncover intimacy, it is useful to think about the groundbreaking work of the political scientist and anthropologist James Scott.[46] Scott studied interactions in peasant villages and slave cultures and revealed that power is always in flux. He decided that through everyday strategies such as slowing the pace of their work or feigning ignorance even the most oppressed individuals exerted some control over the quality of their lives.

Antebellum African American women and children thoughtfully coped with the difficult circumstances in which they found themselves by relying on similar strategies with Southern white men.[47] Whether or not sex was involved, whether or not the relationships were consensual, intimacy was still possible. In spite of having been exploited by her former master on the basis of her gender and on the basis of her African descent, there remained the possibilities for an improved future for Avenia White. When she used the word love she could have been performing in order to maintain her ties to an influential individual who engineered big changes in her life. Was she disingenuous? No, she was able to discern an opening and assess the likelihood of success or failure in taking a chance on one unlikely man really caring for her and others beside her.

That she and Ballard had a deep personal bond should not be surprising, for slavery did not necessarily define their lives in a way that progressed "singularly and steadily toward racism."[48] The historical record shows that there was often reciprocal regard, warmth, and even caring in settings where whites and blacks became trading partners, shipmates, servants, allies, or lovers.[49] The word love may figure into a longer history between two people who observed and knew one another. That something of considerable import existed between Ballard and White—and the five others he manumitted with her—is strongly suggested by the fact that he freed her in a city where she and the others stood to do as well as could be expected, especially with his occasional presence and financial assistance.

Unmarried mothers of color in antebellum Cincinnati and elsewhere foreshadow future matrifocal urban trends in African American families that scholars have long studied but rarely with white males as part of the equation.[50] Such neglect might be a result of the greater visibility of less savory aspects of white men's behavior.[51] But proximity to white men has long provided African American women and girls with the ability to see what whites said and what some actually *did*.[52] Some white men's generosity is not hard to fathom if, as sociologists suggest, a person's emotions cannot be divorced from social contact with another human being, even one deemed a mere commodity. Though intimacy and love are not always a consequence of sharing space (and a bed) with another human, sharing space has real psychological consequences, some of them thoughtfully or unknowingly cultivated by one or both parties.[53]

That said, no matter the level of intimacy, oppression is always in view in the relationships before us—even if pleasure was part of the equation.[54] However, we risk being too reductive if we fail to acknowledge that not all white men were as exploitative as generally presented, nor was their behavior consistent.[55] And critical here is less what these former enslaved people did to obtain freedom and support than what white men *permitted of themselves*. Some might call such favor white hypocrisy, but how antebellum black women and their children and white men felt about it was probably shaped by other factors: the degree to which they understood not just master-slave relations, but male-female relations and even parent-child relations.

As these relationships are explored, it is useful to look at how interracial sexual unions have been stigmatized across time. The rise of the Cotton Kingdom figures into such a discussion. What follows is a generational portrait of Southern white men who invested emotionally and financially in the lives of enslaved women and children.[56] Some men were so committed to their own bigotry or wives and families as to never consider such investments. There were others who did so quietly but decisively. Among those men is Ballard, the man who freed White, the woman who sent him her "love." In fact, a level of intimacy was so established between him and White that I will return to them again and again as a means of seeing how enslaved people had the capacity to "love."[57] This is the case even though black-white intimacies before the Civil War more often than not took the form of coerced sex and outright rape of black women.[58] Still, sexual ties between white men and African American women, consensual or not, resulted so often in these women and their children being freed and financially supported that they should be studied for their broader significance. White's relocation to Cincinnati and its larger implications are worthy of closer scrutiny.

How do we find meaning in the lives of women like White who sought to ensure their future and that of their children? Their exertions were of paramount importance in Cincinnati, whose economy was tied to river commerce and was subject to frequent droughts resulting in low water and slowed business.

And what do we make of these black women when their lives are juxtaposed to white women who suffered emotionally during their husbands' absences for myriad reasons, including tending to the needs of black women and children? Indeed, the black-white intimacies in question took a toll on a wide circle of individuals. Much might be said, too, of the intraracial conflict in the African American community as many African Americans in and outside slave territory looked at the favor some freedwomen and children received with both jealousy and anger.

It is then worth it, too, to look at the personalities of freedwomen with whom white men had intimate relations. One such woman whose life I discuss is Louisa Picquet, who was purchased by a New Orleans man, among others, and serves as a model of such women. Curiously benefiting from Victorian ideas of womanhood that were not intended for them, women and girls of color like her with past or ongoing ties to Southern white men often acted forcefully, a trait long associated with women of color.[59] Aware of their privileged position in slave society, women of mixed race in particular emerge as being as complicated and contradictory as the men who once owned them.

Due attention is also directed to the children of antebellum white men and enslaved women of color, among them the descendants of Samuel Townsend, a white planter who left $200,000 to ten children from five enslaved women.[60] As the Civil War approached, growing legal restrictions on free African Americans in the lower South compelled some

Southern white men to relocate the children and their mothers to free territory. Some hired lawyers to ensure the future of the children. I seek to illuminate the warmth between these men and their children even amid the latter's ongoing struggles owing to racism. Altogether, the prevalence of both financial and emotional ties between unlikely individuals makes clear the paradoxes in American life across time.

1 / Probing a Planter's Hidden Life

For much of his adult life, Rice Ballard occupied the highest rung of the Southern social ladder. As a planter, he was an aristocrat, although a curious one.[1] The oft-told tale of the planter depicts a patriarch, settled in one place, presiding over family and workers. Ballard, by contrast, was frequently on the move. "In any one [city] we cannot [e]specially place him," a newsman wrote in 1848 about his wanderings.[2] The newsman was not alone in noting Ballard's unusual ways. Bacon Tait, a domestic slave trader in Ballard's native Virginia, noticed them as well and even hinted that someone else might be responsible for his movements.[3] "Tell me[,] Ballard[,] is there not some bewitching creature about Louisville or Cincinnati . . . if there is, I congratulate you," Tait once wrote in a letter.[4]

The social mores of the day dictated that Tait leave it there. Few commented on the improprieties of the powerful.[5] He had only recently become a slave trader, a lowly position in the Southern social hierarchy. By the late 1830s, he was a powerful planter, although one who evidently made periodic trips to Cincinnati.[6] There he had established ties with Calvin Fletcher, a merchant and former city councilman who served as a go-between between him and two newly freed black women and their four children.[7] Fletcher doubtless met Ballard through his dealings with a New Orleans mercantile company briefly owned by Ballard's brother.[8] Certainly Fletcher could often be found in his counting room, surveying returns from his New Orleans shippers.[9] A cousin in Indianapolis, also named Calvin Fletcher, thought well of the conscientious Fletcher, who once returned some books mistakenly mailed to Cincinnati.[10] In such an individual Ballard found someone who might be trusted as he set out to free six enslaved people.

What would make a man who owned hundreds of other slaves consider freeing these six? What do his actions tell us about his and others' ability to form emotional connections that challenged the prevailing ideologies of the day? How did he enhance in big and small ways the lives of enslaved black women and children?

Though men like him in the opening decades of the nineteenth century often thirsted for power and position, their quests were sometimes accompanied by a sense of duty and moral obligation to others. Financial gifts to them were especially likely if such arrangements were quietly done and did not involve enormous inheritances or the transfer of slaves, although evidence suggests some white men defied convention on both counts.[11]

Nathaniel Harrison, an unmarried white man living in Amelia County, Virginia, died in 1852, leaving land to three women of color. The land amounted to some twenty-five hundred acres, plus livestock, crops, perishables, and eighty-four bondspeople. One of the women also received an annual $600 annuity for life and the other two, $250 annual annuities. Harrison's household furniture was also divided between these women. And he made provisions for them should they be required to leave the state. The disposal of the estate took place against the wishes of Harrison's white kin.[12]

Among other women and children who benefited from white men's emotional and financial investments was Julia Chinn, a black "housekeeper" who had two daughters with the Kentucky statesman Richard Johnson, a leading personality in the Democratic Party and an agricultural reformer during the 1820s and 1830s. Johnson faced public scorn for his open acknowledgment of his children with Julia. We may also consider Mary Lumpkin, the fair-skinned "widow" of Robert Lumpkin, a Richmond domestic slave trader who owned a jail for enslaved African Americans destined for the Deep South. Lumpkin sent the children he had with Mary to Philadelphia to be schooled. Two of their daughters attended finishing school, and both learned French as a second language. Following his death, Mary decided to rent the half-acre complex on which Lumpkin's jail stood to a white antislavery activist, who built a Christian school for freed African Americans. There are also the cases of Bess, a slave owned by a widowed French Huguenot who, upon his death, left her some of his property; and Doll, a black woman who dined with a white family while sitting beside Shoe Boots, a great Cherokee warrior who was her husband. Finally, Fanny, "a mulatto woman of considerable wealth," left Cincinnati in 1845 successfully to reclaim a house in Mississippi that was illegally snatched from her, and did so with the assistance of a white man who was in all likelihood her lover.[13]

Of those just listed, Fanny points to a particular phenomenon. She was among the black women whose proximity to white men resulted in her migration to Cincinnati, a city where such men were hidden actors in the lives of many freed women and children. The interactions between them must be understood in the context of larger patterns of change. The first decades of the nineteenth century witnessed white men taking full advantage of their predecessors' successful fight for independence from the British crown. In doing so, revolutionary leaders claimed the right to live as they wished, free from governmental interference. Though the most intellectual among them spoke of granting this right to everyone, entangled in their ideas was the plan to tell others what and what not to do.

Their ideas held back blacks, women, and even poor white men until Andrew Jackson's appeals on their behalf.[14] Yet some nonwhites quietly enjoyed certain liberties. One such group was people of African descent, namely, enslaved women and the children they produced with white men. Their special position had long been in view, leaving many troubled.

Another such woman was Kate, who, along with another black female slave, informed a South Carolina community about a planned slave revolt in 1749. The announcement of course upset colonial authorities. The white man who subsequently tried to ensure Kate's personal safety was alleged to have cared for her more than "his own Wife and Children."[15] Perhaps outraged by such behavior, or because he had not been wise enough to avoid it becoming public knowledge, the authorities took action. Kate appears to have been banished from the community for she does not appear in subsequent Carolina slave inventories. While we are able to see the ways in which Kate both resisted and accommodated the expectations of those around her, whether black or white, her account invites a deeper examination of black women's emotional exchanges with white men, a phenomenon that one historian regards as "unusual."[16] They may indeed have been unusual. But more likely they were simply hushed.

Such intimacy has a long history. When chattel slavery replaced indentured servitude as a source of labor in the late seventeenth century, leading to whites and blacks working side by side, laws forbidding interracial unions were quickly enacted.[17] Still, interracial relationships and intimacies continued to occur and, equally worrying to lawmakers and moral policemen, sometimes allowed African American women to obtain a publicly visible level of privilege or favor, usually in the form of being manumitted and inheriting property from their former owners. The political repercussions of their relationships were seen.

That such transactions were hushed should be unsurprising given the long history of stigmatization of "irregular" sexual unions, prostitution, and interracial liaisons, coupled with the increasing surveillance of all such activities in the early modern era but also the growing awareness of one's self-image. During the seventeenth century, scrutiny of individual behavior in England and its American colonies increased, driven often by puritanical concerns about the morality and stability of the family.[18] The policing of personal behavior, especially that of women and girls, was also a consequence of traditionalist, patriarchal concerns over controlling sexual activity in the face of a rapidly growing commercial sector, especially in the maritime realm, which almost inevitably fostered "irregular" liaisons, above all, prostitution.[19] Worse still for the moral guardians of English society was the persistence of interracial sex, or miscegenation, as they preferred to call it, in the American colonies. In the earliest days of English settlement in North America and the Caribbean, interracial liaisons, whether between white men and Amerindians or Africans, was a predictable consequence of the scarcity of European women.[20] Yet even after the redressing of that imbalance everywhere north of South Carolina by the end of the seventeenth century, women of color continued to be valued both as white men's companions and for their reproductive abilities, and interracial unions remained common. As long as such relationships were not flaunted, they were usually tolerated in late colonial and early national America.

The development of "race" as a governing tool in the late Enlightenment period complicated such unions and, and in the opening decades of the nineteenth century, pushed them into the purely private realm. As "whiteness" became a way for an individual to enhance his or her social and economic position, those who were deemed not "white" suffered, and "whites" who persisted in publicly consorting with "nonwhites" paid the price in social stigmatization.[21] White men's growing criticism of interracial relationships figured into strained attempts to build a sense of white *Herrenvolk*.[22] It was claimed that white "race," or family, could never be pure if black and white unions continued. If they did, they were hushed as the consolidation of white male power was made more visible by the 1830s following the Nat Turner rebellion and the removal of indigenous people to the West in that decade. During this period, one could see white men's frenzied bid for power and wealth in Georgia, Alabama, Mississippi, and Louisiana, states in America's then-southwestern frontier.[23] The wealth accruing there was of the sort white men were unwilling to lose because of a favored enslaved woman, one often regarded more as a sexual partner than a mother, which ran counter to accepted notions of white womanhood. A thriving domestic slave market points to, among other things, growing demand for fair-skinned women who were believed to have been "unfit for labor" and even "incapable of mothering."[24] They were perceived as being the counterparts to the often larger and darker-skinned female slaves. Though they were purchased for pleasure, and not breeding, some men quietly developed emotional attachments for such mixed-race women and, if they became mothers, their children. Such attachments were sometimes welcomed by families of African descent in and outside the American South. In 1814, an American visiting Barbados remarked that upon seeing the obvious benefits of being tied to white men's capital, some black parents raised their female children expressly to be white men's "kept mistresses" rather than lawfully wedded to men of African descent.[25] In Southern port cities such as New Orleans and Charleston that had large Caribbean, continental European, and free people of color populations, many parents of African ancestry welcomed white men's solicitation of young women of color as a means of ensuring their daughters' future financial security. Such mixed-race free women of color became *placees*, or common-law wives, of white and Creole men.[26]

Interracial relationships between white men and mixed-race women were so pervasive in New Orleans in the early 1800s that visitors frequently commented on them. Among them was a traveler who saw a white man and a "bright quadroon woman" riding through town together.[27] That this couple was seen together was not as remarkable as *where* they were seen. In cities one could find women who were not only sex partners, but sex workers. The presence of either kind of woman, especially when of African descent, disrupted the social order in distinct ways. Goods and certain services were supposed to be for sale but not sex. White women were supposed to exchange sex for financial security and subsistence under the terms of marriage but not unmarried women, especially enslaved or free blacks.

The arrival of race as a social construction in the modern world made such conflict especially visible in an increasingly urban society. People could generally move with greater anonymity within cities than was possible in rural communities, where individuals knew one another. As the number and size of cities in America increased, the cloak of urban anonymity grew. Still, the scrutiny of the white man and quadroon woman demonstrates the increased monitoring of black and white bodies, a practice that by 1800 dated back more than a century but had now acquired new intensity. At this time the rising cotton planter class also began to craft a unifying ideology that privileged all whites as a means of forming a bond between poor and wealthy whites.[28] Poor white women socialized freely with free black women, with whom they competed for jobs. All this occurred as black women, free or enslaved, were increasingly seen as being sexually degraded.[29] Such a categorization had more pronounced implications for black women in urban spaces through which men traveled for both business and leisure. There, those who chose to could easily purchase and form relationships or have sex with women and girls of African descent known as fancy girls.

The term fancy girl existed as far back as Renaissance Tuscany, where it was applied to Eastern European women. Its growing usage in the United States during the early nineteenth century occurred amid the growth of the domestic slave trade and was tied to the sexual exploitation of female servants, a practice carried over from the Old World. As early as 1819, "fancy girl" was a vulgarism for a man's sexual partner.[30] The allure of such a bondswoman or bondsgirl, who was often of mixed race, was also a result of the near-universal image of African women as sexual and promiscuous creatures. The latter was ironic, given the association of the color white with purity and virginity.[31]

Such women and even girls were found in most American cities but were common in Southern ones. Though scholars have not made much of it, the growth in the number of male slaveholders who could afford a fancy girl was directly tied to the wealth being amassed in the rising Cotton Kingdom. Men whether divorced, widowed, married, unmarried, or with no plans to marry engaged in sex with prostitutes or women purchased to be their live-in mates. One Louisville slaveholder owned a large plantation where he kept "vigorous young mulatto girls" to breed other girls who would some day become such mates.[32] The market for young biracial girls was something of which their nonwhite relatives were aware. The granddaughters of Shoe Boots, a cherished member of the Cherokee Nation, and his enslaved black wife, Doll, were once kidnapped and about to be shipped to New Orleans, possibly to be sold as fancy girls, before being saved by their Cherokee relatives.[33] The demand for such girls was also not lost on the Cincinnati abolitionist Levi Coffin, who once helped rescue two fair-skinned girls "either of whom would soon be worth one thousand dollars" by dressing them in boys' clothing. Amused at having duped their master, Coffin recalled how they laughed and giggled so much at the fuss they had created for white folks that his wife had to separate them lest they be discovered.[34]

Enslaved women and girls purchased as mates were recognizable to those around them, even other enslaved people.[35] A former slave from Tennessee noted that white men "will buy a sprightly, good-looking girl that they think will suit their fancy, and make use of them."[36] This man noted the oppression such a girl faced. However, his commentary is also a riff on the term fancy girl, which continues to have a poetic timbre. Fancy girls are the quintessential tragic "mulattoes" of fiction.[37]

However, the contemporaries of women and girls sold as sex workers or sex partners easily recognized the fancy brand even while expressing shock that it existed. Like domestic traders, casual observers often focused on her appearance, her cultivated manner, and her breeding, all of which shaped her as an "other" both in and outside slave society. A *Chicago Times* correspondent visiting a Memphis slave market, for instance, described "fancies" wearing beautiful dresses made of fashionable light wool.[38] Confirming that these were no ordinary slaves, the writer noted that "the merely curious visitor was not allowed to inspect these slaves who were locked up at night."[39]

The domestic slave trader Lewis Robards sold such bondswomen and bondsgirls in Lexington, Kentucky. While "ordinary" bondspeople were housed in a Lexington theater, where they were forced to walk across the stage in front of potential purchasers, fancy girls were kept in well-furnished parlors on the second floor of a two-story brick townhouse. When a prospective buyer arrived, Robards first served him a drink before taking him upstairs.[40] Robards's fancies were "the talk and toast of steamboat barrooms, tipling houses and taverns," some as far away as New Orleans. Over the mint julep, planter's punch, and other "potent beverages," men exchanged stories about their "inspections" of Robards's fancies.[41]

Illinois senator Orville H. Browning visited Robards's establishment and reported seeing enslaved women who were kept in rooms that were "not only comfortable, but in many respects luxurious." During Browning's visit, Robards made the women get up and turn around to show their "finely developed and graceful forms." Browning was stunned that these slaves were "fine persons [with] easy genteel manners." They sat

FIGURE 1. Jesse L. Berch, Quartermaster Sergeant, and Frank M. Rockwell, two members of the 22nd Wisconsin Volunteer Infantry Regiment, with enslaved eighteen-year-old "mulatto" woman rescued from a Lexington, Kentucky, brothel. They took her to Wisconsin but not before stopping to have a daguerreotype made of themselves posing on either side of her. (Photo G98S-CWP, Courtesy of U.S. Army Military Institute)

with "their needlework awaiting a purchaser," which he claimed to have found "shocking," possibly because he thought people of African origins could not have the comportment of the white elite.[42] Demonstrating that whites were hardly in agreement concerning women and girls of African descent, some prospective purchasers deliberately sought educated and cultured fancies and sometimes did so without relying on the services of domestic slave traders.[43] One prospective slaveholder in Washington, DC, posted advertisements seeking "a handsome, intelligent mulatto; a good plain cook, waitress, seamstress and laundress, about 17 or 18 years old."[44] Like slave traders, prospective buyers exaggerated the need for housekeeping abilities in the girl or woman for whom such tasks would become a secondary matter, as the emphasis on appearance and youth made unmistakably clear. Yet no matter how refined and educated some of these girls and women were or appeared to be, they were generally considered vulgar creatures. Desire for women of African descent was so intertwined with slavery as a social institution that sex with black or mixed-race women became an essential part of the trade in human beings.[45]

Understanding the full range of experiences of these women and girls has been hampered by lack of evidence. There was no column on the U.S. Census form to track how many enslaved women and girls were sold as fancies. Because most slaveholders did not want to leave evidence of delicate matters, when the fancy girl turns up in the historical record, she does so principally in domestic slave traders' records, ledgers, and correspondence.

The papers left behind by Ballard demonstrate as much. Ballard was in the right place at the right time in 1831. The surplus of slave labor in the upper South, the legal closure of the international slave trade in 1808, and the rising Cotton Kingdom created the perfect conditions for a domestic slave trade. By 1833 Ballard had partnered with Isaac Franklin and Franklin's nephews James Franklin and John Armfield. Isaac and James in New Orleans and Natchez sold slaves gathered in Virginia by Ballard and Armfield. They took in more than $400,000 in the first year of their partnership.[46] Indicative of their ambitions was the advertisement they placed in one Alexandria newspaper promising to pay higher prices than any other firm.[47] The elder Franklin eventually revamped the costly and time-consuming system of walking slaves in coffles overland and purchased as many as three brigs, including one he immodestly named *Isaac Franklin*.[48] By removing the middleman—a ship's owner—he, his nephews, and Ballard made bigger profits.[49]

The four men regularly corresponded about their sales. Some of their letters also contained details about their sexual relations with the women they were attempting to unload, among them, ones who would be marketed as fancy girls. James once described his plans for an enslaved woman he called "fancy maid Martha."[50] "I shall open my fancy stock of Wool and Ivory early in the morning," he wrote, describing his desire for sex with Martha. That Martha was a woman of African descent was discernible in his reference to ivory, a term that conjured up a trader's inspection of a slave's teeth and the continent itself. Martha's blackness was also clear in his mention of wool, which referred to the woolly quality of African hair. Her blackness was evident, too, in his use of the word maid, an occupation typically associated with African Americans. Martha's standing as a first-class slave was nonetheless evident, for James invoked the word fancy and wrote "fancy maid Martha" considerably larger than the other words in his letter.[51]

That these bondswomen were regarded as more desirable than the average slave was a widely held belief traders found very useful. Isaac once proudly described the sale of a woman he called "Yellow Girl Charlott." This slave had been purchased from "some Branch of the Barber [Barbour] family," he said, adding that "the respectability of that family will have great effect" on her sale.[52] In mentioning the Barbours, Franklin confirmed that an owner's social prestige could be mapped onto the body of bondswomen.[53]

Ballard himself kept records of every man, woman, or child he bought. He also regularly recorded payments for the transport of women to his home. In one case, he paid $6 to a "boy for bringing home woman."[54] It is unknown who these women were, although it is not hard to guess their race. Given that proper white women did not travel unaccompanied by a male relative, they were likely enslaved women he had hired to do housekeeping, maybe more, as he was not in a hurry to get married.

The descendant of Englishmen who initially settled in coastal Virginia before relocating to hilly Spotsylvania County, and in some cases, later to Kentucky, Ballard was driven.[55] The prolonged agricultural slump in Virginia required as much. While the state's economy had been largely built on tobacco, overcultivation had led to soil depletion and dwindling yields.[56] By the early nineteenth century, planters and farmers frequently freed their bondspeople because they could no longer feed, house, and clothe them. Others, in keeping with the rise of humanitarianism, did the same on moral grounds.[57] Still others, like Ballard, saw opportunity and profit in the traffic in human lives.

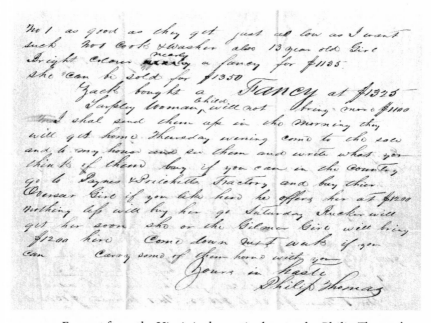

FIGURE 2. Excerpt from the Virginia domestic slave trader Philip Thomas's July 1859 letter to fellow trader William Finney discussing "fancy girls." (Courtesy of William A. J. Finney Papers, David M. Rubenstein Rare Book and Manuscript Library, Duke University)

As early as 1832, while still in Virginia, Ballard was exploring the possibility of becoming a planter in the lower South. That year, he received a letter from William Hewes, a New Orleans agent. Hewes mentioned that the relatives of the former owners of an estate were certain that Ballard would "on examination, be pleased" with the property, located in the Louisiana parish of Terrebonne.[58] The plantation comprised 4,014 acres, of which 800 to 1,000 acres were already cleared. A railroad would soon pass within five miles of the property, and the tracks would cross over a canal on the property, which had a bayou on either side. The advantages of waterways and the railroad were obvious. The buyer was assured of having easy access by land and water that would aid him in getting sugar or his crop of choice to New Orleans, about seventy miles away.

No surviving evidence suggests that Ballard purchased the Terrebonne plantation. But in March 1836, while still residing in Virginia, he began shipping cotton grown in Mississippi to Liverpool and Manchester, and by fall of that year, he was living instead in Natchez.[59] Those foreign sales, his time in Richmond, and his travel to New Orleans expanded his world and allowed him to move beyond being a mere domestic slave trader, a profession upon which elite Southerners frowned. The open selling of slaves in auction facilities and their long-distance overland trek in coffles contradicted the benevolent image of the South that the elite sought to project.[60] White aristocrats also generally thought traders were lacking in education and ill bred. The experiences of a British geologist who visited the United States in 1834 illustrate this point. He shared a stagecoach with another man who used the foulest language and appeared to the visitor as "a compound of everything vulgar and revolting."[61] After the passenger stepped down from the stagecoach, the Englishman asked the driver for his name and was told that he was John Armfield, Isaac Franklin's nephew.

If birds of a feather flock together, Ballard may have been no different from Armfield. When some of his cotton was once left to rot by the side of a river, Ballard was furious and told a plantation manager—a woman—as much. Catherine Prince apologized but also let Ballard know how much his admonishment had hurt her. "Mr Ballard," she wrote. "I could not blame your plain language. . . . [I]t alarmed and distressed me much."[62]

Ballard's directness was applied in his dealings as a planter. The move to Natchez was advantageous. There he could pare down his interests in slave trading while making a go of it as a planter like Isaac Franklin, who had begun his own transition into planting.[63] Ballard eventually had an interest in properties in Warren, Claiborne, Adams, and Madison Counties, most of them near the Mississippi River to allow for easier shipment of his cotton.[64] His widening social circle included John Anthony Quitman, governor of Mississippi, and the Kentucky statesman Henry Clay, whom he doubtless met through Samuel Boyd, a Mississippi judge with whom he entered into a partnership to purchase plantations.[65]

But being a proper planter required a man to have a wife. Prospective brides in his native Virginia knew as much. In spring 1838, Bacon Tait told Ballard about several women in Virginia who were still pining for him, although some had stopped waiting. "Miss Mary Matter was married about ten days ago to Mr. Elijah Baker," Tait reported.[66] Seeing his options declining, Ballard sent greetings via Tate to another woman, evidently also named Mary. "You desire that your respects be made," an amused Tait replied, adding, "Are you ignorant of the fact that on the 10th last month Miss Mary took unto herself a husband named Mr[.] John Priddy? So no more of Miss Mary."[67]

Isaac Franklin had more success.[68] Demonstrating how affluence trumped his own seedy past as a domestic slave trader, in spring 1839, at the mature age of fifty, Franklin married Adelicia Hayes. A graduate of the Nashville Female Academy and the daughter of a Presbyterian minister, Oliver B. Hayes, Hayes was a catch.[69] Suggesting the social significance of their marriage, the wedding was announced in two Nashville newspapers.[70]

Franklin himself settled into the life of an aristocrat, though one who also traveled frequently, in his case between plantations in Louisiana and his famed Fairvue plantation in Gallatin, Tennessee.[71] Before his death in 1846, he took to a Louisiana dance floor to join his daughter Laura at one of her polka dance lessons. He shared this in a letter to his father-in-law, who longed for a visit from him. But Franklin could not travel at that moment. "Ade[licia]," he said, "will not hear of it."[72]

Adelicia obviously had some measure of control over him that contradicts the image of Southern white women as docile. Either that or Franklin was not telling the truth. He had lied about other things. In August 1839, two months after he married Adelicia, a Gallatin slaveholder named Jesse Cage asked William Cotton, a farmer in eastern Kentucky, to keep an enslaved woman owned by Franklin named Lucindy and her child until further notice.[73] Cage stated the girl had to be removed from Fairvue because Franklin had just married "a very pretty and highly accomplished young girl."

With Cage's assistance, Franklin evidently concocted a story about Lucindy's past. Cage told Cotton that if he was questioned, he should say that Franklin hired someone to deliver her and the child to Cotton because she had not been sold, presumably in New Orleans or Natchez:

> Knowing you to be a smooth hand on cuff, as Ballard says, and not wishing anything known of the removal of the girl, I had told that man that brings the girl that she belonged to you, that you was an old trader[,] that she remained unsold on your hands last spring and that she came up in company with some of Mr. Franklin's people from below and that you had wrote me to employ some person to take her to Louisville on the stage at your price.[74]

Cage's letter illustrates that as the century matured, Southern white men went to great lengths to hide their relations with enslaved women of color. Lucindy was probably one of several bondswomen of mixed race that his Gallatin neighbors reported seeing on his Fairvue property prior to his marriage.[75] More to the point, Franklin's eagerness to get her and her child safely out of his wife's sight strongly suggests that the child's paternity was so evident that Adelicia would have no difficulty recognizing that it was the result of relations between Isaac and Lucindy.

While being prostituted in Louisville, a port town through which many men traveled, may have been in the cards for Lucindy, it is more likely that another scenario was imminent. Franklin possibly planned to relocate her and the child. Franklin's mention of a "stage," or stage-coach, and Louisville suggests she and the child would eventually travel by that means to Louisville, a city from which one could easily continue via steamboat to the lower South or numerous points north and west, including Cincinnati. No matter her destination and that of her child, their experience was unfortunate. Interviews with former bondspeople conducted between 1936 and 1938 as part of the Works Progress Admin-istration project contain numerous accounts of others like her who had sex willingly or forcibly with their white masters. Scholars used these interviews cautiously because whites predisposed to racial prejudice often conducted them. However, some interviewees unflinchingly recorded the trauma endured by enslaved women and girls, among them ones of mixed race. One former slave from Kentucky recalled "a light colored gal [who was] tied to the rafters of a barn. . . . [H]er master whipped her until blood ran down her back and made a large pool on the ground." Mary A. Bell, a former slave from St. Louis who was of "very light complexion" and had "very long and straight" hair, said the two people to whom she was hired out were not nice to her.[76]

Lucindy, too, had not escaped suffering, but her relocation suggests she may have also received some measure of favor, the sort that owed to earlier intimacy between her and Franklin. Lucindy may have been one of the numerous unmarried women of color named Lucinda residing in Cincinnati from 1860 to the end of the nineteenth century.[77] That all of them, including those of mixed race, were unmarried domestic workers and not wealthy kept women reveals the limits of white men's generosity. Some bondswomen could certainly find themselves alone and vulner-able like Cynthia, a woman observed by the nineteenth-century Afri-can American abolitionist, author, and former enslaved man, William Wells Brown. While being hired out by his master to work on a riverboat, Brown witnessed a slave trader placing her in his stateroom. The trader promised Cynthia that he would take her back to her St. Louis home if she would give in to his "vile proposals." She did, and he took her back, only later to sell her.[78]

A pregnant woman named Virginia who once wrote Ballard from a Houston slave "jail" met a similar fate. She appealed to him for help in preventing her sale and that of her two children.[79] Evidently her proximity to powerful white men had given her considerable courage. Unafraid, she denounced the unnamed man who was trying to sell her and his own children. In fact, revealing her own sense of worth even in this dire situation, she asked Ballard the following:

> Do you think . . . that its treating me well to send me off to strangers in my situation to be sold without even having an opportunity of choosing for myself[?] [It's] hard indeed and what is still harder [is] for the father of my children to sell his own offspring yes his own flesh & blood.[80]

Her letter uncovers many things, among them, her boldness in announcing the father of her children in the private space of a letter addressed to a man who himself had almost certainly fathered half-black children. She thus uncovers sexual relations that routinely happened, even if they were rarely discussed, between enslaved women and white men in the plantation South. Her letter also reveals that her oppressor was someone Ballard knew, probably Mississippi judge Samuel S. Boyd. "My god[,] is it possible that any free born American would hand his [character] with such a stigma as that . . . to sell his child that is his image," Virginia wrote about her tormentor, whom she called "the Old Man."[81]

Virginia blamed a gossipy "rascal" woman, perhaps another slave, who had indeed shared some of Ballard's potentially damaging secrets, for her plight. Admitting that she herself had willfully participated in this conversation, Virginia asked for Ballard's pardon. "I hope you will forgive me," she said, promising to never "let anything be exposed." But even then, she stated she would indeed continue telling others if "forced from bad treatment." Evidently concerned about her plight or the potential inconveniences she might cause him and her children's father, Ballard asked C. M. Rutherford, a Louisville domestic slave trader in Texas, to keep him apprised of her situation.[82] Rutherford sent a letter to Ballard two months later announcing that Virginia and one of her children had been sold, but the eldest child, a girl, had not.[83]

Virginia's ordeal resembled that of Maria, a slave Ballard owned. J. M. Duffield, a Natchez resident, wrote Ballard to inform him about Maria and her child.[84] Duffield wanted to purchase Maria, who had been beaten severely. In fact, Duffield stated that he feared she would die and asked if he could buy her "only to free her." Whether or not he was dealing with Ballard by means of flattery, he asked that his request be honored as another "memorial" of some earlier "generosity." As if anticipating a favorable response, Duffield announced that he had taken it upon himself to make arrangements to send Maria's daughter, who was evidently his child, "northward" to be "educated, and there forever to reside."[85]

Duffield serves as further proof that white men of this generation acted inconsistently and deliberately in their efforts to enhance and protect certain enslaved individuals, specifically, women and children in whom they had earlier had sex and along the way invested some measure of emotion. Such investments were made while these men safeguarded their patriarchal and racial dominance. It is certain that Duffield had not planned to protect all enslaved people from abuse or see to it that all enslaved children be freed and educated. But he was concerned about two in particular.

So great was Duffield's concern, he went as far as to cautiously identify the man who had abused Maria: Judge Boyd, Ballard's business partner. But wishing to be careful, Duffield stated he had written "the Old Man," presumably Boyd, to inquire about Maria, but committed to discretion, he sent the letter in a way that would "fall in[to] his hands and none other."[86] That he did reveals his interest in protecting Boyd from any fallout, no matter how close he had come to killing an enslaved woman.

But even Boyd joined this generation of men who acted unpredictably. While he seems to have exploited Virginia and Maria, he treated at least one enslaved person with more regard. Boyd reportedly fathered a child named James with an enslaved woman.[87] Having a "favored" position in his father's eyes, James apparently even ate at the dinner table with Boyd and his family rather than with other slaves.[88] Boyd's wife was so incensed at the favor shown him that James was sent to live on another plantation Boyd owned.[89] One of his white half sisters, however, later hired James to manage one of their father's properties.[90]

Black Americans were property to be sold, put to work, and sexually exploited. Yet some people of African descent—namely, certain women and children—received some favor even as they endured oppression. The degree to which Ballard's behavior was also unpredictable is unmistakable in his earlier status as a domestic slave trader willing to abandon an entire shipment of bondspeople to the ravages of cholera to that of a slaveholder open to manumitting some enslaved people, even those whose suffering was a consequence of his indifference. He must have allowed Duffield to have access to Maria.

Lucindy's, Virginia's, and Maria's experiences figured into a range of Southern white men's behavior toward enslaved women with whom they had sexual relations. Some such women and girls found ways to cope psychologically with their enslaved state and sexual exploitation, even flaunting the favor they received. Helene, one such woman, lived so much like a free person in France that she demanded her freedom upon her return to the United States. Upset by her actions, her master called her "a drunken, worthless wench."[91] But he complied with her wish and freed her. One of the more extreme cases of white men's bond with such women and girls, however tenuous in the face of societal pressure, involved a white New Orleans bank cashier who reportedly was so in love with a woman of color to whom he was married that he went to a physician and had some of her blood transferred into "his veins and then went to the court and swore he had colored blood in him" in order to circumvent laws banning interracial marriages.[92]

Some Southern white men's sense of duty and moral obligation to certain African American women allowed the latter, when freed, to prosper and move into the middle and upper classes outside slave territory. Among the wealthy African American women in Cincinnati were Mary Parris, Kesiah Boyd, Louisa Gaines, May Wilson, and Catherine.[93] These individuals had real estate and personal property holdings worth $5,000 to $25,300 without any visible income or occupation.[94] Many other white men were less circumspect. "In our Queen City of the West, I know of hundreds of mulattoes who are married to white men," Eliza Potter, the Cincinnati hairdresser, recalled, adding, "and some . . . are so independent they will be thought nothing but what they are." In saying this, Potter shed light on the ways in which some women of color's relations with powerful white men generated confidence in them.[95] Although some were clearly wealthy, white men's inconsistent behavior guaranteed that most freedwomen and children of color never fully escaped the anxiety that characterized black life across time, because "a family dependent on a woman's wages almost always lived in poverty."[96]

Some Northern whites accepted the responsibility of caring for such enslaved people. As Ballard was settling Avenia White and Susan Johnson and their four children in Cincinnati, he acted one way publicly while often maintaining another position privately. Indeed, in one of the rare instances that he presented himself as a resident of Louisville, Ballard signed a 1845 public petition in which he and other presumably white male slaveholders reminded the state's elected representatives that their actions regarding the issue of emancipation should reflect the wishes of their constituents.[97] Even more incongruous, five years later a census taker noted that his Louisville home held six enslaved people, among them a 27-year-old woman, a 6-year-old boy, and a 5-year-old girl, all fugitives of mixed race.[98] Perhaps

To the People of Jefferson County.

Understanding that the Representatives elect of the city of Louisville, stand pledged to introduce into the next Legislature, a Convention Bill, the main object of the friends of which is believed to be Emancipation: it is proposed, that the Voters of Jefferson county shall instruct their Senators and Representatives on that subject; they are, therefore, all, without respect of party, requested to meet at Jeffersontown, on Saturday next, Aug. 30, 1845, in order to express their sentiments on that subject.

It is the clear and explicit understanding of the unders gned, that the subject of Convention above, shall be brought before the meeting, and no subject proposed or discussed, which can, in the slightest degree, involve Whigery or Democracy, nor any thing party or personal. The undersigned maintaining the full right of the people to instruct their Representatives, deem this an occasion, the importance of which imperiously calls for an expression of the popular will.

AUGUST 27, 1845.

Edward D. Hobbs, Chairman,	Leaven L. Dorsey,	James W. Graham,
W. H. Pope, Secretary,	James Bate,	John T. Bate,
J. L. Martin,	Jacob Blankenbaker,	L. Young,
James Brown,	Jacob Reel,	Samuel Hart,
Alexander Veech,	R. C. Ballard,	H. Arterburn,
Luther Howard,	W. C. Bullitt,	Stephen Ormsby
John Herr, Jr,	Joseph Funk,	W. H. Pope,
A. G. Jeffries,	David O. Conn,	R. Tyler,
John Womack,	R. T. Bate,	H. Tucker,
Lewis M. Taylor,	John O. Ross,	B. D. Harris,
Peter Funk,	W. T. Hite,	William C. Arterburn,
W. L. Thompson,	C. Arterburn,	E. S. Terrill,
John Harbold,	F. Stuckey,	George F. Miller,
Allen Tyler,	George Phillips,	John Mackey
Robert Fisher,	G. B. Bate,	Henry Ayres.
John Shrader,	A. S. Frederick,	
Jacob Gaar,	R. S. Murray,	

FIGURE 3. The 1845 Jefferson County, Kentucky, petition signed by the Southern planter Rice Ballard and prominent residents, reminding their state legislature to respect the will of their constituents on the issue of emancipation. Folder 411, Rice Ballard Papers, Southern Historical Collection, Wilson Library, University of North Carolina at Chapel Hill.

their final destination was free territory, possibly Cincinnati. If so, Ballard may have been assisting them in full view of his family.

Ballard's position on slavery was hazy when individual African Americans, not just black women and children, were concerned. In one instance, he was called on to help an enslaved man. In 1854 Delia, an African American servant who later worked in his Louisville home, asked him to buy her still enslaved husband.[99] How he responded is unknown. Regardless of his response in this instance, his charitable actions sat uneasily beside his reprehensible ones. Discretion was in order when men like him bestowed favor on enslaved women.

The boom-or-bust economy that typified the nineteenth century presented other challenges to everyone, even wealthy men like Ballard. Unlike Britain, which by the mid-nineteenth century had a largely stable economy and banking system in which liquid capital could quickly be raised, such funds were less readily available in the United States. When profits were made on the sale of goods and services, they were usually swiftly reinvested in land, buildings, tools, and other property, including slaves.[100] The anxiety generated in this uncertain economic environment, especially in the years following the 1837 recession, can be seen in a January 1838 letter Ballard received from Joseph Alsop in Virginia, warning him that a mutual acquaintance was trying to "defraud" Ballard out of his portion of a particular investment before he went on to ask for a $500 loan.[101]

This kind of letter was often before Ballard as he made plans to marry. Eight months following its composition, Ballard received a letter from a Louisville man, Joseph Pierce, who reported that he had found a "very fitting little" buggy and harness for $280.[102] Ballard was apparently in need of such a buggy because he planned to settle the woman he would marry two years later in Louisville. Bacon Tait seemed to be among the few who knew that he had found a bride and was eager for more information. "I wish you would come out and tell me what the gal said to you at last," Tait wrote in a November 1838 letter. "[If] I guess, will you tell me *por favor* whether I guess right or wrong?" He also advised Ballard to be careful: "Ladies have hearts as hard as the steel pan. . . . Their tongues are sweet little lying varmints."[103]

Tait said this even though he longed for the social stability and status that would have come from marrying into a distinguished family like Isaac Franklin had. In August 1839 Tait informed Ballard that he had seen John Armfield in Alexandria: "Until last Saturday I had not s[a]t at table in a private house with ladies for more than twenty years. [O]n Saturday last I was sitting with Mr Armfield when tea was announced. There was no way of escaping." Tait added, "Happiness my friend is only to be found in the domestic circle. I beg you sincerely not to become an old bachelor. I speak from experience and declare this is an insipid life."[104]

Tait expressed concern for Ballard even while chatising his friend for his secretiveness. He knew about a prospective bride but not a pending wedding. Someone else knew more. "I am pleased to hear you talk of marrying as you know, I have often advised you to marry and settle your self[.] Rice[,] you feel as near as any child I have," wrote Samuel Alsop in September 1838. Alsop was a Fredericksburg farmer and the father of Joseph.[105] He must have been a close confidant, maybe even a father figure to Ballard, for even his son did not know of the latter's pending marriage. That much can be ascertained from the letter Ballard received seven months later from the younger Alsop.[106] "Your letter of the 16th April past containing the first intelligence we had of your marriage. . . . I take this the first opportunity of tendering to you and your fair lady my congratulations," wrote Joseph. "We shall be much pleased to become acquainted with her. . . . You took me somewhat by surprise as I had not had any intimation of any such intention from you recently nor heard it from any one else."[107]

Ballard's secrecy was not all that sometimes irked his friends and acquaintances. So was his decision to have the wedding not at a plantation in the lower South, where he was amassing his wealth, but in Louisville, a location that was inconvenient for some guests. William Glover, an English commission merchant based in New Orleans, sent his regrets for not being able to make the trip.[108] Wrote Glover, "I find it will be utterly impossible for me to accompany you up."[109] Glover, however, suggested Ballard might sit beside his cousin Dolley who was leaving on the *Vicksburg*, a steamer on which Ballard presumably had plans to travel.[110]

After the wedding, which took place sometime in April 1840—the exact date is unclear—Ballard and his bride traveled for three months. Perhaps so as to not entirely distance himself from his relatives and his Virginia friends, the Ballards traveled to his home state. He spared little expense during the trip. Wanting to put his best foot forward, servants were even hired along the way. In one hotel, he paid $83.33 for food for "self and Lady" and $37.50 for three servants, as well as $6.75 for drink. All of this and more was spent in a hotel where he and his wife lodged for twenty-five days.[111] They also visited White Sulfur Springs, Virginia, a resort where they made the acquaintance of Henry Turner, a Philadelphia grocer.[112] "My Dear Sir," Turner began a letter sent after he and his wife had met Ballard and his bride at the resort, "I hope Mrs. Ballard had enjoyed herself since we separated. We have missed her agreeable company much."

A year and a month following the wedding, the Ballards welcomed a daughter into their lives. Ballard shared the news with Joseph Alsop, who wrote back, "Wish you both much happiness with your first born."[113]

Alsop next asked whether the Ballards had plans to visit Virginia that summer. He closed by stating, "Write to me on the receipt of this. . . . Let me hear from you frequently." Alsop's words suggest that Ballard was obviously still wary of sharing too much with others, or when sharing anything, doing so with much thought. His circumspection was something even the woman Ballard had married found troubling.

2 / The Wife and the "Old Lady" Speak

Having married a planter, Louise Cabois Berthe probably envisioned that she would have a particular life. She would live principally on a plantation, in Mississippi, the state in which she was born.[1] In order to escape the monotony of her rural life, she might take trips to New Orleans or travel to Europe.[2] She would acquire a worldly outlook or, barring that, a securer one because she had seen her husband's growing wealth. She had seen similar wealth accruing to her birth family.

The Berthes had been among Mississippi's earliest settlers. Her father resided in Natchez as early as 1818, a year after Mississippi formally became a state.[3] Within three years, he married her mother, Catherine Blanton. One of six siblings, four from her mother's previous marriage, Louise was born in 1822.[4] The family lived comfortably. Her father, James, managed the sale of local estates and owned a Natchez mercantile company that sold fresh tea, brandy, and "Negro hats, shoes and caps."[5] He also oversaw local estates and was a partner in a firm that shipped cotton from Natchez to New Orleans.[6] For someone seeking to establish himself as a planter, the man she married doubtless realized it would be beneficial to have her father in his circle. By 1860 James owned property in Chicot County, Arkansas, where her husband also owned a plantation.[7] The marriage doubtless solidified a bond between two men.

Louise quickly discovered after her marriage that she would spend most of her time in Kentucky, not Mississippi or Louisiana. Further, she was in Louisville, a city, not a rural community.[8] Louise had been placed in such circumstances because of her husband's personal ties to two black women and their children whom he had recently freed in nearby Cincinnati and his familial ties to one of the area's earliest settlers.[9] Seeing the benefits of its position by the Ohio River, a group of settlers under the protection of Virginia militiamen, among them her husband's late uncle, were drawn to this part of Kentucky and by 1780 had obtained the privilege of settling there.[10] The river was a boon for these early residents even as Louisville's location on the river's fall line posed problems for those traveling between Pittsburgh and New Orleans.[11] Before the first locks were constructed in 1825, anyone traveling by water had to come ashore to get beyond the rapids.

Although it did not enjoy the success of Cincinnati, which was not plagued by a fall line, or Lexington, which had a railroad by the 1830s, Louisville had become an urban center by the 1830s.[12] In fact, in 1832 a city councilman complained that the city was "greatly infested . . . with robbers, felons, pick pockets, and swindlers and vagrants" who were "resorting to houses of prostitution, grog shops, and gambling houses."[13] Visitors also grumbled about the way Kentuckians "attacked" their meals.[14] They complained, too, of those who spit in public after chewing tobacco and rolling their tongue around snuff.[15]

This chapter explores the hardships endured by Louise and the black women and children Ballard freed in Ohio. Ultimately, it demonstrates how some of the restlessness evident in a still-young nation was due in part to Southern white men who quietly invested themselves in black women and children. That they did so permits us to learn more about the contradictory nature of the human spirit in American society. Though white men were never in danger of losing their authority, their weaknesses were clearly in view. Some dared to be concerned about certain enslaved people, often causing distress to their white relatives.

In the early days of their marriage, Rice Ballard seems to have given Louise nearly everything a newly married woman would desire. She acquired the material things that accompanied the life of the elite. There was the brand-new dinnerware set of twenty-four plates, twelve dessert plates, two water pitchers, and a dozen fluted tumblers. She also had a fifty-one-piece set of cutlery and four yellow baking pans.[16] She received two bottles of cologne and twelve yards of hand-woven fabric, doubtless to be sewn into a new garment.[17] And Ballard purchased a two-horse wagon. [18]

Before the year ended, however, Ballard made a purchase that served as confirmation that Natchez would not be Louise's home or that of the three children to whom she would give birth. On October 1, 1841, he paid for a year's worth of toll travel in Kentucky.[19] The pass was designed

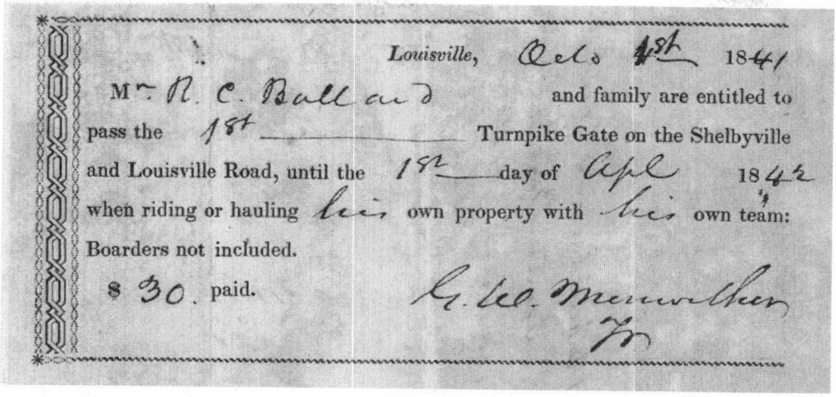

Louisville, _Oct 1st_ 1841

Mr _R. C. Ballard_ and family are entitled to pass the _1st_ Turnpike Gate on the Shelbyville and Louisville Road, until the _1st_ day of _Apl_ 1842 when riding or hauling _his_ own property with _his_ own team: Boarders not included.

$ _30_. paid.

FIGURE 4. Receipt permitting Rice Ballard's family turnpike access on certain Kentucky roads. Folder 352, Rice Ballard Papers, Southern Historical Collection, Wilson Library, University of North Carolina at Chapel Hill.

for the Ballards to travel extensively on toll roads in the interior of the state, away from navigable waterways. Such trips likely included occasional visits to his distant relatives. For longer distances, the Ballards traveled by river.

Ballard's solo travel to and from his family's Louisville home was tied to the seasons. He journeyed north to Kentucky during the spring as the rivers rose with the ice and snow melt. If he waited too long, the heat of summer could create drought conditions that slowed or stopped river traffic. Illustrative of how steamboat owners marketed to the public was an advertisement in a New Orleans newspaper announcing that the _George Washington_, a speedy vessel, left at 10 a.m. on Wednesdays for Louisville and Cincinnati and all landings in between.[20] This steamship offered the passengers who met it at the foot of Poydras Street "superior accommodations." Ballard often traveled on vessels between the Mississippi and Ohio Valleys.

Early in their marriage, Louise, who was twenty-three years her husband's junior, was tolerant of his travels. If she wanted, she could boast that they owned homes in many places, even if she only saw some of them occasionally.[21] Before his death in 1860, in addition to several properties in Mississippi, her husband had two plantations in Louisiana and one in Arkansas.[22] None was her principal residence.[23] That Louisville was her home is evident in the recording of her name and those of their three children beneath her husband's at this residence in the 1860 Census.

Suggestive of the relatively modest life she and the children led in Louisville, their home was valued at $30,000 and the family's cash holdings at $35,000. Neither was a trivial amount. However, both reflected a different lifestyle from that possible farther south. For example, Ballard's Arkansas plantation, enslaved people included, was valued at $400,000.[24]

To understand the stress that existed in the Ballard's Louisville home, it is helpful to examine letters that he received from Louise between late 1847 and 1848, shortly after she gave birth to their two youngest children, twins. This was an event that Ballard did not stay around long to celebrate. Further suggesting his indifference is that the twins, both girls, were not immediately given names. The extent of Louise's suffering because of this departure and other absences was shared with him.

"Dearest Husband," began a letter to Ballard in mid-November 1847.[25] "It is several days or three weeks since you left and we have not heard from you yet. Are you sick or have you so much to attend to that you have not had time to write?" Louise added that she had already sent three letters to him because she had promised to write weekly, but she had not received a reply. Her anxiousness arose because of this and because one of the twins was colicky. "[She] was perfectly lifeless three times. . . . I do not think I have ever seen trouble until I seen my dear little child so near dieing [sic]," Louise reported of her baby.[26]

Reflecting her interest in her children's well-being, in the same letter Louise described the reading ability of their eldest. Ella, now six, was reciting passages from *Little Lessons for Little Learners*. Ballard had earlier presented the book as a gift to Ella, suggesting that he was not wholly indifferent to his children's lives. Overjoyed by this, Louise wrote, "Ella says tell Farther [sic] she can read in the book he gave her," adding, "I am much [pleased] with her improvement and think she learns fast."[27]

But Ella's progress did not allay Louise's suffering. She reiterated her concern about Ballard's absences and his failure to write: "My patience is most worn out about not getting a letter sooner but I must make many allowances."[28] Her words exposed the ways in which white wives in her day contended with lives that were far different from the ones that they had led as unmarried belles. Susan Middletown, a South Carolina mistress, summed up the woes of such women:

> The realities of my life and the situations in which I have been placed have been so strangely different from what my character and the early promise of my life would have led me to expect. Anxiety, responsibility and independence of thought or action are what are

peculiarly abhorrent to my nature, and what nevertheless has so often been required of me.[29]

Though permitted some measure of independence in the private sphere of the home, many unmarried white women were distressed by their narrow lives. Even the most educated were expected to spend more of their time in the private sphere of the home, not in public spaces.[30] In 1851 Gertrude Clanton, a young Georgia woman, postponed a visit to a friend and explained away her delay by saying it was her father, not her, who said she was "too unwell" to travel.[31] Maria Bryan, another woman in Georgia, similarly was prevented from a longed-for trip, but in this instance it was because her brother refused to accompany her. He told her he could not do so because he was tending to "pressing business."[32] Ballard's frequent and prolonged absences generated similar anxiety in Louise, who was relieved to discover that his delay in replying in late 1847 was legitimate. A mule on an unnamed plantation had kicked him. "I was sorry to hear of your being lame . . . ," Louise hurried to write in reply. "You must be careful."[33] In his letter, Ballard also told her that he was lonesome. She confessed that she felt the same, adding, "It will be very tryeing [sic] to be separated until next spring." She asked him to try to come home sooner.

Louise shared next that she had had a disturbing dream, one that Delia, a servant in their house, had too. Louise surmised that the dream was an omen that someone was "very ill." She did not tie the dream to Ballard's farm accident but instead changed the subject, informing him that she had received letters from relatives in the lower South. She encouraged Ballard to visit her half sister Catherine to ease his loneliness, for letters from Catherine had eased hers. Louise closed by sharing news about the twins. "They are noticing very much for such young children," she wrote. She disclosed, too, that, Ella, was also well. "She hopes to read to you in the book you gave her when you come." Louise ended with a conventional closing: "Your wife Louise C. Ballard."

Louise revealed herself as being as lonesome as her husband claimed to be. At the time of their exchange, he was actually in possibly intimate contact, at least at a distance, with an enslaved woman he owned. During summer 1847, Lucile Tucker, the woman in question, sent Ballard a letter from Bainbridge, Georgia.[34] In it, Tucker stated that she was earning good money in an unstated profession. Instead of seeking financial assistance, Tucker requested her freedom. With beautiful penmanship and perfectly spelled words in a letter that was possibly dictated, Tucker wrote, "I wish you could have emancipated me when you was last in New Orleans for that is a matter I deserve to have arranged as early as possible and if you could do it without putting me to the expense of returning to New Orleans, I should much prefer it for life you know is very uncertain and you might die before I can see you."[35] She closed by writing, "Remember me to Miss Louisa."

The level of intimacy between Tucker and Ballard and possibly Louise revealed in this letter is hard to miss. Her mention of New Orleans indicates Ballard had purchased or spent time with her there. She seemed to know his wife as well, who is listed as "Louisa," a diminutive of her first name, in the 1870 Census.[36] Tucker had doubtless met Louise on one of Ballard's plantations during one of the latter's infrequent visits. While the injunction "Remember me to Miss Louisa" was a pleasantry, it also allows us to see how her lowly state was not absolute. There was evidently enough closeness between them that this bondswoman had asked to be remembered by his wife. Such closeness had also given her the courage to demand her freedom.

Tucker's livelihood in Bainbridge was tied to waterborne commerce. In the southwestern corner of Georgia, Bainbridge sits beside the Flint and Chattahoochee Rivers, which flow into the Apalachicola River, which in turn empties into the Gulf of Mexico. These waterways were important thoroughfares for travelers seeking to avoid the mountains when heading west to and beyond New Orleans. Sitting astride them, Bainbridge, a former Indian trading post, seems to have reaped the economic benefits. Tucker likely prospered from the incoming traffic. She was one the numerous female entrepreneurs who capitalized on the many "unattached" male travelers. One such entrepreneur was "Old Rachel," a black woman who owned a cake shop in Bainbridge. She also operated a dance house on Saturdays for the "Kulud ladies," probably a prime spot for prostitution.[37]

Whether Ballard prostituted Tucker or allowed her to earn money in another line of work, she had established a cordial enough relationship with him to earn the privilege of keeping some of her earnings. Judging by the tone of her letter, Ballard and Tucker seem to have had an understanding. By allowing her to work and live independently in Bainbridge, he had positioned her to earn more than enough money to live on her own. Such an existence emboldened her to request something more critical: her freedom. In fact, in this letter, she bluntly stated that being freed was "a matter I deserve to have arranged as soon as possible." Her words suggest that Tucker regarded her manumission not as a privilege but as a

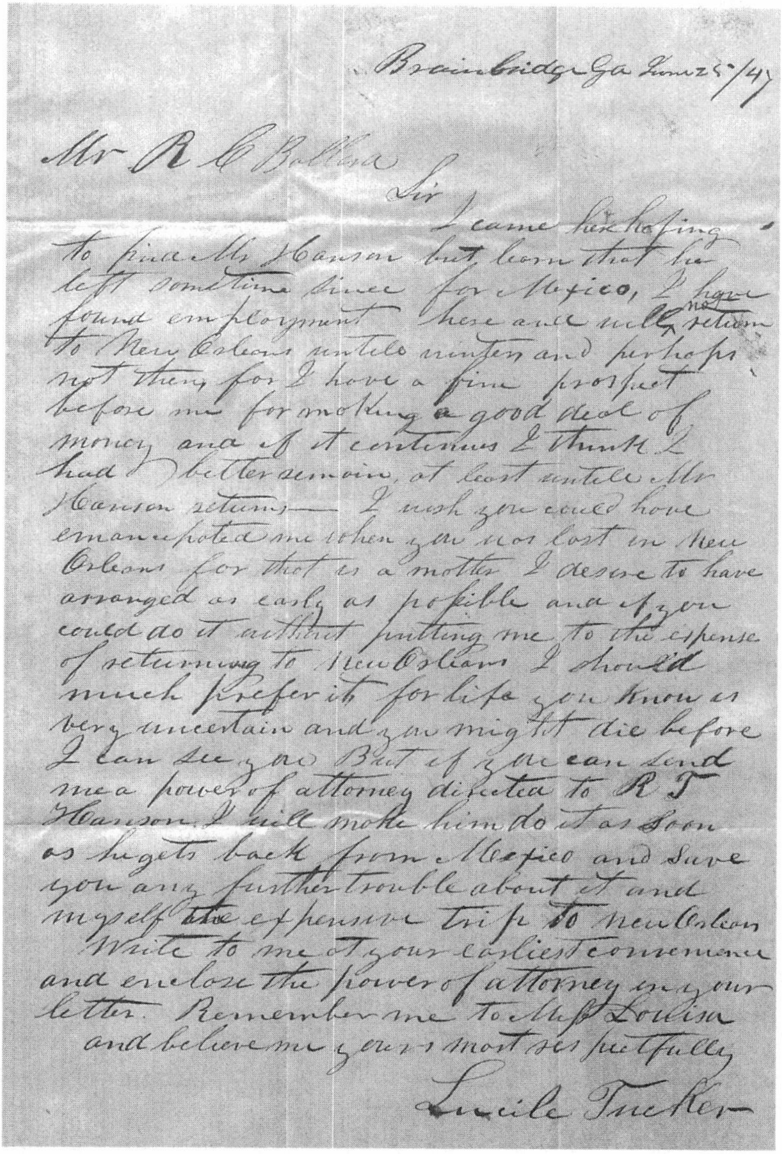

FIGURE 5. The June 25, 1847, letter that Bainbridge, Georgia-based enslaved woman Lucile Tucker sent her master Rice Ballard, requesting her freedom and that he "remember" her to "Miss Louisa," in all likelihood his wife, Louise. Folder 113, Rice Ballard Papers, Southern Historical Collection, Wilson Library, University of North Carolina at Chapel Hill.

right. One can also infer from her words that she was reminding him of a commitment made earlier.

Tucker's confidence was likely related to her ability to enhance her life, perhaps through shady means. Other women of color, especially those working on their own, often entered local economies through prostitution in the United States and Caribbean, disrupting the social order.[38] Whether free or enslaved, these women's worldviews changed according to their economic and legal autonomy. Laws that had made African Americans mere chattel were now exposed for their flimsiness and evidently contributed to these women's resistance. Seeing white men's inconsistencies, some bondswomen became braver. Though Ballard could be ruthless ("We had better loose [sic] them all and begin again than loose ourselves," he had stated to Isaac Franklin regarding the abandonment of slaves during a cholera epidemic in Natchez), Tucker saw something unorthodox in him and asked for her freedom. Virginia, the bondswoman in the Texas jail, had seen something similar in him and asked for his help, if not her freedom, once calling him "an [honorable] and high minded man" although her words may have been mere flattery given her desperate situation.[39] Still, her use of such words and other words in her letter demonstrates empathy between people no matter the power imbalance between them.[40] Like literate white Americans, African Americans turned to certain phrases to reveal their awareness of the rank and ordered way of modern life.[41] That enslaved women did both is significant, as they revealed the limits of laws and customs intended to subjugate blacks and women alike. They revealed, too, their ability to elicit positive responses from powerful white men owing to their earlier dealings, coerced or not, with such individuals. Virginia, Lucile, and other women, among them Delia, the Ballards' Louisville servant, made appeals because he had done more than have coercive sex with some of them. He had displayed more than indifference. He had displayed concern.

Whether Ballard freed Tucker is unanswerable. Nonetheless, her letter uncovers a measure of intimacy between him and her that is missing in the conventionally worded letters from his wife, Louise. The closeness between them was so great it had given her the courage to ask for much more than the privilege of working on her own. She did so because, despite the power imbalance between him and her, men like him were sometimes capable of responding compassionately to the less powerful. Even Louise, his wife, discerned as much.

Ballard's absence had provided her with a bit of power, as it had for the enslaved Lucile, demonstrating again the limits of laws intended to render marriage and slavery in absolute ways. Illustrative of Louise's authority is her announcement in a December 1847 letter that she allowed a nursemaid to attend church while she looked after the twins whose names she had recently registered in an official birth record.[42] She had named one of them Ann Carter Ballard, the other Charlotte Berthe Ballard. Regarding the latter, she stated, "I had wish[ed] to have one of them called for my family." But Louise was still curious about his comings and goings: "[Where] are you . . . ? Have you commenced your new gin on your Louisiana place and Negro quarter[s]? I often feel as if I should like to know what you were doing on each place. When you write give me all the news."[43]

Here Louise was speaking more directly than she had previously. Her appeals for greater candor suggest that she sought a more intimate bond with her husband, of the sort that he shared with other women, black ones among them. In fact, she was stating outright her wish to know more about his life. She invited him to be open with her, stating emphatically: "[D]on't be scarse [sic] in what you have to say. . . . My letters are written just as I think and talk. Write me soon and don't write so seldome [sic]."[44]

But Ballard continued to write infrequently. His reticence may have owed in part to his efforts to liquidate the domestic slave trading firm he owned with the Franklins and Armfield. The elder Franklin's death in 1846 necessitated doing so.[45] Ballard also had other worries related to his financial dealings. His constant travel delayed his responses, leaving some of those with whom he did business as frustrated as his wife. Upon learning from the newspapers that Ballard was in New Orleans, one creditor wrote him, "Write . . . and make me happy in knowing that you are still in the land of the living."[46]

Meanwhile, Louise's concern for him never waned. For example, she chastised him in an 1848 letter for not taking better care of himself. "You are so often imprudent and [make] your self [sic] very sick," she wrote.[47] Hoping mention of the children would make him more responsive, she told him that Ella, their eldest, repeatedly spoke of him, once stating, "Ma lets go down on the Plantation to see Father." In the same letter, demonstrating her autonomy, she asked him to send a female slave to work as her nursemaid because of evident troubles with a white one:

> [I]f you . . . have a woman that [has] a young child and gives a good deal of milk on either of your places . . . bring her up when you come as [there is] such an uncertainty of keeping a white woman. They so e[a]sily get spoiled and I would much rather have a good Negro of my own [although] I have one now. I am

unhappy at any time she might leave me and the children might suffer.[48]

Feeling empowered, Louise did not use a sentimental closing such as "Your wife" but instead curtly signed this letter, "Louise C. Ballard." Her request made plain that no matter their suffering, mistresses helped maintain the racial hierarchy of antebellum America, both inside and outside slave society.[49] Because she was white and a woman, Louise believed she was entitled to some comfort at the expense of an enslaved woman, one who would probably be separated from her own child or children. Illustrative of such separations is the report by a black abolitionist of an enslaved man who fled to free territory with an eight-month-old child after seeing his wife presented as a "waiting-maid" to a young white mistress who did not want the "incumbrance" of her husband and baby.[50] The enslaved man was told to select another wife. Instead, he ran away, taking his child with him.

Many Southern white women indeed had some say over enslaved people's lives, some acting angrily when African American women they suspected of being the bedmates of their male relatives, coerced or not, were concerned. One man left instructions that his bondswoman Delphine be set free upon his death.[51] In an 1854 lawsuit initiated by Delphine, his wife refused to carry out this wish because Delphine was rumored to be carrying her owner's child when he died.

If Louise expressed her suspicions about Ballard's intimate ties to black women, freed or enslaved, in writing, Ballard failed to preserve them. Even if she did in conversation, she doubtless did not press the issue. As a married woman, she was protected financially, something she dared not risk losing. Also, to desert him would have left her socially stigmatized.[52]

Not all white mistresses made peace with their husbands' infidelities and other manifestations of the power imbalance in married life. In her position as a seasonal hairdresser to the wealthy visitors to the resort town of Saratoga Springs, New York, Eliza Potter observed that many white couples were emotionally distant from each other. She saw one who man "treated his wife . . . with the greatest attention before the eyes of others, but alone" never exchanged a word with her.[53] His wife, Potter said, eventually had an affair with a man in Paris. Others were more assertive. As early as 1687, when the Reverend James Blair asked "several times if she would obey her groom," "the most powerful man" in Virginia until his death in 1743, Sarah Harrison, a white woman, reportedly said, "No obey." The minister continued the ceremony without eliciting the expected response.[54]

But most white women felt compelled to remain silent or record their suffering privately. The diary of the childless Mary Chesnut, a Charleston woman, is famously known for making clear the degree to which white plantation mistresses struggled to contain their anger at their husbands' dalliances with female slaves.[55] Mixed-race enslaved women may have especially bothered Chesnut, who remarked on one in this bitter diary entry:

> So I have seen a negro woman sold. . . . [She] . . . overtopped the crowd. . . . She was a bright Mulatto with a pleasant face. She was magnificently gotten up in silks and satins. She seemed so delighted by it all—sometimes ogling the bidders, sometimes looking quite coy and modest, but her mouth never relaxed from its expanded grin of excitement. I daresay the poor thing knew who would buy her.[56]

The girl Chesnut described may have been marketed as a fancy girl. Like the slave traders who made fancies seem larger than life in their letters and ledgers, Chesnut wrote "Mulatto," with an uppercase M, indicating her awareness of the allure of a particular type of bondswoman. She was one who "overtopped the crowd" while ogling male buyers. For Chesnut, this enslaved woman was most disturbing because she appeared gratified by the attention to given to her. She was sure the girl was aware of white men's desires and how to play on them to her advantage. Irritated by this behavior and by the clear evidence of race mixing, she recorded her frustration in her diary.

Writing about her woes in a diary was Chesnut's way of resisting the "cult of the southern lady," which demanded submission and restraint.[57] Nonetheless, other mistresses took more extreme measures, some selling bondswomen and girls when they threatened their authority.[58] Lucy Delany, one enslaved individual, was sold by her mistress for "getting too proud and putting on 'white airs.'"[59] Another mistress sold an enslaved girl named Celestine specifically because her son liked to "play and fool about her."[60] Raising children alone or overseeing the daily details of running one's household was one thing. Condoning depraved behavior in one's household or watching an enslaved girl's haughtiness was something else entirely.

Sensing Louise's angst, Ballard gave her permission to look for a bigger house in Louisville. But Louise told him that searching for another one would not be an "easy matter."[61] She did promise to call on a local realtor. Meanwhile, he continued to busy himself with other matters, mostly financial ones related to his planting interests. Characteristic of his business correspondence is a letter from J. T. F. Cox, manager of one of his Mississippi plantations, who in an April 1847 letter sought Ballard's thoughts on how much he should plant. "I finished planting yesterday. . . . I planted fast," Cox stated, not mentioning the obvious, that it was slaves who had done the planting.[62]

At the time of this letter, Ballard was heading to Louisville. To further placate Louise, he brought china with him.[63] The cotton commission merchant who had facilitated the purchase wished Ballard a "safe and pleasant journey home."[64] That the merchant referred to Louisville as Ballard's "home" suggests that some of those around him regarded the place where his wife and children resided as his true residence even though he was frequently elsewhere.

* * *

From the moment they were purchased, Avenia White and Susan Johnson seemed to have had a place in Ballard's life. White's name is the very first listed on a schedule of 262 slaves he purchased in 1832. Johnson's is third.[65] Ballard did not resell these women like he did other slaves. Their names do not appear among the 212 who were shipped from Virginia to the Deep South in 1832. Nor are they listed on his 1833 or 1834 shipment ledgers. Paternity may have been one of the reasons he was holding on to them.

Sandwiched between White's and Johnson's names on the 1832 slave schedule is that of a boy named Preston. This child was probably White's son because his name appears directly below hers. Slave agents and traders noted relatives of slaves this way.[66] Preston's name also appears in other places in Ballard's records. An entry in his 1833 expense book shows $5.00 dollars were spent to buy "a suit of clothes" for this child. This was no small amount of money to be spending on a single boy, especially an enslaved one. Ballard also paid $1.50 for a pair of shoes for Preston.[67] While slave traders routinely purchased or had clothing sewn for slaves they planned to sell, these entries for Preston appeared on lists in which Ballard recorded the purchase of household goods, which is curious given that Preston was born before—exactly how long is unclear—Ballard bought him and his mother.

Preston appears to have fit into Ballard's life in a special way, as did another male child. In Ballard's book there is a scribble on a blank page that reads, "Susan Johnson was delivered a boy child 21 May 1833

4 o'clock in the morning." No other births were recorded in this book, which suggests that this one was special, like Ballard's relationship with his mother and Preston's mother, who seems to have been the one to whom Ballard was most drawn. The 1840 U.S. Census lists White as being between the ages of twenty-four and thirty-six, which means, if her age was accurately reported, that she could have been born as early as 1804 and as late as 1816. The family of Nathaniel White, an agent who helped Ballard gather slaves in Virginia, was almost certainly Avenia White's first owners.[68] Ballard likely met her while out gathering slaves. She may have been the woman for whom a boy was hired to bring her home.[69]

Ballard's records provide no clues about White's physical features or those of Johnson. That these two women were possibly of mixed race is a reasonable conclusion in light of a proposal Isaac Franklin once made.[70] Franklin told Ballard to make "the Old Lady and Susan" earn their keep by running a brothel. He was almost certainly referring to Avenia White and Susan Johnson. Instead, Ballard left Virginia for Natchez in 1836, taking these two women and their children with him, probably on one of the ships Franklin owned.[71] Leaving them with his kin or friends in Virginia would have been unthinkable given the hard times in the area. Few wanted extra mouths to feed, even ones that could cook and clean. With these enslaved people beside him, he made his gradual transition into planting.[72]

After arriving in Natchez, White and Johnson and their children were not kept inside a "squatty frame building" where three roads met just east of the levee, like the other slaves. They escaped, too, being among the men dressed in navy blue suits with brass buttons and plug hats who "marched beside another . . . in a circle" for prospective buyers. They also escaped being among the women who were dressed in calico with white aprons, ones who had pink ribbons on their carefully braided hair.[73] Instead, they followed Ballard to a long two-story frame building where domestic slave traders stayed temporarily.[74] Once he had acquired a local residence they bided their time with him on a plantation near or in Natchez.

Sometime in summer 1838, Ballard transported White, Johnson, and the four children to Cincinnati. Black women and children for whom Southern white men had shown some measure of concern arrived in this city during a time when the country's frontiers were pushing westward. They traveled by boat, first up the Mississippi and next the Ohio, sometimes sitting in a galley where passing scenery could be taken in as long as the weather permitted. Black men, enslaved or free, were also on board to work as waiters or servants who dashed ashore to gather wood for the ship's boilers.[75] The women and children would have also spent time in Ballard's stateroom during the journey. It was not an unusual practice for white men to have women of color in their rooms, though most were traveling with slave traders in the opposite direction, above all, to the market in New Orleans. The former enslaved man and boat worker William Wells Brown once noticed a trader who kept a particular bondsgirl beside him while his other slaves were stowed elsewhere. Brown remembered that the girl was "was not in chains"; she was beautiful and "had been on the boat but a short time before the attention of all the passengers, including the ladies, had been called to her."[76] White and Johnson and their children possibly received similar attention and more.

Upon their arrival in Cincinnati, many local whites were doubtless unhappy to see them. From the city's earliest days, white Cincinnatians, some of whom were from the South, tried to discourage black settlement.[77] The "black laws" passed as early as 1804 and mob attacks on blacks that began in 1829 confirm the prosperity found here was not intended to be shared with nonwhites, who did not make up even 5 percent of Cincinnati's population at midcentury.[78] However, like other border communities in the United States well into the next century, Cincinnati had a different racial history from nonborder communities because of the ways in which black-white interactions unfolded, even with racist attitudes generally in view.[79]

Freedwomen and their children's ties with white men had been shaped by a bigoted and gendered system. That system sometimes buckled in Cincinnati because it was home to hundreds of mixed-race people, many of whom resembled their masters' white children. These were the children no one in the antebellum South seemed to want to claim; they were those who seemed to "drop from the clouds," as Mary Chesnut once lamented.[80] But following their manumission another drama began, one revealing that the children had not just dropped from the clouds. They and their mothers were people with long-established ties to Southern white America.

Ballard had not intended to marry either White or Johnson. Although it seems fairly certain he visited Cincinnati "on business" frequently and may have settled them there in order to remain in contact and to check on their well-being, even to maintain a sexual liaison with one or both of them, he probably hoped that they would start life anew without him even though doing so would be difficult. Before the Civil War, and prior to the formation of ghettoes, African Americans were by and large dispersed among

Cincinnati's white residents, including Irish and German immigrants.[81] However, blacks still congregated in certain areas because of local racism. They could be found in an east end neighborhood or on the waterfront, called "Bucktown" and "Little Africa," respectively, by their contemporaries.[82]

The six people initially freed by Ballard lived in neither place but instead near the white-dominated central business district. So did other African American women, suggesting they had arrived under similar circumstances, which is to say, they were freedwomen and children who had earlier benefited from some level of intimacy with Southern white men. Indeed, by midcentury women of color headed a third of black households. Their average age was twenty-four.[83] Most of these women lived in the central business district, where one of two avenues of employment for women of color in their day could be found: domestic work. Those who pursued the other, prostitution, tended to live closer to the riverfront, where they could benefit from the presence of transient men.[84]

Planning to pursue the former occupation—as Ballard expected them to earn money to supplement the funds he sent—White and Johnson lived some distance from the waterfront, on Elm between Fifth and Sixth Streets.[85] Frances Bruster, a black woman, held the mortgage on the house in which they lived.[86] Ballard had earlier made Bruster's acquaintance in New Orleans, and he must have decided that her house would be a fitting residence for the six people he planned to free.[87] She agreed because she could benefit from his patronage.

However, possessing a bit of independence owing to her closeness to Ballard, White almost immediately wanted to leave Bruster's house. In fact, she found another a house that would soon be vacant. It rented for $13 a month, vastly more affordable than boarding with Bruster, which cost about ten times that amount. There were many obstacles before them, however. All of this news was shared in White's first letter to her former master. In it, she also shared other woes.

"Mr Ballard, Sir, I write you a few lines," she began, before reporting that she, Johnson, and the children were in good health but "somewhat depressed in spirits."[88] He had moved them to Cincinnati during the summer, an unfortunate time.[89] Regional droughts created problems for the city at this time of year, causing the Ohio, Mississippi, and Missouri Rivers to fall as low as eleven inches, so low that all but a few steamboats refrained from traveling.[90] This bottleneck caused serious disruptions to the movement of goods and people and wrought major damage to the city's economy, which was dependent on waterborne commerce.[91] He

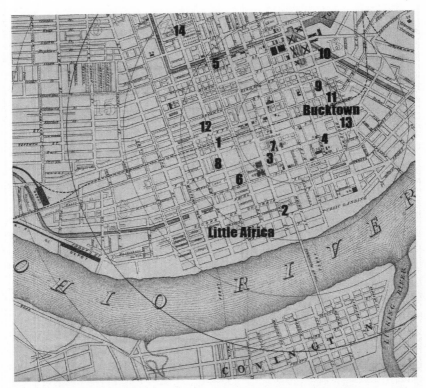

1. France Bruster's house, late 1830s	8. Eliza Potter's home, 1860s-postbellum
2. Calvin Fletcher's produce business, 1830s	9. "Colored" school
3. Calvin Fletcher's home, 1830s	10. "Colored" school
4. Dry goods store, Dennis Hill's workplace	11. 1841 mob attack
5. Dennis Hill's home, 1830s	12. Levi Coffin's home, 1847-postbellum
6. Henry and Louise Picquet's home, 1850-1867	13. Dumas Hotel
7. Carlisle Bldg., Henry Picquet's workplace	14. Colored Orphan Asylum

FIGURE 6. Key sites in Cincinnati and environs, 1830–postbellum. Adapted from Map of Cincinnati & environs, J. T. Lewis, topl. engineer. Scale [ca. 1:10,560]. Cin[cinnati], O[hio]: Middleton, Wallace & Co., Lithrs, [between 1855–1859]; Original map held at Map Collection, University of Chicago Library; Henry Louis Taylor Jr. and Vicky Dula, "Black Residential Experience" in Henry Louis Taylor Jr., ed., in *Race and the City: Work, Community, and Protest in Cincinnati, 1820–1970* (Urbana: University of Illinois Press, 1993); and Eliza Potter, *A Hairdresser's Experience in High Life* (New York: Oxford University Press, 1859 and 1991).

also relocated them during a time that was generally difficult across the country. The recession that had begun in 1837 was well under way.

Because of the reduction in waterborne traffic, local businesses were reluctant to hire additional workers. With job prospects dim, White asked Ballard for monetary assistance. She did not state how much money or for how long. Having spent much time with him, she may have wanted to give him leeway to act in the manner in which he felt most comfortable.

If times were hard for a rich white man, they were harder for a poor black woman. As White announced in her letter, Bruster's boardinghouse was not close to "business." While she might have been referring to the riverfront where she and Johnson might pick up washing and ironing from hotels, it was an unsavory area. She more likely meant Bucktown, the center of Cincinnati's black middle class on the city's east end.[92] Here, especially on McAlister Street, was a collection of black-owned homes and businesses.[93] By the end of the year, a brick house on McAlister near Fourth Street in the area was available and advertised as being "suitable for a small family."[94] This house or something like it in this neighborhood would have been ideal. If taking in sewing or laundry from clients in this area, White and Johnson would not have had as much difficulty carrying a bundle of clothing while holding the hands of young children as they would have if walking to and from Bruster's more distant home.

Ballard did not reply to White's letter. Being a wealthy white man had made him the more mobile one. He could have been traveling when it arrived. If this was the case, his silence was unintentional. Then again, he may have simply balked at her complaints. He had already been generous in freeing them. Moreover, there was a more urgent matter before him: setting up a home in Louisville.

Undaunted, White sent him another letter, this one dated October 25, 1838: "Mr Ballard I am compelled to write you again." She wrote that the river was still low. However, there was better news to report. She was now taking in sewing and laundry, presumably in order to be at home with the children while Johnson was working as a live-in domestic by the week. Their earnings were not, however, enough to meet their needs. They needed beds, she said. They also needed money to buy wood for fuel because the nights had grown cooler. Their funds were so limited, according to her, they had to borrow $8 from Bruster, who sent a hello. White, herself, sent "love." She ended the letter with a postscript: "PS Harvey has been very sick. He is now recovering."[95]

Mention of Harvey—presumably one of Johnson's children if we are to rely on the 1840 census, which lists White as having only one child—was

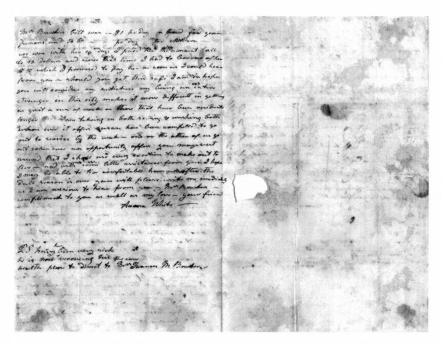

FIGURE 7. Excerpt from freedwoman Avenia White's October 25, 1838, letter to her former master Rice Ballard. Folder 25, Rice Ballard Papers, Southern Historical Collection, Wilson Library, University of North Carolina at Chapel Hill.

done in a clever manner, at the end of her letter. Assuming the last idea mentioned is the one most remembered, putting Harvey's name here was strategic. White was using the children to get Ballard's attention.

Ballard did not respond to this letter either. She grew desperate. So did Bruster, who within a month of White's second letter wrote Ballard. It is worth noting her penmanship resembles that of White's two earlier letters and one White sent the following month, suggesting she had written White's letter, which might account for their formal tone. In her letter, Bruster announced her own troubles. She said she lacked $300 to make the final payment on her mortgage and would be "under ten thousand obligations to" him and "anything that concerns" him if he would lend her $100. She asked him to send it in care of Calvin Fletcher, the local merchant and former Cincinnati councilman who acted as a liaison between Ballard and the women and Bruster.[96] If he did not, she said, the "children will be deprived of a home." She ended her letter, "Avenia and the little boy are well[.] She has written you twice[,] once to Louisville. The last letter she directed to Natchez."

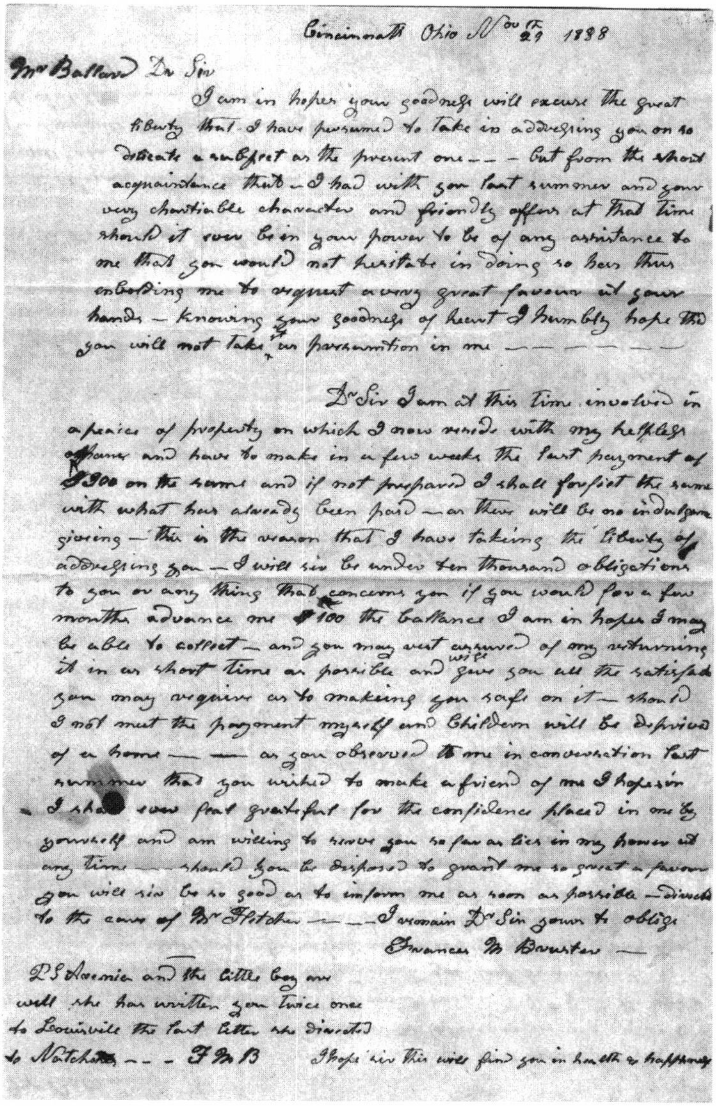

Cincinnati Ohio Novr 29 1838

Mr Ballard Dr Sir

I am in hopes your goodness will excuse the great liberty that I have presumed to take in addressing you on so delicate a subject as the present one --- but from the short acquaintance that I had with you last summer and your very charitable character and friendly offer at that time should it ever be in your power to be of any assistance to me that you would not hesitate in doing so has thus emboldening me to request a very great favour at your hands – knowing your goodness of heart I humbly hope tha you will not take it as presumption in me ———

Dr Sir I am at this time involved in a peice of property on which I now reside with my helpless family and have to make in a few weeks the last payment of $300 on the same and if not prepared I shall forfeit the same with what has already been paid – as there will be no indulgence giving – this is the reason that I have takeing the liberty of addressing you – I will sir be under ten thousand obligations to you or any thing that concerns you if you would for a few months advance me $100 the ballance I am in hopes I may be able to collect – and you may rest assured of my returning it in as short time as possible and will give you all the satisfaction you may require as to makeing you safe on it – should I not meet the payment myself and Children will be deprived of a home —— as you observed to me in conversation last summer that you wished to make a friend of me I hope sir I shall ever feel greatefull for the confidence placed in me by yourself and am willing to serve you so far as lies in my power at any time --- should you be disposed to grant me so great a favour you will sir be so good as to inform me as soon as possible – direct to the care of Mr Fletcher --- I remain Dr Sir your obliged

Frances M Bruster —

P S Avenia and the little boy are well she has written you twice once to Louisville the last letter she directed to Natchez --- F M B

I hope sir this will find you in health & happiness

FIGURE 8. Excerpt from a November 29, 1838, letter written by Frances M. Bruster, a Cincinnati African American woman, to Rice Ballard. Her penmanship resembles that in four letters from Avenia White, who resided for a time with her. Folder 25, Rice Ballard Papers, Southern Historical Collection, Wilson Library, University of North Carolina at Chapel Hill.

Bruster herself surmised Ballard had missed their earlier letters owing to his travels and that no matter the power he had over black women like themselves, he cared. He had planned to remain in touch with at least White because he made it possible for her to contact him. She and Bruster had the addresses of both his Louisville and Natchez homes. A man who provides such information is a man who wants to be found.

Bruster was now capitalizing on Ballard's evident sense of obligation to the women and children, especially White and the "little boy." Her letter ultimately points to the extent to which some Southern white men were prepared to act on behalf of the women and children they had freed. They found them homes and even created opportunities for them to network with locals. In their case, they had a contact in Fletcher.[97] With this connection to Fletcher, White and Johnson's network went beyond Cincinnati's African American population. They were two degrees away from a white merchant and former politician. That he was all of these things further confirms Ballard's intentions to secure a better future for the women and children.[98]

There is no surviving evidence of Ballard's reply to White's or Bruster's letters prior to this point. A more anxious letter, this one by White or her and Bruster, was addressed to him on December 30, 1838. In it she or they repeated the news that Harvey had been sick and added that Johnson was now ill. Cold weather was the likely cause. Upset about this and more, White told Ballard, "I am sorry to have to trouble you so much but my present necessities are so great at this time that I am compelled . . . to get Mr Fletcher to advance me ten dollars to get me some wood."[99]

Perhaps moved by her pleas, or ashamed of how Fletcher might regard his silence, Ballard finally replied. In a letter dated January 28, 1839, Fletcher acknowledged the receipt of $150 from Ballard, $50 of which was immediately delivered to White. Fletcher assured Ballard that "the wom[e]n and children appear to be getting along very comfortably."[100] Grateful for his assistance, however much delayed, White sent her former master a letter of thanks on January 20, 1839. She noted that Harvey was "mending slowly" under a doctor's care.[101]

White's letters reveal as much as they hide about the six people on Elm Street for whom Ballard had ambivalent but ongoing feelings. These former bondspeople were obviously people he cared for, though he did so uneasily, as suggested by his asking Fletcher to verify the women's status and Bruster's need for $100.[102]

White appears to have not written Ballard again for another year and a half, or perhaps there is a gap in his surviving correspondence. It is likely, though, that she did not have to write because Ballard periodically visited Cincinnati, allowing her to communicate with him in person.

On February 2, 1840, she sent him the final letter that he preserved. In it she announced that the house in which she and Johnson had lived, presumably the one Bruster had tried to pay off, had been sold.[103] This development was distressing, but something else bothered White even more. A local woman named Mary January was trying to destroy her reputation.[104] White maintained that she was "innocent of everything" that this woman had "so maliciously reported." She went on to claim that January herself was the shameful one: "I never condesend [sic] to associate with a woman like Mary January's character."[105]

January may have been a sex worker who accused White of being the same. Isaac Franklin had earlier suggested that Ballard employ her and Johnson in a brothel, and poverty may have driven White to desperate measures.[106] She was now in a more difficult situation, for she did not want to lose Ballard's favor or financial support. She had to make sure he always believed the best about her own character. January threatened to destroy his faith in her.

January's accusation fit into a longer list of worries for her, some related to Cincinnati's proximity to Kentucky, a slave state. Such proximity carried the constant threat that catchers might kidnap and reenslave her, Johnson, or their children. Many white Northerners, some aided by black spies situated along the Ohio River, were eager to reenslave free people of color.[107] White's anxiousness may have been compounded by her separation from Davy White, Carter White, Sally White, and Sam White, four enslaved individuals who were probably her relatives who were also purchased by Ballard in 1832. Ballard's records show that these slaves and others whose last names were White were shipped south while she was kept behind in Richmond with Ballard.[108]

There was also the issue of racial tension.[109] African Americans sensed the significance of Cincinnati's position on America's frontier, but perhaps only those like the widely traveled Eliza Potter, who once boasted about her desire to travel and see "the *Western* world," truly appreciated the significance of the city's geographic position, as had white Americans and Europeans.[110] Among the other migrants hurrying to the city were Irish and German immigrants, their numbers increasing in the 1840s preceding and following revolutions in the latter and potato famine in the former.[111] Between 1840 and 1850 Cincinnati's population increased from 46,338 to 115,434. It was third behind only New York and New Orleans in volume of commerce.[112] British visitors of note to the included Charles Dickens and Frances Trollope, though the latter once complained that the so-called Queen of the West wanted for "domes, towers, and steeples."[113] While Trollope was concerned about aesthetics, African Americans like White had other worries. Though the Bucktown and Little Africa communities where local blacks congregated seemed isolated from one another and from black populations across the United States, they were in fact joined because of ongoing racial oppression. Black steamboat workers often brought local blacks news from enslaved relatives. Many such communications took place at the Dumas Hotel, which acted as a sort of black post office where information was exchanged between local African Americans and those in slave states.[114]

The racial hostility African Americans experienced here and nationally had long been nuanced by ethnic loyalties, a fact borne out by Cincinnati's 1841 mob attack, which largely involved Irishmen who typically came from rural areas, thus bringing fewer skills to urban economies, unlike Germans, who often came from towns and arrived with marketable skills.[115] White's final surviving letter was written in 1841, just six months before this riot, which lasted for several days. Aside from an 1834 attack in Philadelphia, it was known as the "most violent and disgraceful" before the Civil War.[116] Bruster, who now lived in Bucktown, doubtless saw the violence or its impact up close.[117]

Cincinnati was a haven of sorts for African Americans, but living there required resilience. Racism there, as elsewhere, was notorious, as one African American man from Baltimore insinuated in an 1833 letter to *The Liberator*, an abolitionist weekly:

> Find them where you may, in Philadelphia, Cincinnati, Richmond, Charleston . . . in free or Slaveholding state, you find them with few exceptions . . . the same degraded, demoralized race.[118]

White also had to contend with Cincinnati simply being very different from the rural environment to which she was accustomed.[119] Pigs ran wild, eating waste that residents dumped into the middle of streets. The city had a poor drainage system that was overwhelmed when it rained, washing rubbish downhill from higher streets.[120] These drainage and debris issues so plagued the city by the late 1830s local leaders introduced proposals to clean it up.[121] Like Louise, Ballard's wife, White saw firsthand the crude behavior of urban dwellers who were learning to cope with others whose backgrounds were very different from their own.[122] White men in particular could be so rowdy that a local racecourse built extra seating specifically for local white belles to "check immorality" in this setting.[123]

African Americans as a whole faced other challenges in Cincinnati. Some had come from cities such as New Orleans that had a three-tiered social order: whites, free people of color, and slaves.[124] In Cincinnati the social order consisted of whites, people of mixed race, and dark-skinned blacks.[125] Whereas in the South those of mixed race often made economic inroads, taking some of the better jobs—because they had been given the chance to learn a trade while enslaved—in northern cities they and blacks were generally discriminated against by local whites. And while many blacks were able to unite on the basis of kinship bonds, such bonds, as White learned through her experience with Mary January, could never be assumed.[126]

Her many worries were compounded by her realization that Ballard was getting married and probably needing every cent for his "white" family. Before she signed off in her final surviving letter, she wished him success, "and all the happiness in this world," adding, "[If] you have forgotten me I hope you have not forgotten the children." Then she wrote that he should write her in care of "Mr. Dennis Hill." She ended her letter, "Your most humble [servant] A. White PS Elizabeth is well and going to school."

This letter is significant for additional reasons. As had Virginia, the pregnant woman in the Houston "slave" jail (and Lucile, the enslaved woman in Bainbridge, Georgia), she used sentimental language to get Ballard's attention.[127] She did as much while being both humble and confident. Indeed, as did his wife, White addressed her former master in a commanding way. She seemed to be reclaiming some part of herself that had been denied by men who had denigrated women like her even while demonstrating concern. To convince him that she was in fact an upright woman, she stated that she had conducted herself in a way that garnered the respect of others. In order to lend weight to her claims of respectability, she even invoked the name of someone whose prominence in Cincinnati's black community marked him as a man of moral stature: Dennis Hill, a local black porter.[128] Though this was a relatively humble position in the larger society, a porter was among the most prestigious occupations open to African American men in mid-nineteenth-century America and made Hill a member of the city's black middle class. White hostility had relegated African American men to menial labor and seasonal jobs. Just 10 percent of Cincinnati heads of black households worked in skilled positions by 1836.[129] Even those arriving from the South with skilled occupations like silversmithing were routinely forced into other work. But men who worked in service and domestic industries, like barbers, waiters, and porters, were often leaders in the African American community.[130]

Hill was not merely a porter. During the 1830s, he was president of the Cincinnati Union Society of Colored Persons and thus part of the local abolitionist movement. That he provided a fixed address for White to receive letters was significant, for doing so put her and Johnson within his circle of association. Moreover, the handwriting in this letter is different from that of White's earlier letters. Hill not only provided a fixed address, but he may have written it.[131]

That men like Ballard placed women like White in a city with political allies like Fletcher and Hill is significant. Though society dictated one behavior publicly, these men often did something else privately. They publicly consolidated their power while privately addressing the entreaties of women and children of color.[132] Having spent considerable time with White and Johnson and their children, Ballard developed an interest in their future. White signaled as much in the postscript of her final surviving letter when she mentioned that Elizabeth, who was almost certainly one of Johnson's three children, was in school. White understood, as most of those aspiring to a higher position did, that education was one of the routes to a better and more respectable life.

After this letter, White seems to disappear from surviving historical records. She is not listed in censuses or Cincinnati directories after 1840, suggesting she died, got married and assumed her husband's surname, or returned to the South. Surviving records suggest all three scenarios are possible. After possibly passing as white, White may have been a once-married Virginia-born woman named Elizabeth A. Ward (who may sometimes have gone by the name Avenia Ward) noted by census takers who resided in Greene County, Ohio, in 1850, which was about fifty miles away.[133] Ward had four children who were all born in Ohio. Notably, she had no male head of household, and her marital status was left blank. Further, she had no apparent occupation, raising questions about the source of the $50—about $1,476 in today's currency—that she possessed.[134] It is also interesting that Xenia, the city where in 1856 white abolitionists would open Wilberforce University for African Americans, is located in Greene County. Racially tolerant whites were evidently among this county's residents, something Ward would have appreciated if discovered to be of African descent.[135]

It is also possible that White returned to the South to live near Ballard. On May 19, 1852, R. F. Morgan, manager of a plantation in which Ballard had a financial interest, wrote him a letter announcing the death of a woman.[136] This news was at the beginning of the letter, suggesting its importance to Ballard, who asked to be kept informed of her condition because she had been ill for a while. Ballard's plantation managers and overseers tended to begin their letters to him with news about the status of crops and the weather before moving on to information about the health and condition of his slaves. Morgan reported that the deceased had experienced "bloody flux which she was unprepared to stand." The deceased woman may have been White because the first letter of her name began with a capital A; the next two letters are indistinct.

It is also worth noting that Ballard kept two curious receipts dated within a year of White's final letter. One showed that he paid $5 for the "passage of Negro girl from N. Orleans" to Natchez.[137] The second showed that he paid $5 for another black woman to make the same trip five months later. This second receipt also lists $15 paid for himself and a servant. Given that a distinction was made in the second instance between the "Negro girl" and the "servant," the "girl" was probably not a slave, and moreover, one who traveled regularly with him between New Orleans and Natchez.

This girl may have been White. There were other women whose ties to Southern white men were so strong that they returned to the South after having been freed and resettled. Levi Coffin recounted his dealings with a twenty-one-year-old woman of mixed race who had been freed by a white uncle and sent to Oberlin College in Ohio for schooling. She soon asked to be sent back to Louisiana. It appears she had been the mistress of a white New Orleans merchant who had given her dresses and jewelry. Her beau also sent money to Ohio, which distracted her further.[138] She eventually left for New Orleans and her benefactor. She was not unusual in pursuing a white man of wealth. Another who did this was Jacqueline Lemelle, who had a de facto marriage with a white man and who found a way to continue living with him in Louisiana even after being manumitted.[139] Lemelle's daughter followed in her mother's footsteps, entering into a relationship with a prominent white New Orleans man that lasted throughout her life. The relationship resulted in several children, one of whom lived as a white woman in Natchez.

If the "girl" in question was White, how long she remained with him in the lower South prior to her death is unknown. She may have returned alone, allowing her son to remain in Ohio where he could be educated. Such an act appears to buttress the Southern defense of slavery as a superior system because slaves seemed to live more securely in the South than wage earners in the North. But this logic is shortsighted because of the fragile nature and highly variable definition of "freedom." White may have felt more "free" in a place where she could secure financial support for herself and her child. She reveals the ways in which freedom was never a "philosophical absolute" but rather something that was "locally and ideologically conceived," a position that Harriet Jacobs also took.[140] Though their experiences were vastly different—Jacobs fled from her master who both subjected her to sexual harassment and prevented her from marrying the African American man she loved and hid for several years in her grandmother's attic before escaping from the South—both women realized that "freedom" can encompass far more than the narrow range of civil liberties generally associated with the word. Jacobs could see her children and look out a window, hoping for a better day.

Even in the face of escalating laws preventing their settlement, numerous freedpeople chose to live in the lower South where enslaved or free relatives and others—including white men—could reside with or near them. As Emily West has written, in the years leading up to the Civil War some women successfully petitioned to reenslave themselves or to live in the South.[141] One-fifth of the ninety-eight reenslavement requests that she studied can be linked to single free women who were apparently involved in intimate relations with white men, since other motives for voluntary enslavement, among them, love of spouse or family, poverty or debt, were not mentioned in their petitions. These petitions affirm the degree to which Southern white men were hidden, sometimes not so hidden, actors in the efforts of such women, even those who never left slave territory, to enhance the quality of their lives.[142] In fact, during the 1850s when the passage of residency and enslavement laws intensified in the South, both "black women and white men used complex negotiations under new laws in an effort to achieve their economic and possibly emotional aims."[143]

While speculating on White's fate, we should not lose sight of Ballard's behavior. Whether or not the woman to whom Morgan referred was White, the facts of the matter are (1) Ballard obviously requested that he be kept apprised of her health, and it was of such importance to him that Morgan opened his letter with the news; and (2) even if she was not White, she was a black woman about whom he cared a great deal and not his wife. In short, although "Avenia White" disappears from the record, Ballard does not seem to have altered his behavior, suggesting his ongoing distraction by her or someone else. He never regularly spent time in his Louisville home. As late as 1857, three years before his death, he was still frequently visiting the Deep South. That year W. A. Ellis, a Louisville pork merchant, asked him to return to Louisville because Louise was associating with a questionable crowd. In a letter of March 1, 1857, Ellis wrote, "Your dear children I feel for very much. . . . [T]he older they get the worse it is for them as they are more liable to be injured by the wickedness of an unnatural Mother."[144] Two months later, Ellis wrote Ballard again, saying, "I fully believe if you will come up soon . . . the influences can be broken off and much good done."[145]

Ballard's absences had an impact on his daughters as well as his wife. Ella, his eldest, once blamed his constant travel for his not receiving her letters in a timely manner. "You think because you don't receive them I don't write to you," Ella stated.[146] Still, like her mother, Ella was concerned about her father and once commented on his health: "Pa, you are getting old and you ought to take more care . . . of yourself for if you get sick down there, there would not be any person to nurse you."[147]

Ballard at last was himself concerned about his health. At the time of his death he had in his possession an 1857 advertisement for a Tennessee resort owned by John Armfield.[148] This resort sat atop Cumberland Mountain near a spring with alleged health-restoring properties.[149] Ballard explored homeopathic cures, too, for an unnamed illness. He also searched for a physician to work at his Louisiana property where he was apparently residing in mid-1858.[150] Yet he died in Louisville on August 31, 1860, in his early sixties.[151] In their study of southern life before the Civil War, Elizabeth Fox-Genovese and Eugene D. Genovese stress that both faults and virtues figured into what it meant to be southern, particularly the southern gentleman who used classical and Christian concepts like duty, fame, honor, courage and dignity but also frankness and pride to define himself.[152] There is little in Ballard's papers to suggest that he ever obsessed over such things, although he may have indeed been proud of some of his accomplishments.[153] His social standing had decidedly improved as he aged, as suggested by a $3,227 financial gift he made in 1848 to a Natchez orphanage.[154] News of this donation was reported in local newspapers.[155] One of the articles described a portrait painted in his honor for the donation. His eyes were said to be "pleasant, intelligent, and mirror[ing] a great force of character." Unbothered by such attention, he reportedly agreed to sit for the portrait only when he learned the artist was someone he regarded as an "intimate friend."[156] Although wary of others, he clearly managed to make an impression. When it was erroneously reported that he had died in a river accident, the writer of yet another news article reported that he was "truly pleased" to learn it was only rumor.[157]

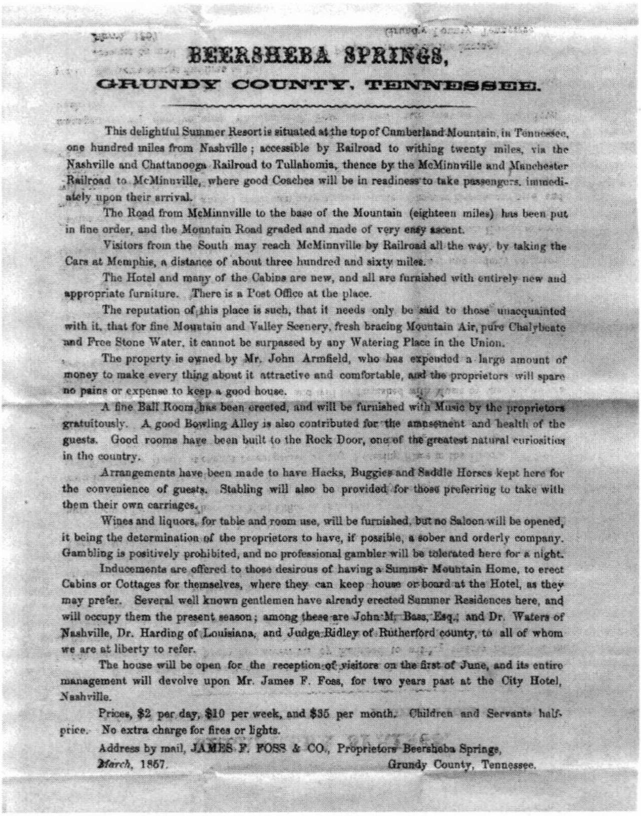

BEERSHEBA SPRINGS,

GRUNDY COUNTY, TENNESSEE.

This delightful Summer Resort is situated at the top of Cumberland Mountain, in Tennessee, one hundred miles from Nashville; accessible by Railroad to withing twenty miles, via the Nashville and Chattanooga Railroad to Tullahomia, thence by the McMinnville and Manchester Railroad to McMinnville, where good Coaches will be in readiness to take passengers, immediately upon their arrival.

The Road from McMinnville to the base of the Mountain (eighteen miles) has been put in fine order, and the Mountain Road graded and made of very easy ascent.

Visitors from the South may reach McMinnville by Railroad all the way, by taking the Cars at Memphis, a distance of about three hundred and sixty miles.

The Hotel and many of the Cabins are new, and all are furnished with entirely new and appropriate furniture. There is a Post Office at the place.

The reputation of this place is such, that it needs only be said to those unacquainted with it, that for fine Mountain and Valley Scenery, fresh bracing Mountain Air, pure Chalybeate and Free Stone Water, it cannot be surpassed by any Watering Place in the Union.

The property is owned by Mr. John Armfield, who has expended a large amount of money to make every thing about it attractive and comfortable, and the proprietors will spare no pains or expense to keep a good house.

A fine Ball Room has been erected, and will be furnished with Music by the proprietors gratuitously. A good Bowling Alley is also contributed for the amusement and health of the guests. Good rooms have been built to the Rock Door, one of the greatest natural curiosities in the country.

Arrangements have been made to have Hacks, Buggies and Saddle Horses kept here for the convenience of guests. Stabling will also be provided for those preferring to take with them their own carriages.

Wines and liquors, for table and room use, will be furnished, but no Saloon will be opened, it being the determination of the proprietors to have, if possible, a sober and orderly company. Gambling is positively prohibited, and no professional gambler will be tolerated here for a night.

Inducements are offered to those desirous of having a Summer Mountain Home, to erect Cabins or Cottages for themselves, where they can keep house or board at the Hotel, as they may prefer. Several well known gentlemen have already erected Summer Residences here, and will occupy them the present season; among these are John M. Bass, Esq., and Dr. Waters of Nashville, Dr. Harding of Louisiana, and Judge Ridley of Rutherford county, to all of whom we are at liberty to refer.

The house will be open for the reception of visitors on the first of June, and its entire management will devolve upon Mr. James F. Foss, for two years past at the City Hotel, Nashville.

Prices, $2 per day, $10 per week, and $35 per month. Children and Servants half-price. No extra charge for fires or lights.

Address by mail, JAMES F. FOSS & CO., Proprietors Beersheba Springs,
March, 1857. Grundy County, Tennessee.

FIGURE 9. Advertisement for Tennessee resort owned by John Armfield, Rice Ballard's former domestic slave trading partner. Perhaps owing to health issues, Ballard retreated here shortly before his death in 1860. Folder 411, Rice Ballard Papers, Southern Historical Collection, Wilson Library, University of North Carolina at Chapel Hill.

Louise remarried in 1863. Her new husband, James Purdy, a New York lawyer, was twenty-three, twenty years her junior. Doubtless at his instigation, he and Louise sued the federal government for $52,000 for losses incurred by the removal of cotton from one of Ballard's Louisiana plantations during the Civil War.[158] They must have been successful with this suit and other efforts, as Purdy's estate was worth $200,000 seven years later.[159] But either Purdy died or the marriage was short-lived, because Louise was listed sixteen years later as Ballard's widow in a Louisville directory.[160] But some portion, however small, of her husband's wealth had been shared with at least two black women and four children. And this was not unique, as the next chapter reveals.

3 / "The stain on it": Exploring the Disposition of "Favored" Black Women

The record is vague as to why John Williams, a man approaching fifty, parted ways with his wife. Or why he was the one left with their three children, all boys, the youngest nine.[1] Williams decided to look for a new companion, but this one he would not marry. He would buy her. In 1841 he headed east from his home in New Orleans to Mobile, Alabama. While enslaved women could be found for sale in large numbers in New Orleans, he possibly decided that looking for her in Mobile was a better option. There he was unlikely to run into someone he knew who might share news of his new acquisition on the heels of a divorce. Mobile afforded him anonymity at the point of purchase and the opportunity to let neighbors become accustomed to this woman, who could be passed off as a housekeeper.

When he arrived at the Mobile facility where enslaved people were sold, his eyes landed not on a woman but someone closer to a girl. Louisa Picquet was her name. Just fourteen years old, she was of fair complexion. Her hair, however, was short because the owner she had recently irked cut it. Still, her hair was of "good quality" by the white normative standards of the society. Such standards, but also her youth and beauty, enabled her to be marketed as a fancy girl, a bondsgirl of the highest class. Years later, Picquet recalled there had been many like her in Mobile that day. "Plenty of them," she said, as if to make a commentary on the demand for her kind, kept in a separate room away from enslaved men and less desirable women.[2]

When it was Picquet's turn to be sold, the auctioneer assured would-be purchasers that she was not only "good-looking," but a "good nurse" who was "kind and affectionate to children" and "never used to any hard work."[3] The bidding soon exceeded $1,000. Albert Clinton Horton, who within five years would become the first lieutenant governor of Texas, bid $1,400.[4] Williams countered with $1,500, which no one topped. [5]

When he went to fetch Picquet, she was almost immediately instructed by one of the auctioneers to undress to assure Williams that he was getting his money's worth. The practice of allowing men to examine, even to have sexual relations with, enslaved women and girls of color prior to purchasing them was widespread. Williams was so taken by Picquet, however, he declined to inspect her.[6] Before they departed, she told him that she wanted to retrieve a floral muslin dress she owned. He told her to leave it, that he would buy her "plenty of nice dresses."[7]

They traveled by boat to New Orleans. Along the way, Picquet recalled that he confessed that he was "getting old" and after seeing her, decided that he would spend his final days with her. He assured her that if she behaved herself, he would treat her well. If she did not, "he'd whip [her] almost to death."[8] Within six years, Williams was on his deathbed. Picquet recalled that it was a cold night. She helped him to a chair that was close to the fire so that he could warm himself.[9] Beside him was a table on which he began to write.[10] "He told me he was goin' to die, and that he could not live," Picquet remembered.[11] Williams said that he would give her "something for the children."[12] He then disclosed his intention to leave her "the things in the house, the beds, and tables, and such."[13] He pledged, too, to free her and the two surviving children she had produced with him (another two had died). He had one condition, however. He wanted her to go to New York. He figured that if she told no one that she was of mixed race, she could easily pass as white and find a white "mechanic—someone who had a trade, and was able to take care of" her and their children.[14] Picquet chose instead to go to Cincinnati, partly because she knew freedpeople there from her childhood days in Georgia and partly because she lacked the funds to go farther. "I had just enough money to get there, and a little bit over," she recalled.[15]

When she arrived in Cincinnati, she, like the women discussed in the previous chapter, represented a certain kind of freedwoman, one who possessed the ability to do things other people of color could not owing to her earlier ties to Southern white men. Such women and children were not only relocated but also chose to migrate to that city, pushed by a host of factors, including kinship, ease of access by river, the chance to obtain work not easily available in slave territory, and to attend school.

The details of Picquet's life are given in an 1861 memoir written by the Reverend Hiram Mattison, a Buffalo abolitionist. Mattison's wish to share Picquet's story some years after her arrival in Ohio was driven by his desire to draw attention to the horrors of slavery, which in his mind included immoral interracial relationships such as the one in which Picquet had found herself. It did not matter that her former master had freed her. To Mattison, Williams's actions were inexcusable and representative of the evil behavior in the South. So intense was his anger at white slaveholders and their exploitation of women and girls like Picquet that he published the book himself.

The narrative Mattison published reflected the world that Picquet once inhabited. She had been a fancy girl, even though the term does not appear in any surviving record concerning her life. There, however, can be little doubt as to her status in the marketplace: she was sold as a teenager for a price that far exceeded that of most female slaves in her age group. She became the sexual companion of a white man who fathered her four children. She resided for a time in New Orleans, a city where fancies lived in great numbers.

This chapter turns to Picquet and other African American women and girls to continue examining black-white intimate unions before the Civil War but focuses more closely on the mind-set of the women and girls who entered into these unions by choice or force. Like the women and girls mentioned thus far, Picquet and the others discussed in this chapter consciously and deliberately profited from nineteenth-century ideas about womanhood that were not intended for them. In and outside urban spaces in which they moved or were taken, they were the beneficiaries of the obvious changing meaning of womanhood and motherhood. Black women were said to be promiscuous and thus fitting sex partners or sex workers. Depending on a prospective buyer's needs, their reproductive capabilities were considered either a financial boon or a burden. Indeed, some white men wanted sex, not more children. Their selfishness and cruelty were in keeping with other outrages endured by African American women and girls over the years.[16] However, though shaped in demeaning ways, some enslaved African American women and girls assertively and creatively exploited their condition. But when studied closely, it becomes apparent that such girls and women cannot be reduced to a common denominator. They were individuals who maneuvered strategically to survive and maximize the possibilities of their circumstances. Their ability to do as much reveals another way in which slavery has been America's greatest historical problem.[17] The institution

LOUISA PICQUET,

THE

OCTOROON:

A TALE OF SOUTHERN SLAVE LIFE.

BY REV. H. MATTISON, A. M.,

PASTOR OF UNION CHAPEL, NEW YORK.

NEW YORK:

PUBLISHED BY THE AUTHOR, Nos. 5 & 7 MERCER STREET.

1861.

FIGURE 10. Cover of freedwoman Louisa Picquet's biography, which was written and published by the Buffalo abolitionist and Methodist minister Hiram Mattison. Louisa Picquet, *The Octoroon, or, Inside Views of Southern Domestic Life* (New York: The Author, 1861). Courtesy of Manuscripts, Archives and Rare Books Division, Schomburg Center for Research in Black Culture.

was filled with contradictions. These women's white contemporaries often saw the limits of their own power and glimpsed power in oppressed women, even girls.

As with Avenia White and Rice Ballard, it is a challenge to see the possibilities for intimacy between Picquet and John Williams. Because we are mostly privy to what happened *after* Ballard freed White and Johnson and their children, Picquet's life gives us a better understanding of what happened between enslaved women or girls and the men who owned them *before* the former and their children were freed. Unlikely behavior, including real intimacy, can be seen between Picquet and her former master according to the story relayed by Picquet herself. If, as Williams declared on his deathbed, Picquet was fair enough to pass for "white," she presumably could have fled to freedom with her two equally "white" children without waiting for his death. But she chose not to, perhaps out of fear of the unknown. Conversely, he, rather than freeing her and their children before dying, could have sold them all and given the proceeds to his "white" children or to his brother, from whom he had borrowed the money to buy Picquet, a debt that remained outstanding at the time of his death. But he did not.

Whatever their motives, Picquet and Williams reconciled themselves to life together for six years. A divorced white father of three who was growing older and a girl of African descent who bore him four children had to figure out how to share the same space. To be sure, given the power imbalance between an enslaved woman-child of color and the white man who owned her, she had to relinquish much even in his final hours. She helped him from his deathbed to sit closer to the fire to warm himself when she could have refused or pushed him to the floor.[18] Perhaps in acknowledgment of Picquet's assistance then and earlier, Williams promised to free her and their children. This was a huge gift. Other gifts, less momentous ones occurring in their daily lives, were important, too.

Even though he possessed the privileges and power that came from being white and male, in order to make life in his household tolerable for him and them, Williams had to treat her and their children with some measure of kindness if he was going to get part of what he hoped for in purchasing her: companionship and a caretaker for his children. Such considerations reveal the scope of white men's concerns for enslaved people.[19] Given the abuse that Piquet frequently suffered, to conjecture that love figured into her and Williams's relationship, something *almost* thinkable for Ballard and White—she sent him her love—would be unwarranted.

Caution is required in the reading of all historical sources, among them interviews with former bondsmen and bondswomen. It is plausible to say, as some have, that because Mattison narrated Picquet's tale, her power and voice were mediated and diminished.[20] Yet her participation in this literary project was calculated, as were her interactions with Williams.

Whereas her time with Mattison was regulated by a regimen in which she answered questions and offered information about her life in order that they might complete the book, her life with Williams required an entirely different, less orchestrated set of tactics that, too, unfold like the hidden transcript of other oppressed people about whom James Scott has written.[21] She carefully carried out prescribed tasks—cooking, cleaning, and raising the children—attending to her own whenever possible. She also gave more of herself, and not just sexually. Williams did the same. Like the relationship between Ballard and White, the favor Picquet and her children received from Williams rested largely on what he permitted from himself, even if her wishes were considered.

In the end, Picquet's spirit was not broken by her experiences with Williams. Throughout her life she was self-possessed. She is thus a fitting model of certain antebellum black women who benefited from white men's generosity. Such generosity gave her the courage to speak confidently, even angrily about her ordeal. Telling of this attitude is the following exchange between her and Mattison, the abolitionist, about her sale in Mobile to Williams.

> Q: "You say the gentleman told them to 'take you out.' What did he mean by that?"
> A: "Why, take me out of the room where the women and girls were kept; where they examine them—out where the auctioneer sold us."
> Q: "Where was that? [Was it in] the street . . . or in the yard?"
> A: "At the market . . . where the block is."
> Q: "What block?"
> A: "My! Don't you know? [It is the] stand . . . where [slaves] get up."[22]

The paradoxical world both she and Mattison inhabited enabled her brazen response. She had been enslaved, but she had access to things for which white women longed: "plenty" of dresses and, more important, shelter and food for herself and her children. Indeed, Picquet exhibited the "sass" heard from many other oppressed women of color across time.[23] Suggesting the assertiveness of such women, even those who had not had coerced sexual relations with white men, was a bondswoman who chastised a Union soldier for stealing her quilts during the Civil War. She asked him why he did it if he was fighting for "niggers."[24] Consider, too, an enslaved girl who had reportedly been raised to conduct herself "like a lady," according to the Swedish reformer Frederica Bremer.[25] Her former owners had allowed her to learn how to embroider and play the piano. Bremer also reported that they had "treated her ... as if she had been their own." Her former owners eventually detected that the girl's disposition eventually grew "too high for her."[26] To humble her, she was taken to jail to be sold. There is also the case of Julie Tillory, an African American who resided in the South during the postbellum period. When asked by a northern missionary working for the Freedmen's Bureau why she would prefer to leave her former master's plantation where she had food and shelter, Tillory replied, "To 'joy my freedom."[27] Acting similarly was Dink Watkins, another freedwoman, representative of African Americans who were unwilling after emancipation to stay in marriages informally arranged by their former masters. In refusing to accept such a situation, Dink told a North Carolina court, "I am my own woman and I will do as I please."[28] Like Picquet and Mattison, there was a pronounced imbalance in the distribution of power between these black girls and women and the whites to whom they spoke, even though they were sometimes aligned, in the broadest terms, on the issue of slavery. This imbalance did not prevent black women like Picquet from speaking their minds.

Black women who spent considerable time with white men intuited that they might have some of the liberties these men claimed. They were capable of making the best of a bad situation owing to their master's proximity and sometimes of turning it into some advantage. Likewise, the resilience of the human spirit doubtless enabled many of them to adapt to their circumstances. Picquet certainly took advantage of her earlier status as a special kind of enslaved person and spoke boldly, even rudely. Throughout the exchange quoted above, she acted as if she knew more about slavery than an abolitionist and a minister. And of course she did.

Mattison eventually abandoned the question-and-answer format of the memoir in order to steer readers to the parts of her life that he felt were most important. Because she needed him, she wisely worked with him. She had done the same with Williams. What follows are more details from her narrative, which allow us to see more of what Williams had engendered when fostering a level of intimacy with her. Her and her children's resulting manumission deepens our understanding of the complexities of black-white intimacies, as well as race and class affairs in and outside the Old South.

* * *

Picquet was the daughter of an enslaved seamstress of mixed race named Elizabeth who was in fact still alive at the time Piquet met Mattison. In fact, Picquet wanted to use the proceeds from the book's sale to purchase her mother, who was still enslaved in Texas.[29] Elizabeth gave birth to Picquet in 1828 in Columbia, South Carolina.[30] The white man who owned them was Picquet's father. This led to problems in his household. Two months after she was born, his wife noticed that Picquet bore an uncanny resemblance to the child she had given birth to two weeks earlier. She ordered her husband to remove Elizabeth and her young child from their home. "Then I was sold to Georgia," Picquet told Mattison.[31]

If the sudden departure of a fair-skinned child from a home announced more than that of any dark-skinned child that a household had witnessed both exploitation and domestic tension, the arrival of such a child and her mother to a new household broadcast the same. The bondspeople residing on a cotton plantation in Monticello, Georgia, sixty miles southeast of Atlanta, probably decided as much about Elizabeth and her infant upon their arrival. A white man named "Mr. Cook," their new owner, owned the property.

Elizabeth nursed Picquet and the child to whom Cook's wife had recently given birth and eventually became a cook. As she grew older, Picquet herself tended to the Cooks' children.[32] While living in Georgia, her mother became pregnant by Cook, who not only sexually abused Elizabeth, but whipped Picquet. His disagreeable disposition was obvious to others. Cook liked to throw lavish parties but did not like to pay his bills. In 1841 creditors arrived and claimed his plantation. They also took the warehouse he owned. Cook sent his wife to live with her sister in another part of the state. With Picquet, her mother, a fair-skinned blue-eyed enslaved woman named Lucy, and Lucy's four children beside him, Cook left for Mobile.[33]

The arrival of the eight individuals may not have appeared too unusual in Mobile, which, like New Orleans, had a reputation as a city in which race mixing occurred. The first capital of French Louisiana in 1702, Mobile was distinguished by its large number of free people of color, among them Afro-Creole residents of French and Spanish descent who were fair-skinned.[34] While living in Mobile, Cook impregnated Picquet's mother again. As had been the case with the child she had carried in Georgia, she lost this baby. There would be yet another pregnancy. This time Elizabeth gave birth to a boy she named John.[35]

Picquet soon discovered that she and her mother and Lucy and Lucy's children lived in a particular milieu, one in which Southern white men frequently took black women or girls as their sexual partners. After Cook hired out Picquet and the others to work for local residents, she encountered another person in this very situation. While working as a domestic servant in one home, Picquet observed a frequent male visitor who owned a "very light" girl from Charleston.[36] He did not share a home with her but "kept her boarding out" so as to not draw attention to himself. Picquet discovered their living arrangement from a young enslaved man of mixed race who served as this visitor's driver. Upon discovering that she, too, was of mixed race and not white, the driver was attracted to Picquet. He began to visit on Sundays and soon asked her to marry him. She mulled over his proposal, recalling, "I liked him very well."[37]

Perhaps because he was interested in Picquet, too, a white servant who also worked for her beau's master grew jealous and told their master that Picquet's young man was actually interested in the Charleston girl, who was sent to New Orleans where she almost certainly was marketed as a fancy girl.[38] Picquet's beau was whipped. Seeing this sequence of events, Picquet and her beau decided that they would escape. According to Picquet, an "Englishman, or Scotchman," told her beau that given his complexion, he could easily escape to free territory and that he should take Picquet with him. Revealing the degree to which she had her own mind, Picquet refused, for one reason: her beau could not read or write. Because of his illiteracy, she was afraid that they would be discovered to be people of color. Picquet did talk to him for two hours before bidding him farewell, however.[39]

Picquet's awareness of the opportunities to improve her life was evident not only in her decision to not leave with her beau, but in the telling of this story. For example, she announced the skin complexion of the girl from Charleston and her beau or provided those details after being asked. She thus revealed the hardships but also the advantages of people of mixed race, especially females. Because she and the Charleston girl had fair complexions, they were desirable to men, both white and black, and therefore vulnerable to the exploitation that often accompanied that desirability. On the other hand, some of them could pass as white and possibly escape to free territory.

Interestingly, Mattison failed to make much of either fact because doing so would reveal the degree to which Picquet herself bought into prevailing ideas concerning power in people of mixed race, a status Mattison himself deplored as it announced immoral behavior between white men and women of color. Noting how Picquet capitalized on her unfortunate condition to enhance her life would not further his goals of condemning Southern white men and the institution of slavery. If he drew attention to her views, Picquet and other enslaved women and girls would seem to be accomplices in, rather than victims of, one of the most degrading, morally repugnant, and exploitative aspects of slavery. Rather than present them as individuals who were consciously attempting to control their destinies, something he was doubtless aware of, Mattison remained silent. He needed Picquet to conform to the role he envisioned for her, not an unequal partner in a relationship in which she sought to maximize her well-being.

Throughout her narrative, Picquet presented herself as someone who constantly assessed how powerful or weak she *really* was in relation to each person she encountered. Avenia White did something similar, revealing how such careful thinking figured into their ability to establish or resist intimacy with white men. Recall White's worries about Mary January, the woman who slandered her. It is impossible to know how White and January measured up beside each other. For example, both women may have had fair complexions, giving them relatively equal social advantages. Or one of them may have been dark-skinned and thus less privileged socially. But given the amount of time White spent with Ballard, which permitted their evident closeness, White cleverly maneuvered and made appeals to him, often mentioning the children as a means to gain his attention. Picquet found other ways to maneuver. In fact, she was compelled to do as much when Cook, her master, eventually made advances toward her.

Cook did so when he hired her out to work as a servant for a couple who ran the boardinghouse in which he resided. "One day Mr. Cook told me I must come to his room . . . and take care of him," Picquet told Mattison. Without offering details, it was understood that "take care of him" meant more than attending to Mr. Cook's feigned illness. He wanted to have sex with her.

Picquet shared her suspicions with the mistress of the house, who conspired to help Picquet, now fourteen years old, avoid Mr. Cook. When he called for Picquet, the mistress sent one of Lucy's sons, who also worked in the house. Upon seeing this child, Cook demanded that Picquet be sent to him instead. She went but only during the daylight and thus managed to avoid his advances.[40] Aware of Picquet's tactics, Cook reminded her that she "belonged" to him. He then whipped her. "Around your shoulders, or how?," Mattison asked. Picquet replied that he had whipped her around her shoulders. She noted that at the time she was wearing a "very thin" and "low-neck'd dress."[41]

Cook grew desperate. After a night of drinking with male friends, he offered to give her "a whole handful of half-dollars" if she promised to visit him later. Though Mattison never admitted as much, because to do so would reveal that some enslaved African American women and girls did consent to sexual relations with their masters in exchange for something, in this case, money, Picquet agreed to do so. She wanted to use the money to purchase some muslin cloth to make a dress.[42] This was the dress she wanted to retrieve after she was sold to Williams in Mobile. But after she failed to come to his room as promised, Cook beat her once more.[43]

Picquet's troubles in Mobile with Mr. Cook ended when a sheriff apprehended him on behalf of his creditors. Picquet, her mother, her brother, John, who was now two months old, and Cook's other slaves were put up for sale. They had been in Mobile not even a year. It was at the auction facility that Williams saw Picquet and the other bondspeople that Cook brought from Georgia. The soon-to-be lieutenant governor of Texas bought her mother. He also purchased her little brother and three others, including a male carriage driver who later became her mother's husband.[44] Interestingly, some of Lucy's siblings, who were evidently free people, purchased and freed Lucy.[45]

What happens next reveals the frequency with which white men acknowledged black children, even those who were owned by other white men—something that was not uncommon given the proximity of many enslaved women to their master's white male associates and friends. Two white men with whom Lucy had had her children arrived to purchase two of them. "Mr. Moore bought his, and Mr. Hale bought his," Picquet recalled.[46] In addition, a man who owned two of Lucy's sisters purchased her two remaining children. It is worth noting that one of her sisters had been taught to read and write, something of which Picquet was aware and unafraid to mention, although, again, Mattison, made little of the fact. Lucy's sister was even allowed to "learn music" before her death, upon which her master made the other sister his sexual companion. His capacity to care at the same time that he exploited his female slaves was elsewhere evident in his traveling to Mobile with Lucy's relatives, who might have been raped or resold into slavery themselves. While his own interests were uppermost in his mind, in accompanying them he provided protection against serious risks.

Picquet herself was purchased by her final owner, the newly divorced John Williams. As she and Williams walked away, Picquet's mother cried and prayed aloud to "the Lord" to go "with her only daughter."[47] Feeling helpless to calm her mother, Picquet left with Williams. She was just fourteen.

During her time in New Orleans Williams exploited Picquet sexually but also tormented her through his possessiveness. He sometimes accused her of wanting to be with others when white men appeared to make advances to her.[48] Many attempted to sweet-talk African American women and girls into being their partners, even if they were already "spoken for." For example, one 1820 advertisement in a Natchez newspaper asked for the return of a sixteen-year-old girl of mixed race named Octavia who was wearing a light calico frock and a red-striped handkerchief on her head when she disappeared. Her owner, a Kentucky man, promised $10 to anyone who could help him find her. He seemed equally interested in the person who "seduced her away," and warned that if he could prove that this happened, the responsible person would be "brought to justice."[49]

Williams evidently thought Picquet would be open to such an overture. He grew so suspicious that Picquet began to pray that he would die. There was irony in this, for she had learned how to pray from her former mistress in Georgia. Mrs. Cook read the Bible to her and other slaves. Even following the 1831 Nat Turner rebellion, which was the impetus for many prohibitions on enslaved people, including restrictions on independent religious gatherings, the prevailing racial ideology of the day regarded people of African descent as being unintelligent. This belief led some whites, perhaps including Mrs. Cook, to conclude that the enslaved would not internalize what they heard. There may have been another motive, social control. Many Bible verses instruct readers and listeners to accept their lot in life without protest or resistance because their reward will come in the next life. Mrs. Cook almost certainly picked such verses, although Picquet appropriated biblical instruction for her own purposes. She learned that if she prayed the beatings she received from her master would not hurt so badly.[50]

It is worth noting in reading Biblical verses, Mrs. Cook shared something else that stayed with Picquet: the sinfulness of adultery. Her mistress pointed to Lucy, the blue-eyed bondswoman, as an example of an adulteress, although she never revealed white men's role in Lucy having four children. Mrs. Cook's self-righteousness suggests again the degree to which white women helped maintain the racial hierarchy in the Old South, oppressing African Americans as did men.

Revealing the extent to which she had internalized what she learned about adultery from the Bible, Picquet regarded her relations with Williams as living in sin. On the day he died, she dressed up and went to church. Doing so allowed her publicly to express her independence and also to make amends for behavior that, although coerced, she nonetheless regarded as immoral.

She headed to a Methodist chapel where a minister who had known of her situation presided. At one point, he referred to Williams as "her husband." Evidently even he acknowledged that an enslaved woman had access to some of the privileges of married white women, revealing the complexities of race and class in New Orleans. Even Southern whites struggled to describe the "favor" of certain enslaved women and girls. Picquet, however, was more open to acknowledging the truth about her situation. "He wan't my husband," she said to herself then, and later to Mattison.[51] She was right. While she had exchanged subsistence for sex, given Louisiana's miscegenation laws, Williams could not give her the full legal protection of matrimony, a fact borne out shortly after his death when his brother arrived. He ordered Picquet out of the house in which they had lived, saying he would not pay the rent.

While she pondered her options, Picquet longed to see her mother, who she had heard from just once in the six years she had been with Williams. In fact, Williams read the one letter from her mother, who was still owned by the Texas lieutenant governor. In the letter, her mother requested sugar and tea.[52] Aware of her daughter's living situation, she had evidently decided that Picquet could provide such things. That she asked for minor luxuries possibly reflected her awareness, too, that certain goods were "rewards" for female slaves who engaged, willingly or not, in relations with white men. In asking for tea, Picquet's mother also disturbed stereotypes. While tea in the Western world was originally a fashionable drink associated with the highly cultured, it eventually became an item of mass consumption in Britain and America.[53] By the nineteenth century, the elite championed it to decrease alcohol consumption, which was becoming an urban problem.[54] Tea therefore continued to be associated with respectability, a quality not typically associated with African American women. Still, this Old World indulgence and ritual allowed an aging, once desirable bondswoman to connect to another kind of life, one that she might have felt she deserved. From a plantation in Texas, she thirsted for a small luxury. "She could always get it in Georgia, if she had to take in workin' and do it at night," Picquet said, before expressing her regret that she was not able to fulfill her mother's request.. "I had no money," she stated. "I could not send her anything."[55]

We may wonder why Picquet did not do as her mother had. Why did she not take in laundry or sewing as a means of earning money? Perhaps because she and Williams had established some sort of rapport that Picquet had helped foster. She was almost certainly wary of any undertaking that might give independence. Although her passiveness can be criticized, she acted strategically because she did not want to upset him. She was probably not alone in having done this. Sella Martin, a former bondsman from North Carolina, recalled that his mother "had a separate cabin set up" for herself on her master's estate, which was "very rare." He added that his mother's duties "around the house were merely nominal."[56]

As was the case with Picquet, we may wonder whether the circumstances of Martin's mother's life were also due to a level of intimacy between her and her master. Martin's mother had a separate cabin in which she lived, and her work duties were light. Neither would have been forthcoming had she displeased him. These visible privileges were related to something occurring behind closed doors. Whatever one thinks of someone who bartered her body in return for privileged treatment, the critical point is that she received something in return, and those around her recognized as much. Martin's son indeed carried the memory of it for the rest of his life.

Martin's mother had to give up something to receive favor, but her owner did, too. That the agreement was manifestly unequal—Martin's mother must have offered much more than she received in return—does not alter the fact that she was a participant in a bargain and that the bargain itself was evidence that white supremacy was not absolute. Something similar happened with Picquet, who nonetheless prayed that her master would die.

Williams indeed grew ill.[57] But she did not leave him. An unarticulated agreement between them resulted in enough trust that enabled her to endure her situation and to enhance his as well. After all, he was a divorced father of three sons. He acquired someone to look after him and his children, and she acquired things—a home, meals, and clothing—that made her life more bearable. In fact, had she been with her second master, Cook, longer, a similar agreement might have been reached. She had already demonstrated her ability to bargain concerning that floral muslin dress. She agreed to have sex with him in exchange for money, although she did not keep her end of the deal.

In Williams's case, it appears she offered her body but also her companionship and labor until he died. That she did not run away with her

children, all of whom, like her, could have "passed," suggests that something kept her with him, probably security. It may have been inertia.
Possibly, too, she resigned herself to suffering. We do not know every
detail of her life, but their relationship was surely typical of many others in their day. Even for many white wives, marriage and subservience
to their husbands was a fate to be endured rather than enjoyed, one to
which they submitted because the alternative—financial insecurity and
all that went with spinsterhood—was worse. Such black-white intimacies and the inconsistencies they revealed were visible to those close to
them who could see the benefits and costs incurred, among them, Helene
Hopkins, a "colored" New Orleans laundress who befriended Picquet.
"She was very kind to me, and used to give me victuals when I did not
know where to get it," said Picquet. Knowing that Picquet's security had
ended with Williams's death, Hopkins told her to leave for Cincinnati
after his brother announced that "by rights," she "belonged to him."[58] At
Hopkins's urging, Picquet left New Orleans, curiously with funds provided by her former master's brother.

Suggesting that an unrecorded agreement existed between her and
Williams, his brother sold the furniture he had given her to a secondhand
store and gave her the proceeds to enable her to leave the South.[59] We
may wonder how she secured the favor of her deceased master's brother.
Quite possibly her faithfulness to Williams elicited his sympathy and
support. Moreover, in helping her and her children he was respecting his
brother's wishes.

After receiving the proceeds from the sale of her owner's furniture,
and following Hopkins's advice, Picquet headed to Cincinnati. She went
there rather than to New York as her master had instructed because she
knew that people she had known in Georgia as a child lived there. Like
Avenia White and countless other women in their circumstances, Picquet realized it was not enough simply to be free. In order to exploit her
life as a free woman, she needed assistance, especially because she no
longer had a male head of household.

Fortunately, by the time Picquet reached Cincinnati the city's black
community had formed several benevolent associations to help new
arrivals, unmarried mothers included. In 1848 fifty African American
women of the city formed the Female American Association to care
for invalid and sick people of color.[60] A year later, the state's legislature
repealed many of the city's black codes.[61] A law was passed in 1849 allowing the opening of black schools, and black Cincinnatians quickly did
so.[62] Picquet's four-year-old daughter, Elizabeth, her only surviving

child—shortly after her arrival, her baby boy died—attended such a school even though racism remained endemic in Cincinnati, as it did throughout the country.

Racism did not prevent African Americans from unleashing their own brand of race-based resentment on each other, adding to the complexities of race and class relations in antebellum America. Cincinnati was a city in which mixed-race people had certain advantages, just as they had in the South. Many advantages turned on skin complexion. In keeping with contemporary views of race and the caste hierarchy of the African American community, people of mixed race tended to marry other people of mixed race, a practice that continued well into the twentieth century. If they married other blacks, it was usually a dark-skinned man marrying a fair-skinned woman.[63] This was the case despite their willingness to assist other African Americans, including their darker-skinned brethren, in the face of outside threats that they themselves confronted. Picquet herself was hyperalert to such things. She met and married Henry Picquet, a man of mixed race from Augusta, giving her the surname by which she is remembered.[64]

Indicative of such marriage patterns by individuals of mixed race is an 1853 letter to the American Colonization Society, which helped free blacks emigrate to Africa as an alternative to enduring racism in the United States:

> I am a colored man with one fourth of African blood, and my wife is about the same. I move from the state of [Tennessee], in the year 1824. to the city of Cincinnati and live there for about ten years and moved one hundred miles north in mercer county [four] years, since then I moved to [Shelby] county where I now reside at present[.] [W]e have six children four sons and two daughters my children live . . . in Cincinnati and are oppose to goin to Liberia and I am sorry for it.[65]

The author of this letter was of mixed race and had married a woman of similar ancestry. Like other African Americans, he had experienced enough white hostility to consider leaving the country. Equally significant, no matter the level of racism he encountered, like Picquet, he possibly exhibited his own racial prejudice by marrying a mixed-race rather than a dark-skinned woman. Picquet's husband might have felt the same about marrying her, and her sensitivity to complexion suggests that she did, too. Their fair skin was not the only thing they had in common. Henry was also the product of a black-white union that resulted in enslaved women and children receiving favor. Indeed, Henry's father was a white Frenchman. His mother, a dark-skinned woman, had been his father's enslaved companion. But after the latter's marriage to a white woman, Henry, his mother, and her four siblings were freed and sent to Cincinnati.[66] Though free, Henry subsequently returned to the South and married a slave woman. There he watched her become the mistress of a white man, this one from Macon, Georgia. Henry's father then helped him purchase his daughter from his wife's new owner. Henry went on to raise the child. Said Picquet, he worked all day "and then [worried with] the child all night."[67]

Henry's child was not as fair as Picquet or her young Elizabeth. Again revealing her hyperawareness of skin complexion was her response to Mattison's inquiry concerning Elizabeth's appearance. He asked whether she appeared as "white" as Picquet. Picquet replied, "Oh yes; and a great deal whiter."[68] She also stated that Henry's child was "the darkest one in the house." But wishing to emphasize her white ancestry, she noted, too, that her hair was "only little bit wavy."[69]

Given her attitude concerning skin color, it is reasonable to wonder whether Picquet herself would have been less compassionate—as was the case with some fair-skinned African Americans in the South who enslaved other African Americans—had she not suffered in the manner that she had.[70] In other words, it is reasonable to ask, what would Picquet have been like if she had possessed all the advantages of some women of mixed race?

She had once resided in New Orleans, with its three-tiered social order, whites, free people of color, or *libres*, and slaves. A free person of color's status rested not just on her legal status, but on her skin. Picquet herself certainly thought that fair-skinned African Americans were of a higher status than those who were "colored" like her friend Helene Hopkins, even if the latter were free. Yet, despite having bought into the caste culture that placed a premium on "whiteness," she and Hopkins bonded like other African American women in New Orleans and elsewhere who forged a kinship networks in and outside plantation communities.[71] However, the bond between these two across complexion and possibly class lines may have been less likely to have formed had Picquet not been in dire straits following Williams's death.

But fair-skinned women like Picquet still had a unique status, no matter their suffering, because they intrigued others. The caricature of the tragic mulatto appeared in numerous mid-nineteenth-century imagined works, some produced for stage. Some such works were midcentury fiction, including antebellum German "urban mystery" novels, which were set in major cities.[72] These urban mysteries evidently filled a gap left by midcentury American novels, which generally focused on rural and frontier regions. Their basic plot was to present the urban space as something recognizably sinister. But this space also revealed the dramatic impact of the New World generally and urban life specifically on German immigrants who shared with other whites a fascination with women of mixed race.[73] For example, one serialized German novel in a New Orleans newspaper described the freed offspring of a white planter and his "favorite" slave:

> The dazzling whiteness of her face would lead a superficial observer to conclude that she was of white ancestry, a fact that a finer connoisseur would doubt on seeing the dark cloudiness of her fingernails and the mother-of-pearl coloration at the corners of her eyes. And in fact Lucy Wilson—for that was the name of this beautiful woman—is the daughter of a planter on the Grand Bayou Caillon, a few miles from Lake Quitman.[74]

Literary descriptions of women of mixed race were not restricted to German writers. In an 1856 novel, Captain Mayne Reid, a British writer, presented the tragic mulatta archetype in a character being chased by a young Englishman who was attracted to "her golden tresses."[75] In noting her physical features, Reid, as did others in the United States and Europe, objectified her. Though aware of such objectification, real-life women like Picquet recognized the advantages it brought. In order fully to understand Picquet's personality in this regard and generally, it is necessary to know more about her life after she fled to Cincinnati.

She and her husband initially lived on Third Street, near Race Street, in the Fourth Ward, which by midcentury encompassed the city's busy central waterfront district. This area had the second highest concentration of people of mixed race in Cincinnati, behind only Bucktown, the heart of the black business community. Picquet and Henry shared their home with her daughter, Elizabeth, and his daughter, Harriet. Sarah, another daughter, was born in 1852 and Thomas, a son, in 1856.

While African Americans made inroads as businesspeople in Cincinnati—for example, the black-owned Iron Chest Company possessed three brick buildings leased to whites—most, like the Picquets, were confined to menial positions. Even though those of mixed race sometimes had better paying and skilled work, this was not always the case. Picquet worked as a laundress and her husband worked as a janitor in the Carlisle Building on Fourth and Walnut Streets, two blocks east and one block north of their home.[76] Pervasive racism had an impact on the quality of the Picquets' lives, although they were better positioned than many African Americans in Cincinnati, some of whom lived in make-shift homes.[77]

Picquet was aware of the suffering of her brethren and said she worked hard to lessen it, in keeping with her religious beliefs. She became a member of Cincinnati's Zion Baptist Church, a fact of which she was proud. As she told Mattison, her church did not welcome slaveholders, as did some others. In fact, her pastor once announced from the pulpit that slave catchers were in the area looking for a runaway named Mary White. As it turned out, Picquet and her husband had taken in White, who was a "real genteel" woman. Almost gossipy, because she herself was deeply familiar with the range of lifestyles for women in her condition, Picquet told Mattison that White "tried to make me believe she was free." Picquet, who had lived in New Orleans and had seen many like her, knew otherwise; White only went out on Sunday evenings, suggesting that she was hiding from someone or something. With the assistance of a local Quaker, the Picquets disguised White and sent her on to Canada. Others in White's circumstance also found refuge in their home. Though she did not state how many she assisted, Picquet said she helped as many as she could.[78]

Seeing such escapes and reflecting on her freedom made Picquet long even more for her mother. In 1859, more than a decade after her arrival in Cincinnati, she decided to find her. She did so through a local man who sent his shirts to her for washing. This man had announced that he was going to Texas. Picquet and her husband discovered that he knew Albert Horton, her mother's master. With his assistance, Picquet sent a letter to her mother, Elizabeth. She received a reply in a letter on "tough blue paper" within three weeks.[79] She learned that her mother still lived on Horton's Sycamore Grove Plantation in Wharton County, Texas.[80] Horton almost surely wrote the letter, as little space was wasted before suggesting that Elizabeth could be purchased. He announced that she could either be bought for $1,000 or swapped for another woman—surely a younger woman who could provide faster service than the aging Elizabeth, who also sent love via Horton from Picquet's brother, John, now a boy of fifteen, who could also be purchased for $1,500. Elizabeth also sent "100 kisses" to Picquet's own son, Thomas.[81]

Not even a week after this letter arrived, another was sent. The pur-chase prices for Elizabeth and John were repeated. Within three months, another letter arrived, this one signed by Horton. He stated that Elizabeth was "as fine a washer, cook and ironer as there is in the United States," and though she was "getting old," he insisted on the amount requested since she carried "her age well." He included a daguerreotype of her and John, who were apparently well dressed.[82]

Picquet set out to purchase her mother. The rest of her memoir describes her attempts in 1860 to raise the funds to do so, in the process describing her unassuming life as a laundress in Cincinnati. The allure and mystique of women of mixed race concealed the ordinariness of many of their lives. However, she was a well-positioned person of mixed race and could move through space in ways denied to most other African Americans, especially the enslaved. She traveled first throughout Ohio, finding subscribers, often in churches. Her efforts were aided by a letter of support from Levi Coffin, who, as did Mattison, attested to her good character.[83]

As she traveled, her past caught up with her twice in surprising ways. On a train from Xenia to Springfield, Ohio, she met a man who asked her, "Were you ever in Mobile?" This traveler remembered her from the days when she was hired out in that city.[84] Picquet subsequently traveled east, to Brooklyn. There another man took notice of her as she sat on a bus. When she got off, he walked with her for a while and finally also asked whether she had ever lived in Mobile. To her surprise, he turned out to be her first love, whom she had not seen since their parting nearly twenty years earlier.[85] He was now the married father of two children and "passing" as white. Excited to share details about his new life, he asked her to wait in a park so as to not provoke the suspicions of his wife. He returned with his two children. One of them, a boy, was darker than the other. "That one has the stain on it," Picquet said of this child, once more revealing her awareness of her unique place in America's racial hierarchy as had, obviously, her old love. In marrying a white woman, he demonstrated a degree of freedom impossible for their darker-skinned brethren. She and her old love shared a laugh and then parted again.

Though she faced difficulties with her fund-raising efforts, Picquet was eventually able to purchase her mother. She publicly thanked her supporters in a letter published in the *Cincinnati Daily Gazette* on October 13, 1860.[86] However, Picquet's gratitude hid the sorrow she also felt. Horton had decided he wanted her brother John to run one of his plantations.[87]

The Civil War began the following year. Henry Picquet became a private in the 42nd United States Colored Regiment.[88] Meanwhile, African

Americans continued to migrate to Cincinnati, although in fewer numbers. Black women continued to outnumber black men, though not by much: 1,900 to 1,831 according to the 1860 census.[89] Fearing that the war might cause these numbers to rise, in 1862 the *Cincinnati Enquirer*, a newspaper with Democratic leanings, printed a sentiment with which many white Cincinnatians probably agreed: "Hundreds of thousands, if not millions of slaves . . . will come North and West and will either be competitors with our white mechanics and laborers, degrading them by competition, or they will have to be supported as paupers and criminals at the public expense."[90]

Such escalating racial tension and an injury that Henry received during the war probably contributed to the Picquets' leaving Cincinnati. In 1865 he received a medical discharge, temporarily forcing his wife to become the sole supporter of the household. Two years later, they moved to New Richmond, Ohio, a river town about twenty miles southeast of Cincinnati, a bastion for white liberals from New England, New York, and Pennsylvania and seemingly a more hospitable place for people of color.[91]

Like many others in New Richmond, whose economy relied on river commerce, Henry went to work on a steamboat. After several unsuccessful attempts to claim his service pension, he began receiving $6 per month in 1885.[92] Following his death in 1889, Picquet received a widow's pension of $12 a month. At the time of her death five years later, she owned her home in New Richmond.[93]

Though she had helped support her family as a laundress, even purchasing her mother from slavery with a memoir she participated in producing, Picquet is remembered most for having once been a white's man sexual partner or an exotic creature. Indeed, the words "Louisa Picquet, The Octoroon," appeared on the cover of her memoir, displaying her as a spectacle rather than a woman who served as proof of the ways in which the distribution of power between antebellum whites and blacks was in constant negotiation. This dynamic had deep implications for certain enslaved women who had more influence over their future than others because of their intimate ties to white men. Williams and his brother could have sold her and her children. Neither man did, revealing again the contradictions between what men of their day said and what they actually did. They thus emerge as complex characters, like many people of color, among them women like Picquet, who in buying into white normative standards that favorably positioned her acted to enhance her own status. Because of the closeness she experienced with white men, she, like other women in her situation, saw the gaps in the authority of such men, creating space for her to achieve a degree of security if not autonomy.[94]

We have no proof that women like her reflected on their experiences with the same kind of energy as modern researchers. Most of them probably did what was needed to survive without prolonged introspection. Some may have had more detachment. But whether they did or not, all maneuvered strategically, appropriating specific tactics for their own purposes, sometimes at their oppressor's invitation. While they did not overturn the racial and gender ideologies that prevented them from fully blossoming as citizens of a still young nation, they chipped away at them, drawing on support from others who shared their condition but also on the social capital accumulated from their proximity to white men.

Picquet's calculated complacency while waiting for her master to die is a particularly noteworthy episode because it displays the confidence born from seeing up close the inconsistencies in human beings, white men in particular. This confidence is also plainly visible in Eliza Potter, the hairdresser of mixed race whose own memoir was published two years before Picquet's. Upon being accused once of aiding a fugitive boy and asked to accompany authorities to a Kentucky jail, Potter refused until she could find a caretaker for her child.[95] After being in a Covington jail for three days and a Louisville one for three months, Potter convinced a judge she had committed no wrong. We might ask why she was pardoned when many were not. Her confidence, born partly from her status as a free woman of mixed race—she was born in the North, not the South—was similar to that of Picquet. Her familiarity with white behavior owing to her profession and extensive travels gave her the confidence to face down the Kentucky authorities despite the obvious perils to her.

As if to emphasize the hydra-headed monster of racism that led even African Americans to discriminate against other African Americans, if given the chance, Potter pointed to a Cincinnati "black" woman who became a slaveholder in New Orleans. According to Potter, this woman was "the most tyrannical, overbearing, cruel task-mistress that ever existed; so you can see color makes no difference . . . those who have been oppressed themselves, are the sorest oppressors. . . . [I]f they can get mulattoes for slaves . . . the first word is 'my nigger.'"[96] Potter also recalled a Pennsylvania man of high standing who reportedly went South to purchase a woman of color as a "housekeeper." Upon becoming his "mistress," the woman "became hard to please."[97] In fact, the woman once whipped the servant's back "almost to pieces." Though we do not know whether she was light- or dark-skinned, this woman is yet another example of how proximity to white men seemed to produce assertiveness, even callousness, in some African American women and girls. Such women were well aware of strategies of survival that could bring them benefits even as they exacted costs on others.[98]

It is quite possible that Mary Chesnut's report of seeing an enslaved mixed-race girl ogle men from the selling block was accurate and not the result of Chesnut's own prejudices. The girl may also have been deliberately trying to make the best of a wretched situation. What appeared to be ogling may have been an effort to size up prospective buyers.[99] She may well have been doing all in her power to find the best master, as would most if not all women and girls in her predicament.

Potter described the attempted sale of another woman of mixed race who was "put up to the highest bidder." This woman reportedly told the man who was bidding on her that she would "never serve him." When he threatened her, she added that "she did not like his looks, and that she had been raised by a lady, and always led a virtuous life." The woman was so enraged that her sale was "put off till the next day." She was eventually sold to a family with two girls who reportedly treated her well and eventually freed her. They even asked a friend of their family to relocate her to Cincinnati.[100]

The woman who talked backed to her prospective buyer, like Avenia White, Louisa Picquet, Lucile Tucker, and many others discussed thus far, had fostered enough familiarity with whites, white men in particular, that she was emboldened to speak confidently, even assertively. Although regarded as promiscuous, she emphatically stated that she was not. When their virtue was challenged, White and Picquet had acted similarly. White insisted she had acted uprightly when a Cincinnati woman slandered her. Picquet sought solace and forgiveness in a church to make amends for being in a sexual relationship that she regarded as sinful. These women's experiences expand our understanding of black-white unions and the personalities of the women coerced into them, as well as the inconsistent nature of race and class relations in and outside America in urban and rural spaces. The next chapter continues to explore such unions by focusing on the children born from them.

4 / "Has anyone heard from Willis?": The Progenies' Crossing

As a new century approached, Charles Osborne Townsend, an African American silver miner and sometime barber living in the hills of Georgetown, Colorado, sat down to write a letter.[1] The recipient was his brother Thomas, a lawyer who resided in Huntsville, Alabama, a place in which both men had once been enslaved. Their white father had owned the land on which they lived and had claimed them as his own. Though enslaved, Osborne, as he often called himself, as well as his siblings occupied an ambiguous space. It was one in which they enjoyed some of the benefits and anxieties of freedom.[2] Even whites around them detected that their young bodies were testing the waters of autonomy in ways that most African Americans would not do until the postbellum period.[3] As Osborne recalled in his letter to Thomas, before the war one of their siblings had jumped over a fence onto the land of "Mr. and Mrs. Tate," their white neighbors.[4] Mr. Tate came running after this child to scold him. The sibling jumped back over the fence to escape Mr. Tate's wrath. The commotion got so out of hand that Mrs. Tate intervened. The child "hollered so that ole Mrs Tate made old Mr Tate leave [them] alone," Osborne wrote, reflecting on the incident.

Mrs. Tate's response might have been an outcome of a charitable disposition. Or it might have stemmed from her ability to see that the child was no ordinary slave. Perhaps he resembled his father. Perhaps she had seen him get away with things other slaves could not. Because he looked mixed-race, it probably did not take much for her to put two and two together. This was the child of Samuel Townsend, who, judging

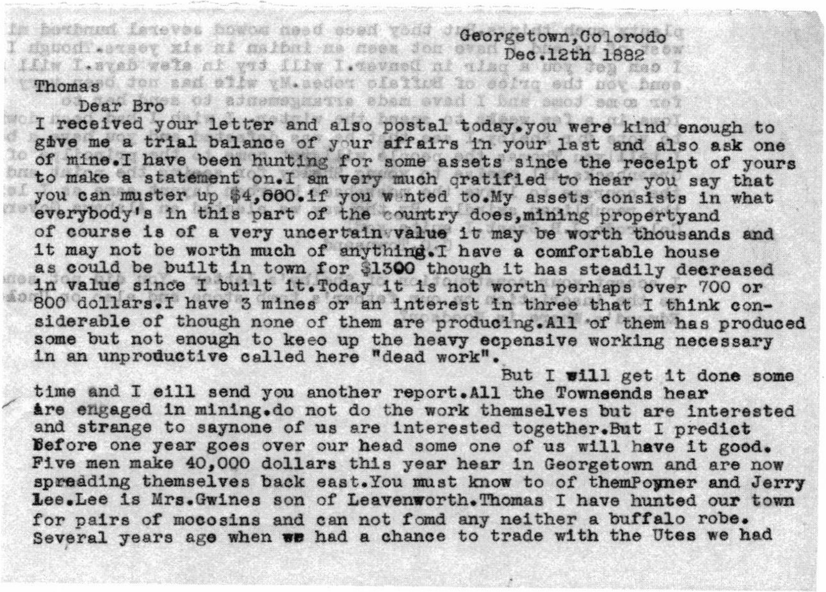

Georgetown,Colorodo
Dec.12th 1882
Thomas
Dear Bro
I received your letter and also postal today.you were kind enough to
give me a trial balance of your affairs in your last and also ask one
of mine.I have been hunting for some assets since the receipt of yours
to make a statement on.I am very much gratified to hear you say that
you can muster up $4,000.if you wanted to.My assets consists in what
everybody's in this part of the country does,mining propertyand
of course is of a very uncertain value it may be worth thousands and
it may not be worth much of anything.I have a comfortable house
as could be built in town for $1300 though it has steadily decreased
in value since I built it.Today it is not worth perhaps over 700 or
800 dollars.I have 3 mines or an interest in three that I think considerable of though none of them are producing.All of them has produced
some but not enough to keep up the heavy expensive working necessary
in an unproductive called here "dead work".
                              But I will get it done some
time and I will send you another report.All the Townsends hear
Are engaged in mining.do not do the work themselves but are interested
and strange to saynone of us are interested together.But I predict
Before one year goes over our head some one of us will have it good.
Five men make 40,000 dollars this year hear in Georgetown and are now
spreading themselves back east.You must know to of themPoymer and Jerry
Lee.Lee is Mrs.Gwines son of Leavenworth.Thomas I have hunted our town
for pairs of mocosins and can not fomd any neither a buffalo robe.
Several years ago when we had a chance to trade with the Utes we had

FIGURE 11. Page 1 of the December 12, 1882, letter that Charles Osbourne
Townsend, a Colorado barber and sometime miner, wrote to his brother
Thomas Townsend, a Huntsville teacher and farmer turned lawyer. MSS 252,
Box 252.054, Folder 01, Septimus Douglas Cabaniss Papers, Special Collec-
tions, Stanley Hoole Library, University of Alabama.

by his subsequent actions, made clear his concern for his children. There
were nine in all, from five enslaved women who were hardly fancy girls
but rather more ordinary slaves. They demonstrate the scope of Southern white men's desire. These women were not the ones for whom men
posted advertisements or traveled to port cities in search of brand-name
bedmates. Instead, men such as Samuel Townsend turned to women
already on their plantations or those of business associates, male relatives, and friends. Some were dark-skinned women. Still, among them
were individuals Southern white men would later free.

In addition to Osborne and Thomas, Samuel Townsend manumitted Wesley, Willis, Parthenia, Caroline, Bradford, Susanna, and Milcha. He also freed Elvira, his housekeeper, who was Thomas's half
sister. Before his death in 1856, Townsend not only sought to free
these children; he also sought to leave them the bulk of the proceeds
from the sale of his estate. That year Townsend called on Septimus

plenty such things.But they hece been mowed several hundred miles South
west of us and I have not seen an indian in six years.Though I think
I can get you a pair in Denver.I will try in afew days.I will also
send you the price of Buffalo robes.My wife has not been very well
for some tome and I have made arrangements to send her to
Iowa in a few weeks to spend the winter. I wish I had been down there
to vote for Shelby.I see that he was defeated and you have a bourbon.
I tell you Thomas the people will yet come to the princilpe of the
Greenbacks.All praise to young Shelby for seeing the point and having
the courage to leave the mossaback bourbon layout same as I left
the republican swindle .By the way we elected an Alabama Governor of
Colorodo,J.B.Grant.I quite you.
                    C.O.Townsend

  I accept your construction of Shelby's letter .You did not send
me the inscription on our father's tomb stone and also on Uncle
Edmond's.Where is Woodson?

FIGURE 12. Page 2 of the December 12, 1882, letter from Charles Osbourne
Townsend to his brother Thomas Townsend. These half brothers are descen-
dants of Samuel Townsend. MSS 252, Box 252.054, Folder 01, Septimus
Cabaniss Papers, Special Collections, Stanley Hoole Library, University of
Alabama

Cabaniss, a Huntsville lawyer, to revise an earlier drafted will,
expressing this wish.[5] At the time Townsend's property was worth
approximately $200,000.[6]

As in previously discussed cases, a Southern white man was a hidden
actor in the Townsends' attempts to survive the rigors and challenges of
life as black people in the years surrounding the Civil War. From the looks
of it, Samuel Townsend established a level of intimacy between himself and
some of his bondspeople that others discerned. Such intimacy contributed
to these individuals' eventual manumission, but prior to that it gave them
the boldness to do things other enslaved people would have been more
hesitant about doing, like trespassing on a white neighbor's land. The ways
in which such children and others were well positioned to do such things is
the subject of this chapter. I earlier examined a portrait of the complicated,
sometimes contradictory Southern men who bedded and established intimate relationships with African American women, who themselves were
often equally complicated, but the voices of the children born from such
relationships were impossible to hear. The Townsend siblings and other
children discussed in this chapter are valuable in this regard. They help us
hear what Harvey or Elizabeth, the children mentioned in the postscript of
Avenia White's letters to her former master, or Elizabeth, the daughter of
freedwoman Louisa Picquet and her former master John Williams, might
have said had they written a letter that survived.

There was, however, one crucial difference between the Townsends and some of the subjects discussed earlier. The former were materially much better off. Nevertheless, the circumstances of their lives as bondspeople and freedpeople mirrored those of other mixed-race children. Despite their more comfortable material situations, they endured racial discrimination not unlike that experienced by the women and children discussed in the two previous chapters. Likewise, they endured because they looked to others, including one another, for strength. That they did so demonstrates that kinship was vital for even the best-positioned African Americans in order to survive white hostility.[7]

As was also true of the subjects of the two previous chapters, Cincinnati figures into the Townsends' lives, though more peripherally. As their father's lawyer attempted to settle matters pertaining to their inheritance, one brother initially settled in Athens, Ohio, a little over 150 miles east of Cincinnati. Here he oversaw his siblings' eventual settlement in Xenia, about 55 miles northeast. There some attended nearby Wilberforce University, at that time just a boarding school. After the Civil War began, the school closed and the Townsends scattered to places as diverse as Kansas, Colorado, Mexico, and Mississippi. Some returned to Huntsville. But one brother went to Cincinnati, where he worked as a waiter on a steamboat.

While rebuilding their lives as freedpeople, the Townsends remained in touch. In fact, the several dozen surviving letters they sent either to one another or to whites interested in their affairs serve as proof that they were the children of a white man that one called "father."[8] Samuel Townsend invested himself emotionally and financially in the lives of these children, aiding their efforts to improve their condition. That he did again reveals the complexities of black-white intimate encounters as well as race and class relations in America.

Like Rice Ballard, the slave trader–turned–planter, Samuel Townsend was from Virginia. And like Ballard, Townsend and his brother, Edmund, amassed considerable wealth in the Deep South as cotton planters. While Ballard's landholdings were spread primarily across Louisiana and Mississippi, Samuel Townsend's fortune, much of which apparently arrived as inheritance from a brother who died before him, was largely built on land in Huntsville, Alabama.[9]

Huntsville's beginnings can be traced to the arrival of Captain John Hunt, a Revolutionary War veteran, in the foothills of the Cumberland Mountains. In 1806 Hunt built a log cabin in this area, which was part of the Tennessee Valley. Five years later the land surrounding his dwelling became the nucleus of the city of Huntsville. In the early days, "improper

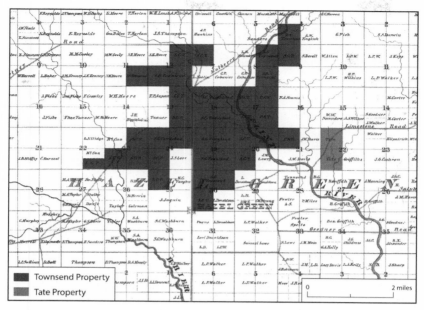

FIGURE 13. An 1875 map of Madison County, Alabama, revealing proximity of Samuel Townsend's land to the Tates'. Courtesy of Geographic Information Systems, City of Huntsville and Cartographic Research Laboratory, University of Alabama.

women," small farmers, card-playing hunters, and racehorse aficionados populated Madison County, where Huntsville sits. A local racetrack, set up beside an area hostel, drew the likes of Andrew Jackson, an admirer of the sport. By 1825 locals were shipping cotton, an increasingly lucrative crop in Madison County, to New Orleans, already a major commercial hub. Efforts were made to build a canal between Huntsville and New Orleans, but the project failed. Another canal was commenced a year later, this one successful. Huntsville then began its initial growth spurt.[10]

Farmers fleeing failing farms in upper South states soon arrived in the area. To them, the fertile land of Huntsville held great promise. That it did was reflected in the rising population of the town's main labor source: slaves. In 1816, some 4,200 slaves made up about a third of the 14,200 residents of Madison County. By 1850, 14,765 slaves comprised more than half of the county's total population of 26,451.[11]

Among those arriving in the 1820s were Samuel and Edmund Townsend, two brothers from Lunenburg County, Virginia.[12] The

Townsends initially settled in Hazel Green, Alabama, just outside of Huntsville. In 1829 and 1832, Samuel Townsend purchased land, totaling 305 acres, in Huntsville proper and continued over subsequent years to buy additional tracts, some as large as 600 acres. His property holdings increased following the 1852 death of Edmund, who had owned two plantations in Madison County and another in Jackson County, Alabama. By the time of his own death in 1856, Samuel owned eight plantations, seven in Madison County and one in Jackson, totaling some 7,560 acres.[13]

Unlike Rice Ballard, who, perhaps to distance himself from his slave-trading past, conformed to the planter's patriarchal image, Samuel Townsend never married. He seems to have sought out at least five enslaved women for companionship and sex. These women would appear to be of little consequence to his life were it not for the fact that we can see that something of huge import took place when Townsend ensured the financial future of ten enslaved children. He even freed three of the women. The other two died before his manumission orders were carried out.[14]

Had they not been identified as people of mixed race, the Townsend children might have been shielded from the widespread prejudice evident in the United States at the time of their father's death. Such prejudices were entangled in partisan politics by the time the century reached the halfway mark.[15] The resulting tension led to the 1854 birth of the Republican Party. Composed of moderate and conservative Whigs and radicals but largely influenced by former Democrats, the Republicans believed that an economy that paid men a wage was far better than one relying on slave labor.[16] The party protested the admission of Kansas and Nebraska as territories in which the slavery question was to be settled on the basis of popular sovereignty, possibly allowing for its further expansion.[17] Before he died Samuel Townsend probably watched such developments with anxiety. While his wealth had been built on slave labor, he had enslaved children whose financial futures he desired to provide for. Prior to his death in 1852, Edmund Townsend had tried to do the same.

Like Samuel, Edmund never married. Like Samuel, Edmund fathered enslaved children with his slave women, in his case, two daughters, Elizabeth and Virginia. Upon his death, Edmund left instructions to give his estate, worth approximately $500,000, to the two girls.[18] Though Edmund made arrangements to manumit Elizabeth and Virginia and took legal precautions before his death to ensure that they received their inheritance, a court voided his will and divided his estate among his white relatives. They then made Elizabeth and Virginia the joint property of

Samuel and John E. Townsend, another relative.[19] After watching this proceeding, Samuel had "a great dread of his children [also] becoming the slaves" of his relatives.[20] In 1854 he secured the services of Cabaniss, a Huntsville attorney. By the time of Townsend's death, Cabaniss had drafted not one but two wills to ensure that the children would be manumitted and inherit his wealth.

Edmund and Samuel Townsend were not unusual. Many other Southern men, particularly during the colonial era, made arrangements to leave property to their mixed-race offspring. This practice was particularly prevalent in states with large free people of color populations like Louisiana. Before the Louisiana Supreme Court outlawed such bequests in 1840, many Southern men made similar arrangements.[21] But Samuel Townsend's white relatives' opposition created so much turmoil that Cabaniss left his practice in 1858 to attend to Samuel's case full-time. Some of the white Townsends were almost certainly upset because, like many if not most white Americans at the time, they believed that Samuel's children were not entitled to such favor. In their view, the social capital they possessed on account of their whiteness would be jeopardized if these half-black children received their inheritance.

After a four-year battle, Cabaniss successfully blocked the white Townsends' claims, but his efforts to carry out Samuel's wishes were interrupted by the Civil War. In June 1861, a chancery court ruled that the children, who were now manumitted and living outside the state, could not make further claims on their father's property because they were residents of the United States, which the Confederacy regarded as a foreign country.[22]

After the war, Cabaniss spent five years paying Townsend's debts, suing his debtors, foreclosing mortgages, and, finally, liquidating the estate. During this period and well into the subsequent decades, he periodically disbursed funds to Townsend's offspring. While the estate was "significantly diminished by 1870," he was able to pay not only Townsend's children, who were called "first class" slaves in Townsend's will, but others, among them the children's surviving mothers, who constituted the "second class." By the time the estate was finally settled in 1896, the children had received $33,719.57, less than a quarter of the intended amount. Some died before "reaping the full benefit from their inheritance."[23]

Prior to Townsend's death and the provisions made for these former slaves, he lived on 1,700-acre property called the Home Plantation.[24] He was hardly alone. Sixty-three bondspeople resided with him, some probably his children. The Home Plantation was the center of Townsend's agricultural operations. There stood barns, tools, a blacksmith's shop, and a cotton gin, the latter two used by Townsend and his neighbors. Among the bondspeople who learned how to shoe horses and sharpen hoes on this property was Wesley, Townsend's eldest enslaved child.[25] Wesley's education in this regard was not unusual for fair-skinned African Americans in and outside slave societies. Color distinction prejudices in the United States typically privileged fair-skinned over dark-skinned blacks in learning skilled trades.[26] Blacksmithing was an especially important trade. Even as the nineteenth century became increasingly industrialized, a growing turnpike system carrying horse-drawn buggies and wagons still existed. Moreover, although railways were connecting urban areas by midcentury, travel in most cities and towns continued to rely heavily on horse-drawn transportation until the internal combustion engine arrived.[27] Finally, many of America's farms continued to rely on horses and mules into the twentieth century. If a man of color was hired as a blacksmith, he stood to do well.[28] Hence, although a slave, Wesley was well positioned on his white father's plantation, a place for which some of the Townsend siblings retained warm memories through their lives. This much can be gathered in the letters they and their relatives sent one another over the years. In one such letter, one of the Townsends of mixed race reflected nostalgically on their former days in the "old home."[29] "I often long for news of my old home and friends," this Townsend also said.[30] Like many white Southerners across time, although for different reasons, the Townsends longed for their old homes if not their old lives. The quieter pace of life in the country was appealing to another Townsend of mixed race, who recalled reminiscing on Sundays about "things that happened twenty years ago in the South."[31]

The affection Samuel Townsend displayed for his children and their mothers, half siblings, and other relatives was apparently such that some of them could fondly recall their lives in Huntsville. That his mixed-race descendants did so permits us again to see the degree to which antebellum Southern white men were hidden actors in the lives of enslaved women and their children, complicating race and class hierarchies. The resulting level of intimacy benefited the children and their mothers in considerable ways, as their manumission and inheritance demonstrates. While he was alive there were less significant everyday benefits, too, as Wesley's blacksmith training and Osborne's anecdote about trespassing on the Tates' property reveal. Townsend's affection and indulgence were not unique in the antebellum South. A visitor to a Hilton Head, South Carolina, plantation saw a group of "six straight-haired, bright-looking mulatto children" ravenously eating boiled sweet potatoes while sitting on the porch of a dwelling.[32] The old black man who fed them said these were his master's children.

It was recognized that mixed-race children happened. And the less powerful did not generally complain, at least not publicly. In fact, lawyers, judges, and others were complicit in Southern white men's sexual activities, at least those like Townsend who were capable of paying for their services.

Samuel Townsend seemed to have the respect of some of his neighbors but also some of the children he freed. In one of his several surviving letters, Osborne chastised his brother Thomas for what was probably an unintended oversight. "You did not send me the inscription on our father's tombstone and also on Uncle Edmonds [sic]," Osborne wrote.[33] Like some of the African American women discussed earlier, the Townsend children had a sense of entitlement because of their relationship to a white man whose regard for them was on display despite their ongoing oppression as enslaved people.

Given Townsend's affection for them, it is curious that he did not free his children prior to his death. A couple of possibilities may account for his delay. First, he was thrifty. Despite his wealth, Townsend lived simply. An inventory and appraisal of his home furnishings following his death revealed he made very inexpensive purchases.[34] Given the volatile economy characteristic of the early and mid-nineteenth century, he may have been concerned about the cost of having his offspring reside in another state. Then again, he may have wanted them nearby because he, like Ballard, desired companionship, although unlike Ballard, he did not have to worry about keeping his liaisons and progeny secret from his wife. Finally, Townsend almost certainly hesitated to relocate his children because he, like many other Southerners, did not believe the North was without its own problems.

Given the near-universal racism of nineteenth-century white American society, both South and North, Townsend probably concluded, quite reasonably, that his children were better off under his watchful eye and protection in Huntsville than they would be as freedpeople in an overwhelmingly hostile environment in the North. That calculus ended with his death, however, at which point remaining in the South became much more perilous for them—not to mention illegal if they were freed—than resettling in free territory. His apprehensions were warranted. As freedpeople they encountered the hardships and racism faced by millions of other African Americans after the Civil War.[35] The behavior of the

Freedmen's Bureau employees, the federal agency charged with aiding former bondspeople's transition to freed, casts particular light on this matter. They were among many whites that struggled over what to do about bodies no longer enslaved, but which were black, or at least were regarded as black.[36] One Freedmen's Bureau agent in Kansas, where some of the Townsends settled, described one of Townsend's daughters as "nearly white[.] [W]ould hardly be taken for an African away from" her relatives.[37] Here was an individual whose job implied sympathy toward blacks, yet who could not transcend the racial prejudices of the era. Townsend's daughter was "black" regardless of her complexion. That she did not appear "black" was not only disconcerting; it threatened the racial hierarchy.

More ominously, as Mary Niall Mitchell has observed, this "nearly white" child heralded what would follow slavery.[38] In these racially ambiguous bodies whites in the North and South perceived a future that would be vastly different from the past. African Americans would seek more of the privileges associated with freedom, privileges that had previously been largely monopolized by whites.[39]

Some whites were fascinated by the origins of such children, as demonstrated by the brisk sale of photographs of mixed-race children that white abolitionists used as antislavery propaganda before the Civil War. Abolitionists hoped that others might realize how immoral behavior in the South led to the birth of white-looking "black" children.[40] However, the photographs also revealed the public's ongoing fascination with biracial bodies, as was also evident in descriptions of mulattas in midcentury novels.

The Southern slave market benefited from the existence of biracial girls who, when older, could give birth to children of mixed race who, if female, could be in turn exploited. That they could underscores the special implications that reproduction had for African American women and girls of mixed race and the instability of race and class relations in the Old South.[41] Their ability to give birth to children who could be enslaved and create wealth but *also* serve as sexual partners and companions who exchanged sex for subsistence, education, and freedom for themselves and their children revealed the inconsistent, even contradictory nature of racial oppression in the South. Again, these children ultimately presaged slavery's demise. Biracial children pointed to the numerous black-white intimate encounters that compelled some Southern white men to refer to some of their bondspeople as "their children" and that compelled the latter to refer to these men as "fathers." Both disrupted long-held beliefs that blacks were inferior and not kin. This phenomenon figured into the complexities and contradictions of the peculiar institution of slavery. For example, the political ambitions of Cabaniss, the Townsends' lawyer, led him to serve in the Alabama legislature from 1861 to 1863. His role as a defender of slavery was at odds with his oversight of the Townsend case. But Cabaniss's willingness to fulfill his dead client's wishes was evident in his continuing work on behalf of the Townsends following the Civil War. In doing so, he joined a network of white men who shepherded certain enslaved bodies to freedom. As Bernie Jones has observed, white slaveholders left money to black sexual partners and children so frequently that Southern judges routinely affirmed such transfers and property, "especially when precedents under the common law could be easily used to do so."[42] In some instances, jurists responded favorably because they demonstrated their moral obligation to care for their black children as they did for their white ones. For example, the Hancock County, Georgia, planter David Dickson left his half-million-dollar estate to his half-black daughter with Julia Frances Dickson, an enslaved woman.[43] Although enslaved, Amanda America Dickson received an education and experienced a genteel upbringing while receiving her father's favor and even that of Dickson's mother. In fact, Amanda became known as the wealthiest black woman in the postbellum South when the Georgia Supreme Court upheld her father's will. So committed was she to her father that before he died she returned to live with him, bringing two children who were the product of her failed marriage to a white man.[44]

These quiet efforts to attend to mixed-race children's futures occurred alongside debates about the future of slavery. These debates involved some of the country's most influential politicians, some of whom were not only aware of biracial children's existence, but were consulted about their fates. In his search for the best place to settle the Townsend children, Cabaniss contacted men who, at first glance, appear unlikely to have any interest in the subject. He asked Stephen A. Douglas of Illinois whether settling them there would violate state law. Not only had Douglas, a pro-slavery politician, orchestrated the Compromise of 1850, which attempted unsuccessfully to settle the issue of slavery's expansion, he reignited debate on the topic four years later with the Kansas-Nebraska Act. He also initially backed the 1857 Dred Scott Supreme Court decision and went on to become the 1860 Democratic contender for the highest position in the land, president of the United States. Cabaniss also reached out to Clement Claiborne Clay Jr., Alabama Senator and distant relative of the Kentucky statesman Henry

Clay, who in turn sought the views of William Seward, a fervently anti-slavery New York senator. With these men's input, Cabaniss crafted a plan to resettle Townsend's children.

A year and a half after his client's death, Cabaniss sent W. D. Chadick, a white Huntsville minister, on a fact-finding trip. The mission: to locate a home for the children. While Liberia, the African settlement where many free people of color had been resettled, was considered, Chadick's destination was Ohio. Again, Levi Coffin, the abolitionist, was well aware of the Southern white men who brought their children with enslaved women north to be educated.[45] Coffin recalled the arrival of numerous "emancipated slaves . . . [who were] frequently brought to Cincinnati by their white fathers."[46] Some of the men Coffin met wanted their offspring to live in Ohio because they believed they could lead happier and more prosperous lives there. Others clearly sought only to relieve themselves of social embarrassment or financial burden and were uninterested in ensuring their well-being. One such man, a Tennessee lawyer, arrived in Cincinnati with two slave boys who were his sons. With the help of a local agent, perhaps one familiar with such situations, the man was directed to Coffin, who was a frequent facilitator of resettlement efforts.[47] The boys' father asked that his children be put in the care of someone who would place them in a "good school and look after their interests." Coffin declined to assume such a responsibility. While admitting he had done as much before, he was overwhelmed with his business and abolition efforts. He also found such chores "troublesome."[48]

Coffin suggested that the boys be taken instead to the Union Literary Institute, an inexpensive boarding school opened in Indiana to aid people of color.[49] The institution was ninety miles from Cincinnati. But the man begged Coffin to take the children himself. Coffin acquiesced only because the lawyer left enough money to defray expenses for their first term and promised to send more. However, he failed to send additional funds and Coffin ended up having to advance money to cover the boys' future expenses. Coffin said he "never succeeded in getting [the money he had spent] refunded."[50] Coffin also aided a sixteen-year-old girl who, in his opinion, was as "white" in appearance as any of his own children.[51] She had come from Mississippi, and her father wanted to have her educated. Because this man left funds and pleaded for assistance, Coffin and his wife enrolled the girl in a Cincinnati public school, one that she could attend because she looked so "white." But the $75 her father gave Coffin soon ran out, and Coffin grew frustrated but not just because of the girl's dwindling funds. She was also unruly, something Coffin attributed to the pernicious effects of slavery on her life.

Coffin wrote her father, demanding more money, and received a reply, though not the one he wanted. Her father said if "abolitionists were too mean to school the girl, they could send her back to slavery, where she would be better cared for," because he would incur no further expenses for providing for her while she was outside the South. Coffin and his wife were only freed from the responsibility of caring for the girl when she "fell into bad company among the colored people," although she eventually married a "respectable colored man" and ended her "improper associations."[52]

As the actions of Ballard, John Williams and his brother, and the Townsend brothers make clear, not all Southern white men so carelessly disposed of their half-black children. The wealthy brother of a judge who lived outside New Orleans kept a woman of mixed race as his common-law wife. The couple had eight children. Privilege abounded in this family, with bondspeople waiting on the mixed-race children. The three eldest were sent East to be educated. They were fortunate. The five youngest were still at home when their father died without a will. Having inherited four nieces and a nephew as his own property, the judge tried to raise them in the manner his brother would have done. Because Cincinnati was a well-known destination for people of mixed race, one of the children, a boy in his early teens, requested that he be sent there to be educated. His uncle contacted Coffin, who sent the youngster to the Indiana boarding school. The child's bills were paid in a timely manner. Coffin also helped the judge bring the other four, all females, to Ohio. "On the arrival of the boat I met the girls at the river, and conveyed them to our house," Coffin remembered.[53]

Using $500 their uncle had sent, Coffin saw to it that the girls enrolled at Oberlin College, two hundred miles northeast of Cincinnati.[54] But one of the four, as earlier mentioned, returned to Louisiana to be with her white lover. Her sisters went on to receive their education at Oberlin, but it was disrupted by the war. Coffin and his wife reluctantly took them in while the school was closed. The couple grew frustrated because the girls were unaccustomed to housework, the kind of work the Coffins knew they could easily find for them, given general white attitudes concerning the abilities of African Americans. As well-to-do African Americans brought up in a privileged setting, these young women probably thought such work beneath them. Coffin noted that they were good at needlework. He was delighted when they eventually found mates and got married. Enchanted, as others had been, with their fair skin, his most vivid impression was that the three were "amiable and beautiful young women" and, moreover, "fair scholars."[55]

Other whites, among them Chadick, had similarly conflicted feelings about the mixed-race children of white men whose financial and emotional investments enabled them to live more comfortable and secure lives than most whites thought appropriate. During his visit to Cincinnati, Chadick was made aware of the city's abolitionist presence by pro-slavery whites who played on his prejudices. He was told that these liberals "stripped" any money arriving freedpeople had. But he noticed, too, the general hostility in the city toward free people of color.[56] He was not alone in having made such an observation. The South Carolina planter and politician James Hammond, who reputedly had incestuous relationships with his enslaved kin, instructed his son to secure the futures of one enslaved woman and her children, saying, "Her second I believe is mine. Take care of her & her children who are both of your blood if not mine. . . . I cannot free these people & send them North. It would be cruelty to them."[57]

Having arrived in Cincinnati with Wesley, Townsend's eldest at twenty-seven, Chadick moved on, taking Wesley with him. Chadick and Wesley visited several other Ohio cities. Chadick ultimately found Albany, a town in Athens County, about 160 miles east of Cincinnati, suitable. He heard that free people of color encountered less racism there because "tolerant" Virginians and Marylanders populated the area. But in his report to Cabaniss, Chadick also mentioned that he found the town's pastoral atmosphere, which doubtless reminded him of the rural South, agreeable. Athens County, he said, was "one of the districts [in Ohio] in which a negro with no more than common sense could do well."[58] Pleased that the county had fertile soil and a climate that he believed was favorable to "Negroes," his logic reflected Southern beliefs that people of African descent were better fit to be agricultural laborers in generally warmer climates than to be workers in other occupations and more urban settings.

Chadick did see to it that Wesley, who was married and had a child, settled there and received training in order that he might quickly provide for himself, his family, and his siblings. Chadick enrolled Wesley, who was illiterate, in an industrial school in Albany, presumably so he could obtain the skills that would allow him to manage his and his younger siblings' business affairs once they arrived. The school had sixty pupils "representing many southern states." Though he could see the importance of education to the Townsend children's future, chances are that Chadick, like many whites, considered vocational training to be more suited to African Americans' supposedly inferior intellect than the liberal arts education they would get at schools like Wilberforce and Oberlin.[59]

Though obviously well positioned in comparison to most bondspeople and former bondspeople, ongoing trials for even privileged free children were unavoidable. They encountered not only racism but also more universal sensations, among them, loneliness. In June 1858, Wesley wrote a letter to Cabaniss, expressing longing for his wife and children who remained in Huntsville. He also inquired about his father's estate and announced plans to search for a job in a blacksmith's shop once the school term ended. While he waited for an answer, his father's white relatives continued to make claims on the black Townsends' estate, delaying the arrival of his siblings. Not until January 1860 were the rest of the Townsend children and grandchildren manumitted: Caroline and her infant child Elizabeth, Thomas, Willis, Osborne, Parthenia, Joseph, Bradford, Susanna, and Milcha, along with the two daughters of their Uncle Edmund. Edmund's son, Woodson, was also freed, as were Wesley's wife, Jane, and his two children, Thomas's half sister Elvira, and her infant child.[60]

All were sent to Xenia, 100 miles northwest of Albany. Wesley relocated there and saw to it that his siblings were enrolled at Wilberforce four days after their arrival. He soon found himself in disagreement with some of them and with whites who attempted to manage their lives. In a letter filled with misspelled but legible words, Wesley told Chadick, "Dear friend Mr Chadick I will write you a few lines to give you som information how we are geting along." Though his penmanship was childlike, his mind was that of an astute young man. He went on to express his unhappiness about paying $800 a month for the property where they lived in Xenia.[61] He suggested that purchasing a house would be a better way to use their stipend.

Wesley had other worries. Some of his siblings almost immediately displayed a sense of entitlement arising from their upbringing. Elvira, Thomas's sister, and Jane, Wesley's wife, wanted money, and when Wesley refused their request they demanded to be returned to Alabama.[62] In a separate letter, R. S. Rust, director of Wilberforce, informed Cabaniss that Willis had also demanded money from Wesley.[63] Indeed, Willis sought to bypass Wesley altogether, for on September 8, 1860, he wrote Cabaniss, asking him for money and instructing him to mail it to him and not Wesley.[64]

The conflict between the Townsend siblings was also entangled with their dealings with whites around them. Their relationships with some were better than with others. Though Rust seemed to be concerned about the Townsends, Wesley found him disagreeable. "I think that our money is all that Mr Russ [sic] wants and is all the use he has for us," Wesley said in a letter to Chadick, adding, "That made me right mad with him."[65] Wesley next reported that his siblings were enrolled in school but that some had colds. Speaking in place of the father who was no longer there, he requested additional funds to purchase "bed clothes," beds, stoves, chairs, a table, and house utensils.

While the Townsend children settled in at Wilberforce, Cabaniss decided that Kansas was the best site for their mothers and the other relatives Samuel Townsend had freed. Land in Kansas was affordable, and those with a small inheritance could thus maximize their investment. On February 25, 1860, barely a month after Wesley's siblings had arrived in Xenia, twenty-nine more of Townsend's bondspeople left Huntsville by train for America's heartland.[66] The relocation of these individuals in Leavenworth, Kansas, presaged the movement of thousands of other rural African Americans from the South in 1879 and 1880.[67]

As these former slaves settled in Kansas, they, too, encountered racism. White Kansans feared the presence of blacks would shift white migration from their state to Nebraska and Minnesota. One land agent questioned whether the Townsends he met even had enough money to buy land. "There is a colored man in this place, named Woodson Townsend . . . who calls on us frequently," the agent said in a letter to Cabaniss, adding, "He is anxious to purchase land here and commence farming."[68]

Meanwhile, over the next year, Wesley tended to the needs of his siblings and two cousins in Xenia. In one letter to an unnamed brother, Elizabeth described an event she and the others attended: "The young men and the young lad[ies] had a social and we enjoyed ourselves." Next, she relayed a bit of gossip.[69] Elizabeth announced that some of her cousins had become religious. "[A] few weeks ago we had a r[e]viv[a]l here[.] [A] good many of my schoolmat[es] profess religion. Sister has profess[ed] religion. Thomas and Milcha [and] Bradford all these have profess[ed] religion," she said, referring to the evangelical impulse known as the Second Great Awakening that swept the nation during the late antebellum period.[70] Revealing a sense of independence that was especially pronounced among the Townsend women and girls, Elizabeth seems to have refused to follow the crowd.

That the girls and women of color who had benefited from familiarity with Southern white men were differently positioned than freed boys and men was revealed in their confident way of speaking. Many of them had worked in homes under the surveillance of whites. There they heard and experienced much. Though rape and other hazards existed, the

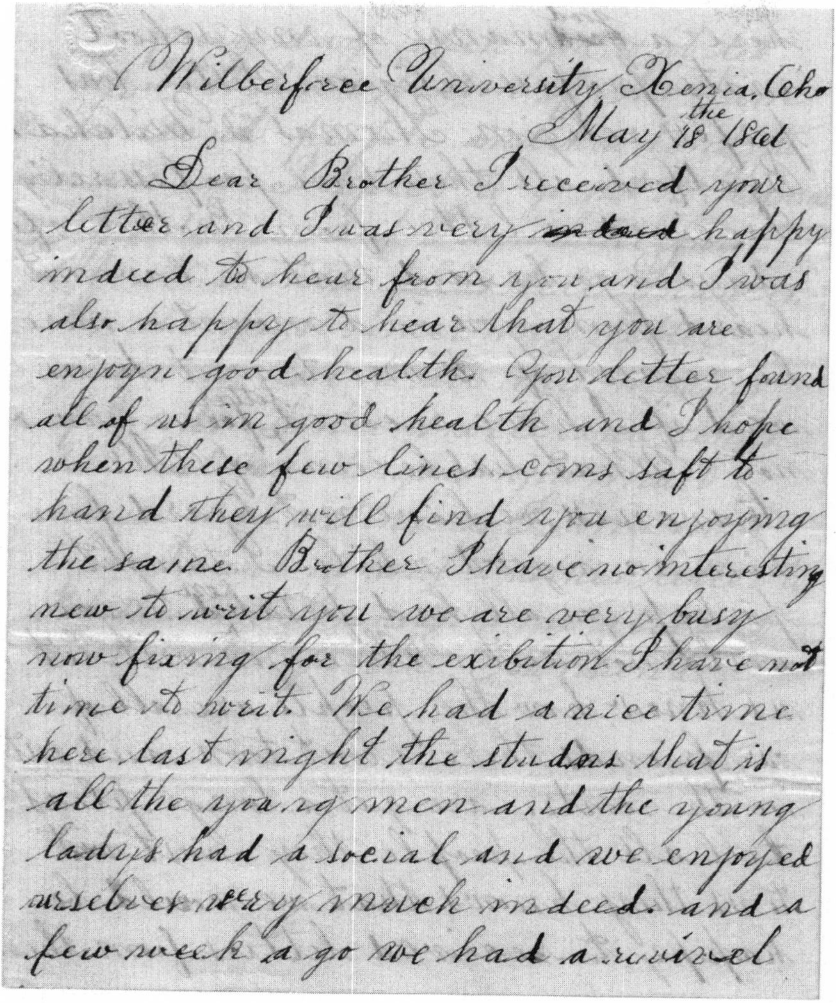

Wilberforce University Xenia, Ohio
May 18th 1861

Dear Brother I received your letter and I was very indeed happy indeed to hear from you and I was also happy to hear that you are enjoying good health. Your letter found all of us in good health and I hope when these few lines comes saft to hand they will find you enjoying the same. Brother I have no interesting new to writ you we are very busy now fixing for the exibition I have not time to writ. We had a nice time here last night the studans that is all the young men and the young ladys had a social and we enjoyed ourselves very much indeed. and a few week a go we had a revivel

FIGURE 14. First page of Elizabeth Townsend's May 18, 1861, letter shortly after the beginning of the Civil War. She is describing activities at Wilberforce, a boarding school–turned–university in Xenia, Ohio. The letter is addressed to her brother Woodsen Townsend. Edmund Townsend, Samuel Townsend's brother, is the father of these two siblings. Notably, she is inquiring about the status of her white relatives in Huntsville. Unlike Elizabeth and several of their freed cousins, Woodson was manumitted and relocated to Kansas—not Ohio. MSS 252, Box 252.054, Folder 01, Septimus Douglas Cabaniss Papers, Special Collections, Stanley Hoole Library, University of Alabama.

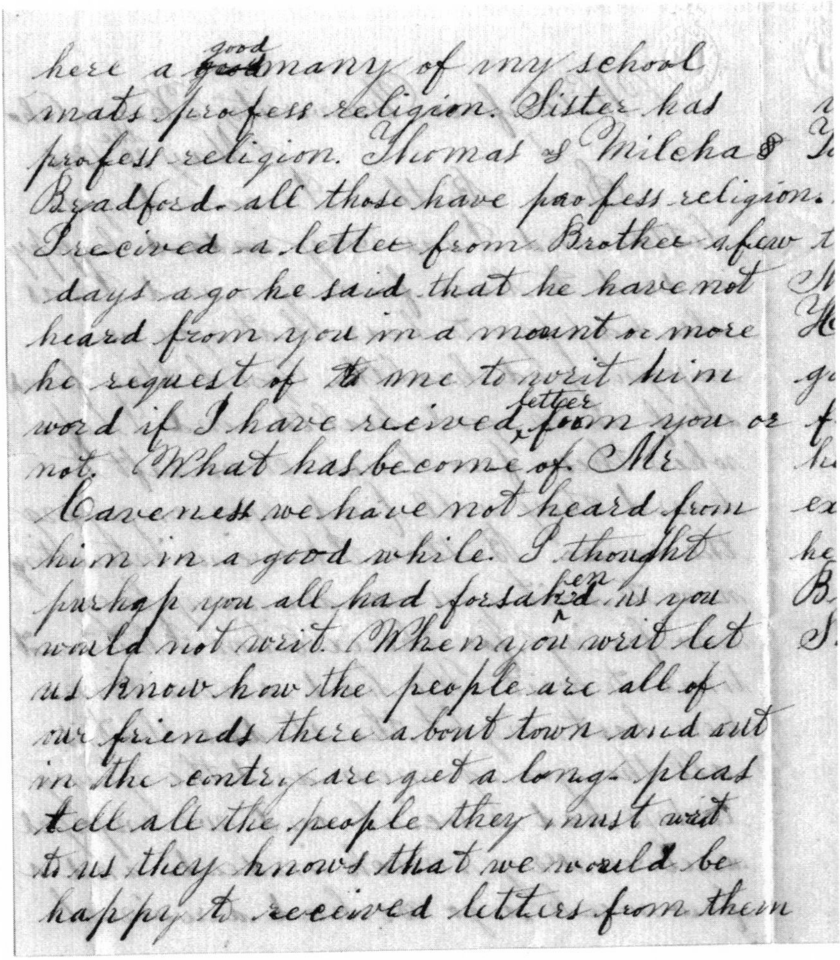

here a good many of my school
mats profess religion. Sister has
profess religion. Thomas & Milcha &
Bradford all those have profess religion.
I received a letter from Brother a few
days a go he said that he have not
heard from you in a mount or more
he request of me to writ him
word if I have received letter from you or
not. What has become of Mr
Caveness we have not heard from
him in a good while. I thought
perhaps you all had forsaken us you
would not writ. When you writ let
us know how the people are all of
our friends there a bout town and out
in the contry are get a long. pleas
tell all the people they must writ
to us they knows that we would be
happy to received letters from them

FIGURE 15. Second page of Elizabeth Townsend's May 18, 1861, letter. MSS 252, Box 252.054, Folder 01, Septimus Douglas Cabaniss Papers, Special Collections, Stanley Hoole Library, University of Alabama.

proximity allowed African American women and girls to see noticeable discrepancies in white men's behavior, enabling some to take advantage of their familiarity with powerful figures and others, too.[71] For instance, Julia Frances Dickson, the enslaved woman who eventually produced a daughter named Amanda with the Georgia planter David Dickson, grew bitter after he had forced sex with her at a young age and reportedly

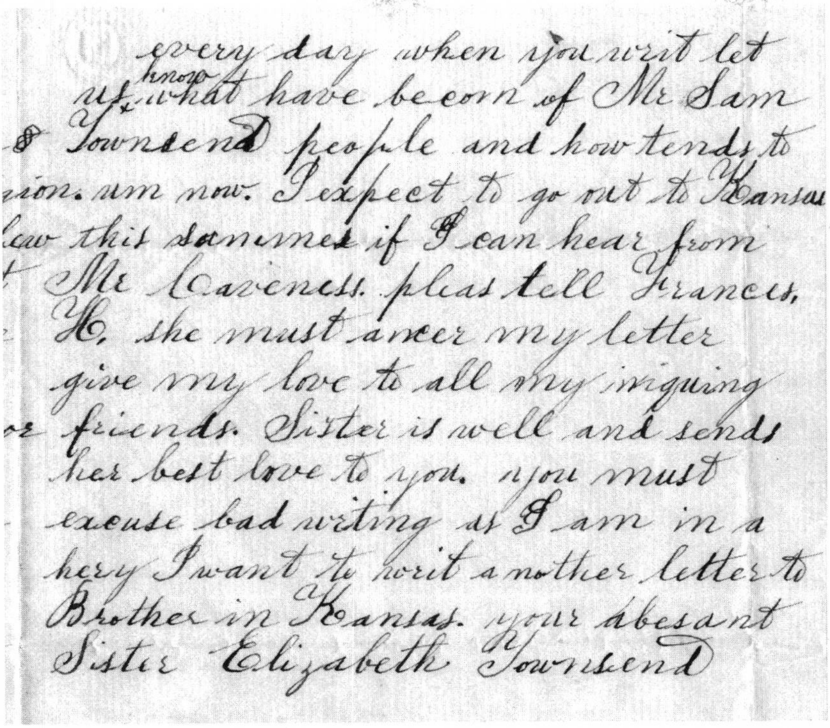

every day when you writ let
us know what have be corn of Mr Sam
Townsend people and how tends to
ion. um now. I expect to go out to Kansas
law this summer if I can hear from
Mr Caveness. pleas tell Francis
H. she must ancer my letter
give my love to all my inquiring
friends. Sister is well and sends
her best love to you. you must
excuse bad writing as I am in a
hery I want to writ another letter to
Brother in Kansas. your abesant
Sister Elizabeth Townsend

FIGURE 16. Third page of Elizabeth Townsend's May 18, 1861, letter. MSS 252, Box 252.054, Folder 01, Septimus Douglas Cabaniss Papers, Special Collections, Stanley Hoole Library, University of Alabama.

"ruled" him and others in his household with an "iron hand."[72] The mothers of the Townsend children may have sometimes behaved similarly. Shortly after being freed, three of the women Samuel Townsend had once bedded were "the greatest trouble" for D. L. Lakin, a Huntsville man hired by Cabaniss to relocate them to Kansas. "I . . . have been forced Several times to Speak to them in tones of unmistakable command," Lakin wrote Cabaniss as he journeyed north on a Mississippi steamboat with them.[73] He had not been compelled to speak so forcefully to their male relatives who were also on board.

As the Townsends forged ahead rebuilding their lives, the Civil War disrupted their efforts. Wilberforce was forced temporarily to close. The Townsend males who were of age served in a "colored" unit fighting on behalf of the Union, and the Townsend women and girls left Xenia to live with their relatives in locations outside the South. Perhaps because of their advantage when compared to other African Americans, they continued to attract the attention of whites around them, some of whom may have been their white kinfolk who desired to see them enslaved again. In May 1861, a month after the attack on Fort Sumter launched the beginning of the war, Wesley received a letter from John Duer, an abolitionist, who asked about their well-being after seeing an advertisement in an antislavery newspaper "inquiring after the former slaves of Samuel Townsend."[74] Duer asked Wesley to "keep quiet" on an unnamed matter—doubtless related to their inheritance—until he heard from "a gentleman who is a 'friend' of colored people." Duer was probably referring to a member of the Quaker community. He added that he hoped the Townsends would "reap substantial benefit" from their father's estate but warned that doing so "will require great care and energy."[75]

Before the war ended, some of the siblings returned to Wilberforce and again found themselves under surveillance by whites, even well-meaning ones, who struggled over what to do with bodies that revealed the great inconsistencies in white supremacist ideas. These were children who had obviously gained an understanding about their own self-worth in relation to a white man of means. Around such children, many whites proceeded carefully. It had earlier been true of Mrs. Tate, their Huntsville neighbor, and now J. K. Parker, a local white man.[76] At the request of Rust, Parker monitored them at the school. Parker initially hesitated, suggesting that such a task was inappropriate because he hardly knew the Townsends. "Being an entire stranger I felt embarrassed [to do this]," he stated in a letter to Rust.[77] Parker added that the Townsends had told him that they were accustomed to managing their own money. Perhaps under pressure from Rust, Parker eventually agreed to monitor the children's expenditures. His report on the expenses of Susanna, one of the Townsend girls, illustrates his oversight. He noted every penny that had been spent by or on her in this manner:

"1 circular	$10
1 hat	$6
Gloves	70 cents
Shoes	$2 .00
Calico .28 yards x 28 cts	$2.24
Stockings 60 x 50	$1.10
10 yds muslin 371/2	$3.75
Hoops	$1.00

$26.69[78]

NAMES.	RESIDENCES.
JAMES C. NAPIER	Nashville, Tenn.
GEORGE W. NESBIT	Cincinnati.
STREETER NESBIT	Cincinnati.
LEWIS OVERTON	Xenia.
CHARLES M. PARKER	New Richmond.
ALEXANDER PIPER	Kirk's Ferry, La.
H. M. RANKIN	Chillicothe.
THOMAS RANKIN	Louisville, Ky.
SANFORD REDMAN	Portsmouth.
CHARLES H. RUST	Xenia.
RICHARD H. RUST	Xenia.
JAMES A. SHORTER	Washington, D. C.
JOSEPH P. SHORTER	Washington, D. C.
EDWIN SMITH	Greenville, Miss.
JAMES D. SMITH	Greenville, Miss.
ROBERT SMITH	Greenville, Miss.
WILLIAM SMITH	Greenville, Miss.
JOSEPH SMITH	Louisville, Ky.
GEORGE M. D. SUMNER	Nashville, Tenn.
THOMAS F. SUMNER	Nashville, Tenn.
LAWRENCE TALLIFERRO	Xenia.
SHIRLEY C. TILLMAN	White Sulphur Springs, Va.
JAMES W. THOMAS	Xenia.
CHARLES W. THOMPSON	Pacific, Mo.
JOHN H. THOMPSON	Pacific, Mo.
WILLIAM B. THOMPSON	Rome, Ga.
CHARLES TOWNSEND	Huntsville, Ala.
JOSEPH B. TOWNSEND	Huntsville, Ala.
THOMAS TOWNSEND	Huntsville, Ala.
WILLIS TOWNSEND	Huntsville, Ala.
DANIEL TOWNSEND	Cincinnati.
ISRAEL TOWNSEND	Cincinnati.
JOHN TRABUE	Louisville, Ky.
LEVI WALKER	Franklin.
DELEMACUS WARREN	New Orleans, La.
AMOS A. WILLIAMS	Paris, Ill.
CHARLES A. WILLIAMS	Paris, Ill.
HENRY M. WILLIAMS	Paris, Ill.
CORNELIUS WILSON	San Francisco, Cal.
JOSEPH P. WILSON	Boston, Mass.
WALTHALL G. WINN	Pittsburg, Penn.
ALBERT G. WOODSON	White Sulphur Springs, Va.

FIGURE 17. Four of the Alabama planter Samuel Townsend's mixed-race sons are listed on this page of Wilberforce University's 1860 yearbook. Courtesy of American Antiquarian Society.

He added that a doctor's bill needed to be paid but that the children "had no money."[79]

Parker's announcement invites deeper scrutiny of the circumstances surrounding the Townsend children's experiences in Xenia. Had they misspent their funds? Had they been given too little on which to survive? Had someone taken some of it? We have no concrete answers to these questions. It is possible that they, being reckless or inexperienced, had not managed their funds well or that Rust took advantage of them, as Wesley alleged. What cannot be doubted is that whites, even presumably sympathetic ones like Rust, did not appear to support the Townsends' efforts to maximize the promises of freedom, at least from the Townsends' perspective. Children of mixed race who remained in slave territory saw similar attitudes. Shortly before the Civil War, George Davis, the son of a white man and a "black servant girl" who resided in Boyd County, refused an offer by two white abolitionists to help him escape to Canada.[80] Davis did not leave owing to his status as the "well treated" and "trusted servant" of his father. Like the Townsends, he benefited from his proximity to a man who was still alive and had invested emotionally and financially in him. Their cases were not unusual. Edd Shirley, a former resident of Monroe County, Kentucky, was the son of a white man and a "colored" woman. Though Shirley was sold twice, his father eventually purchased him, revealing attachment on the part of the former.

Children like the Townsends, Davis, and Shirley were obviously positioned more favorably than other enslaved, even free African Americans.[81] After the war and the abolition of slavery, such positioning had special implications for those who had earlier intimate ties to white men.[82] Their sense of privilege emboldened them—again, the women and girls especially—to speak with unmistakable assertiveness. Consider the letter Elvira sent to Cabaniss. Elvira, who left Ohio for Leavenworth, where she married her cousin Woodson, wrote on September 10, 1865:

> It is necessary that I should know the condition of our affairs; of what has been done with Samuel Townsend estate, and our interest therein. The new state of affairs gives us the power to enforce remedies and we shall do it. Either through the military commanders, or the Freedmen's Bureau we can obtain our just rights, and call any and all parties to a strict account.[83]

Of all the Townsends, Elvira seems to have been especially assertive, probably because she was not only the daughter of one of the slave women with whom Samuel Townsend slept but also his housekeeper. Such proximity probably resulted in a greater level of intimacy and familiarity between her and him than the other Townsends.[84] In challenging Cabaniss, she was not only drawing on her earlier experiences, but testing the shifting terrain of American society brought about by the war.

However, in her letter Elvira was unnecessarily confrontational. While he was pro-slavery, Cabaniss had not abandoned the task of settling the Townsend's estate. Some of the letters from the Townsend siblings to Cabaniss and to each other confirm that he traveled to Kansas to check on some of them. In a September 1866 letter, Willis informed Cabaniss: "I received a letter from Osborne the other day telling me that you had been out to see them in Kansas," adding that he sought news regarding the "estate of our Father."[85]

Willis was more even-tempered than Elvira when addressing Cabaniss, who sometimes appears in their letters as a wishing well around which they gathered, asking for money that should already have been in their hands. To be sure, not all were pleased with his efforts. Elvira's husband, Woodson, was especially irked. He was jailed in Kansas for an unspecified crime during the war and believed Cabaniss should have done more on his behalf. "I think that the [guardians] of Samuels Townsend esstate has treated me mean very mean," Woodson charged.[86] Doubtless the prolonged delay in receiving their inheritance generated tension in the family, for Woodson's anger was also directed at his cousins, who he accused of trying to steal his share. He even believed that Cabaniss was aiding their efforts. Wrote Woodson, "I do not know of what interest it is for you to swindle me out of my money and give to Uncle Sams children. I think that you are trying to kep me in here [in prison] till Uncle Sams estate is wound up."[87]

Woodson's ordeal wrecked his marriage. Elvira told him defiantly, but inaccurately, that she had enough money to live without him, providing further proof of her self-confidence and, by extension, the boldness so frequently exhibited by black women familiar with and willing to take advantage of the inconsistencies in white patriarchy when disrupted by familiarity, sentiment, and even attachment. She remarried in 1866, announcing to Cabaniss that she had married a "good" but "poor" husband.[88] They resided in St. Joseph, Missouri, where he had difficulties earning a living. She therefore demanded that Cabaniss send her some money as he "promised" to do. Elvira died there in 1868, having received a little over $700 from the Townsend estate. However, her two children, who were raised by her mother in Kansas, eventually received more than $2,000.[89]

When the Townsends' correspondence is considered collectively, one senses a family, like many others in their circumstance, attempting to find its way in a deeply racist country, where their mixed-race status carried only limited currency. Despite their ties to wealthy white men, they and many others endured a great deal of suffering, some of it owing to their own missteps but most of it resulting from the bigotry surrounding them.

The historian Martha Sandweiss's study of the nineteenth-century romance between the white geologist Clarence King and Ada Coleman, an African American woman born a slave in Georgia, reveals similar trials endured by their offspring. Coleman relocated to New York after the Civil War, and there worked as a nursemaid. King, who had long been drawn to women of color, married her in 1882, "passing" as African American himself.[90] For decades, "James Todd," as King renamed himself, explained his long absences from their Brooklyn and later Flushing, Queens, homes, first by pretending to be a Pullman porter and later a clerk for a steel company.

King demonstrated his regard publicly and legally through marriage.[91] King's absences took a toll on Ada and their children. But, as Sandweiss makes clear, for over thirteen years King was committed to Ada "and their children, at no small cost to his own financial and emotional well-being."[92] King's devotion to Ada was revealed in letters he sent her over the years, letters that document a deep and genuine emotional bond between two unlikely bodies. In fact, when Ada made claims on King's estate after his death, according to his wishes, she shared the letters with his white male friends, who kept them so that they would never see the light of day. But, perhaps knowing the issue could end up in court, they did not destroy them. In time, Ada learned that the money he sent to support her before and after his death often came via her husband's friend John Hay, Abraham Lincoln's private secretary and later U.S. secretary of state.[93] Again, the reach of mixed-race children was of considerable import. Many were often a mere degree of separation from prominent figures. Such reach often figured into their everyday lives. Often like their mothers, they moved through space with greater frequency than most other African Americans. Some attended schools. Some married whites. Two of the Kings' daughters were so fair that they passed as white and married white men. Following his death in 1901, his marriage became public knowledge and was the scandalized subject of news reports.[94] Though King was the subject of several biographies in the twentieth century, it was not until Sandweiss's book that Ada Copeland

Todd King emerged as more than Clarence King's "kept mistress."[95] As Sandweiss boldly concludes, she was his wife.

Speaking to the difficulties historians have assessing the sincerity of emotional exchanges between interracial couples of the past, Sandweiss writes, "Public documents record the story that James and Ada Todd told the world, but they did not reveal what they said to each other."[96] For example, while Ada had earlier told census takers that her husband was a Pullman porter from Baltimore, in 1900 she told one that he was a "black man born in the West Indies."[97] Ada evidently struggled to explain the comfortable life her "husband" had given her in a mixed-race neighborhood on North Prince Street in Queens. Sandweiss ponders whether King told her to describe him in this manner or whether she surmised on her own that not all was "as it seemed" with her "husband," so she offered her take on the subject to spare her family unwanted scrutiny.[98]

Unlike Avenia White and Rice Ballard or John Williams and Louisa Picquet, details about the Kings' relationship are revealed in his letters and other sources, allowing us to hear their conversations. In one letter that began, "My darling," King told her to expect a gentleman visitor who would soon bring her money. "I don't care for him to see the children. Always have the parlor looking nice, and when he comes put on a nice dress or a nice wrapper."[99] It appears as if King acted as had Ballard, who years earlier used an intermediary—another white man—to deliver money to his former slave mistress Avenia White and her African American landlady, Frances Bruster. We also see the degree to which this relationship was orchestrated. Like Ballard, King was concerned about appearances. To counter myths concerning the promiscuity of black women, or displaying class-based motives, King asked his black wife to dress respectably. Perhaps Ballard felt similarly when he settled White and Johnson and their four children in a home far from Cincinnati's seedy waterfront. Possibly like King, and no matter his offenses, he demonstrated his awareness of how people of color with ties to men like him continued to face white prejudice. Samuel Townsend's children obviously did as well.

Like the Kings' five children, even those who passed as white, the Townsends suffered systemic discrimination in a society that was generally antagonistic toward African Americans. It was something from which they could not escape, no matter how much money they inherited from their white father. But their determination to move forward in spite of the obstacles before them was sustained not just by their awareness of their promised wealth, but by reaching out to each other.

Osborne Townsend, Samuel's fourth-eldest son, seems to have written most frequently. His letters reveal the kinship that existed in the family. They also reveal the loneliness that he and doubtless many other post-bellum African Americans felt. Growing wealth in this country was no substitute for personal contact with familiar faces. Osborne doubtless felt as much in Georgetown, Colorado.

Tucked at the eastern base of the Snowy Range, Georgetown is fifty-two miles west of Denver. Here, at an altitude of 8,530 feet, locals boasted about the pure mountain air and the area's generally mild climate. The town was named for George Griffith, who with his brother, David, arrived in 1859 from Kentucky and made first discovery by whites of silver in the region. As the prospectors flocked to the town, gamblers, "shady ladies," and other fortune hunters came, too, from states as far away as Massachusetts, New York, Pennsylvania, and Maryland, and from the Deep South.[100]

Doubtless Osborne saw and felt much while living in Colorado, where in addition to prospecting for silver, he plied his trade as a barber, one of the more prestigious professions available to African Americans in the nineteenth century. He may have compared the hills of Huntsville to the mountains around Georgetown, a place he studied carefully. In one letter to his brother Thomas, the brother to whom he wrote the most, Osborne described the dwindling presence of Native Americans in the area.[101] The topic came up owing to Thomas's expressed desire for a robe made of buffalo hide. Osborne noted that he had "not seen an Indian in six years," though he had once traded with members of the Ute tribe who had since been "moved several hundred miles southwest" of Georgetown. However, Osborne said he believed he could find such a buffalo hide robe in Denver. That these two siblings could speak so casually about a buf-falo robe suggests that their everyday concerns departed from the basic material comforts on the minds of many if not most people of African descent in the United States during the nineteenth century and after-ward. Certainly they did not long, as had Avenia White, for a bed. The Townsend siblings experienced many sorrows but many triumphs, too. Interestingly, some longed for long-ago moments. For example, in one letter to Thomas, Osborne said he missed their "schoolmates at Wilber-force" and a "good many of the old times live[d] there."[102]

But their worries persisted. Osborne often inquired about the where-abouts of another brother, Willis, who, the last he knew, lived in Ohio. Osborne might have been especially concerned about Willis because they shared a mother as well as a father.[103] "Wish you could let me know if Willis is in New Richmond," Osborne asked Thomas in January 1876.[104] Osborne eventually ascertained more about Willis in news relayed by another relative. In a letter to her "Uncle Thomas," Carrie Leonteen Townsend, Wesley's daughter, mentioned that "Cousin Alice Townsend from New Richmond" was visiting. Alice was probably Willis's daughter.[105]

Willis had apparently followed his older half brother Wesley to New Richmond. Unlike Wesley, however, he stayed there. After the war Wesley lived briefly in Kansas and while there not only borrowed money from his relatives, but deserted his wife, Jane, when he relocated to New Richmond. In New Richmond he remarried, to a woman named Adelaide, and purchased a house, only to lose it.[106] Strangely, Wesley attributed his inability to pay the mortgage to locals not liking him. He was called a "butternut," a derogatory colloquialism in the southern Midwest communities of Ohio, Illinois, and Indiana for rural Southerners who were different from modern eastern Yankees.[107]

Unhappy, Wesley returned "home" to Huntsville, where he got a teaching job at Huntsville Institute.[108] Still restless, he subsequently relocated to Brookhaven, Mississippi, which was close to the Gulf Coast and New Orleans.[109] There he farmed land and earned enough money to afford a piano in his house and pay for Carrie's piano lessons.[110] Indeed, in her letter to her uncle Thomas, Carrie had equally important news to convey concerning herself: "I am not braging [sic] but you ought to see me play piano. I tell you I make ours sing."[111] Before closing her letter, Carrie mentioned that she was attending New Orleans University. She wondered if her uncle could send her something. "A nice winter dress would be accepted," she wrote, signaling that her tastes reflected those of elite Americans in her day.[112]

Thanks to the prosperity of her white grandfather and her father, she was a member of an emerging African American upper middle class. Her uncle Thomas was a claims lawyer for African American soldiers seeking war pensions and eventually a Huntsville city alderman who resided on Adams Street, one of the "choice spots" in Huntsville.[113] In fact, her uncle was a neighbor of John David Weeden, a white man who had been a colonel in the Confederate army and was a lawyer himself.[114] Like Carrie, other second-generation Townsends pursued educations at institutions of higher learning. Thomas Jr., the son of Thomas, attended Fisk University before transferring to Howard University.[115] As well-positioned black Americans, the Townsends had opportunities to pursue education, obtain solid employment, enter the professions, open businesses, and travel. Each new experience and achievement suggests how far they had come as freedpeople. However, as people of African descent, they still struggled to achieve the full promise of freedom.

Among the advantages the Townsend children and their descendants had was the opportunity to make choices about their career paths, which may explain their desire to live in certain places. Demonstrating this point, Osborne once inquired about Thomas's crops and wondered whether Thomas was overworking himself in Huntsville, farming and teaching.[116] "It is no use to kill yourself trying to get rich," Osborne once said to Thomas, apparently unaware of the irony of such a comment from one who was barbering while mining silver. Before he signed off, Osborne inquired again about Willis, saying, "I have not heard from [him] in years."[117]

Why Osborne had such trouble learning about Willis's situation is unclear. Had Willis deliberately distanced himself from his family? Or did he not want to communicate with Osborne? Whatever the reason, Osborne finally heard from Willis and was reminded that no matter their privilege, they would almost certainly struggle like other African Americans. Willis, who apparently had earned his living as a waiter on a steamboat, a once-prized job typically assigned to fair-skinned black men, had been affected by the decline of Cincinnati's steamboat industry. This decline began during the 1850s, as railroads were built. Prior to the 1850s, no rail line offered competition to the Ohio and Mississippi Rivers.[118] But the low-water seasons permitted developing railroads to gain a foothold by the mid-1850s, and the demand for water transportation declined significantly.[119] From 1860 on, black boatmen were disproportionately affected by steamboat job losses.[120]

But even as Cincinnati's infrastructure lagged because of its poor rail system and the steamboat's decline, the city became a major manufacturing center.[121] From the 1860s on, Cincinnati, which had been hemmed in by a waterfront on one side and hills on the others, mushroomed into a manufacturing center. Between 1851 and 1910, the value of products made in Cincinnati increased from $54 million to $262 million.

In all likelihood, Willis encountered job competition from local whites, who dominated the best factory positions.[122] During this period domestic work and manual laborer therefore became the dominant occupations for African Americans.[123] This labor transition occurred in a space that was more congested than it had been during the antebellum period. Only New York City was more cramped by 1870. Land that was increasingly separated by function led to the creation of street lines and cable railways, enabling whites to flee to valley and hilltop communities while people of color continued settling in the city's basin.[124] A once racially integrated Cincinnati now segregated its residents by race and class. Even black Cincinnatians who had earlier benefited from relations with Southern white men faced such segregation.

Yet during the postbellum years, African Americans continued to migrate to Cincinnati and the state as a whole. Ohio's black population grew from 36,673 in 1860 to 80,000 in 1880. This steady increase contributed to rising white hostility that was less evident in states like Indiana, where fewer blacks settled during the postbellum period.[125] For example, Cincinnati's white printers ignored requests by skilled black printers for admission into their union. Such exclusions also applied to women.[126] As the century progressed, the city's skilled white laborers also ostracized the "small, but significant number" of African Americans who worked in semiskilled positions.[127]

Willis Townsend was not shielded from race-based hostility in Cincinnati, possibly contributing to his move to nearby New Richmond. While he worked as a waiter on a boat shuttling passengers between Cincinnati and Portsmouth, he, as had Louisa Picquet, relocated to this a racially more tolerant river town. During the 1870s, he earned $30 a month, or $360 annually, a solid salary considering the typical American mechanic earned $10 a week between 1873 and 1877, the most severe period of a global financial crisis, the world's first.[128]

In such an unstable economic atmosphere, it was not uncommon for Cincinnati workers to experience lengthy episodes of unemployment or part-time work.[129] Amid such social and economic uncertainty, men of color in particular struggled.[130] "Willis seems to sail under difficulties," Osborne shared in a letter to their brother Thomas, possibly referring to the hurdles Willis encountered in Cincinnati during the mid-1880s and beyond.[131] Either he had not managed his income well or his salary had not been enough to meet the needs of his family. His brother Osborne also felt financially strained as the federal government attempted to direct the nation's economy and money supply.[132] "If I had any money I would send some but declare I haven't," Osborne told Willis. "We produce two million of silver each year but the government takes" any profit in it.[133]

While contending with an evolving economy, the Townsends continued to inquire about their father's estate. Said Osborne in another letter to Thomas, "If there is anything coming to me out of that wreck I want it!"[134] With the aid of a second lawyer that they themselves hired in 1870, some of the Townsend offspring actively pursued their father's money without Cabaniss's help.[135]

In the last quarter of the nineteenth century and beyond, the Townsends encountered many trials, some self-inflicted, others owing to racial bias. This was certainly true of Osborne, whose experiences expand our view of African American life in the Far West and the hardening racist attitudes at the turn of the century.[136] While moving west, some African Americans found employment as baggage clerks, cooks, porters, and even conductors on trains.[137] Some blacks passed as white in order to evade endemic racism, because, as Ariela Gross tells us, the malleability of race and the degree to which race is understood not only by what others see, but one's environment.[138] Race was also determined by one's deliberate actions in the face of bigotry. Illustrating this, Osborne's son Thomas, who was born in Georgetown, was listed as "white" in the 1885 Colorado state census. Osborne was recorded as being "black" five years earlier in the 1880 federal census.[139] In the 1910 census, his son Thomas, now a resident of Deer Lodge, Montana, was listed as a "mulatto."[140] This change in designation may have been a result of hardening racist attitudes among white Americans or something that a census taker noticed in Thomas's appearance or actions as he aged, something that declared he was a person of part African descent. Perhaps owing to his ethnicity, he was unemployed. He also lived in a rented dwelling apart from Gertrude, who may have been dark-skinned and increased the chances of observers discovering that he was in fact of African descent. If so, he revealed the complex strategies that mixed-race men adopted during the postbellum years to maximize their ties to white America. During the antebellum period, it had been advantageous for mixed-race free men of color to marry women of mixed race to maintain their high position in the black community. Some may have done the same in later decades even as hardening attitudes toward African Americans of all complexions required new survival tactics.[141] Having possibly married a dark-skinned woman, the fair-skinned Thomas was compelled to briefly live apart from her.

Thomas's strategy mirrored those his father encountered as the century waned. Indeed, the experiences of Osborne's son contrasted sharply with other well-to-do relatives, including his uncle, the lawyer in Huntsville for whom he was likely named. In the 1920 census, Thomas was a "black" resident of Seattle. With Gertrude beside him, he resided in a rented dwelling with three other individuals, among them, his older brother Charles.[142] The two brothers worked as janitors, suggesting the limited benefits of being the grandsons of a white man.[143] Their relatives had received in a piecemeal fashion a sizable inheritance, but in their case not enough to move them beyond menial positions. White prejudice almost certainly figured into their ongoing oppression.

In the 1930 census, Thomas and Gertrude were still residents of Seattle but were the parents of a son named Thomas,[144] listed as being black. He and his family lived in a house on Angeline Street in a multiethnic, multinational neighborhood that contained a "Negro" couple from Antigua and their two children.[145] Possibly indicative of job instability related to the Great Depression, Thomas now washed cars in a garage.

The migration of people of African descent to Seattle announced great changes in American life, presenting other hurdles in an industrializing world. In the closing decades of the nineteenth century, the country was divided more or less equally between two spheres, rural and urban.[146] As a new century beckoned, more people moved into cities. Between 1860 and 1920, the national population tripled, from 31 million to more than 105 million. During the same period, city dwellers grew ninefold, from 6 million to approximately 54 million people. In 1920, more than 50 percent of Americans lived in cities and towns.[147] At the same time, racism escalated and expanded to encompass Asians and others. A white mob led to the forced removal of two hundred workers from Seattle's Chinese district in 1886.[148] In the opening decades of the twentieth century, strained race relations often kept blacks and Asians out of Seattle's labor unions.[149] In this hostile environment, African Americans continued to bend the "truth" about their identity in order to prosper. While Thomas was again recorded as being a "black" man in the 1940 census, within two years he was listed as "white" on his draft registration card.[150]

Having a grandfather who was a wealthy planter obviously did not provide full protection to the Townsends. Their own actions and other factors, including the economy and discriminatory practices that relegated them to menial work, contributed to their personal woes. Some of the Townsends found life so trying, as had Louisa Picquet and perhaps even Avenia White, they took advantage of their racial ambiguity in hopes of securing some measure of protection from racism.

Other Townsends sought to better their lives by other means. Like Avenia White, William Bolden Townsend, son of Margaret, another Townsend who was freed and relocated to Kansas, recognized that education was vital to getting ahead. William once wrote the following to Cabaniss: There is a request that I have to me of you and if be granted I will consider it . . . a favor to me. It is this[:] you are aware that I am still going to school and I am trying very hard to become some person through and by an education[.] [I]t of course requires money and I have spent all the money that I have carried here."[151] His determination was sometimes rewarded. He went on to be a journalist, educator, politician, and lawyer in Kansas. Yet his education and professional attainment did not shield him from racial hostility—he was forced to flee Leavenworth for his safety.[152] And he was listed as a "colored" lawyer in a 1920 Denver city directory.[153]

The Townsends' experiences as relayed in public documents and their letters should be read with caution. They wrote to each other in order to stay abreast of events in their lives while waiting for news concerning their Samuel Townsend's estate. Had a relative's material condition improved? They would not know if they did not stay in regular contact. Several also stayed in touch with the lawyer Samuel Townsend had hired to see to their financial well-being. In 1884 Nettie Caldwell, a descendant of Townsend's daughter Milcha, wrote a letter to Cabaniss to remind him that he promised he would send her an unspecified sum when she was old enough to select her own guardian. Evidencing the self-determination earlier seen in her aunt Elvira, Caldwell wrote, "I am old enough now to choose one. Please let me know if I choose one, will you send me some money? I don't want to choose a guardian unless you send some money." Caldwell also appears to have been enrolled in school, as she went on to say, "My books this session cost me eight dollars." If Cabaniss had "any feeling for a motherless and fatherless child," he should respond, she wrote.[154]

The direct, even manipulative tone in Nettie's letter cannot be missed. One may chalk her impoliteness up to youth or to something or someone else.[155] Her pushiness possibly bore resemblance to that of the enslaved girl whose owners decided she had grown too high-minded.[156] Despite her hardships, Caldwell seems to have had considerable self-esteem. She was the granddaughter of a white man, and a rich one. And like many other African American females, she could make a point forcefully.[157] This self-assertiveness was also seen in Carrie, the Townsend child who asked her uncle for a winter dress. Caldwell's assertiveness reaped benefits, however. After receiving nearly $3,000 from the Townsend estate, some of which she spent on her education, she seems to have invested wisely. She owned property in Topeka, Kansas, at the time of her death.[158]

The younger Townsends, with their sense of privilege if not entitlement, permit us to try something daring—to position them against whites in America, many of whom acted out of self-interest, too, and in doing so exhibited a very American trait. A sense of entitlement can

FIGURE 18. Portrait of the Kansas African American lawyer William Bolden Townsend, descendant of Samuel Townsend. I. Garland Penn, *The Afro-American Press and Its Editors* (Springfield, MA: Willey & Co., 1891. Courtesy of Manuscripts, Archives and Rare Books Division, Schomburg Center for Research in Black Culture.

be seen across the color line, but blacks who have displayed those traits across time have typically been viewed in a negative light by working-class and elite whites alike owing to pervasive stereotypes: dishonesty, laziness, and "uppity-ness." Privileged African Americans were thus probably hyperalert to their own position and the image they conveyed to others, further revealing the complexities of race and class in America in the postbellum years.

For example, although privileged, Osborne, the barber and sometime miner, was powerless to resist the government's growing ability to determine how much he made. But he was fully conscious of his status and the threat posed to it by the actions and appearances of other blacks, who were under constant surveillance throughout the nineteenth century and long afterward. He once wrote his brother Thomas deploring the arrival of "loose negroes" in Georgetown.[159] Perhaps Osborne, like Louisa Picquet, felt superior to other African Americans. Perhaps he and Thomas were acutely aware of the resentment of others, both white and black, who could see their special position. As the number of educated African Americans increased, literature provided one way to challenge white supremacy and all that went with it: surveillance, segregation, miscegenation laws, and other forms of discrimination. Pauline Hopkins, an African American author, received her share of criticism for presenting characters of mixed race in her fiction during the late nineteenth and early twentieth century. Among her critics was a white female subscriber to *Colored American* magazine. This woman had noticed that with few exceptions, the serial stories Hopkins wrote involved "love between colored and whites." Puzzled and angered, this reader asked the magazine's editors, "Does that mean your novelists can imagine no love and sublime within the range of the colored race, for each other?" The editors allowed Hopkins to respond to this reader:

> My stories are definitely planned to show the obstacles persistently placed in our paths by the dominant race to subjugate us spiritually. Marriage is made illegal between the races and yet the mulattoes increase. Thus the shadow of corruption falls on the blacks and whites, without whose aid the mulattoes would not exist. And then the hue and cry goes abroad of the immorality of the Negro and the disgrace that mulattoes are to this nation.[160]

Hopkins's words announced the degree to which the mulatta as an "imagined" character was based on real women. Though race and sexuality were being policed in "deeply intertwined" ways by the late nineteenth century,

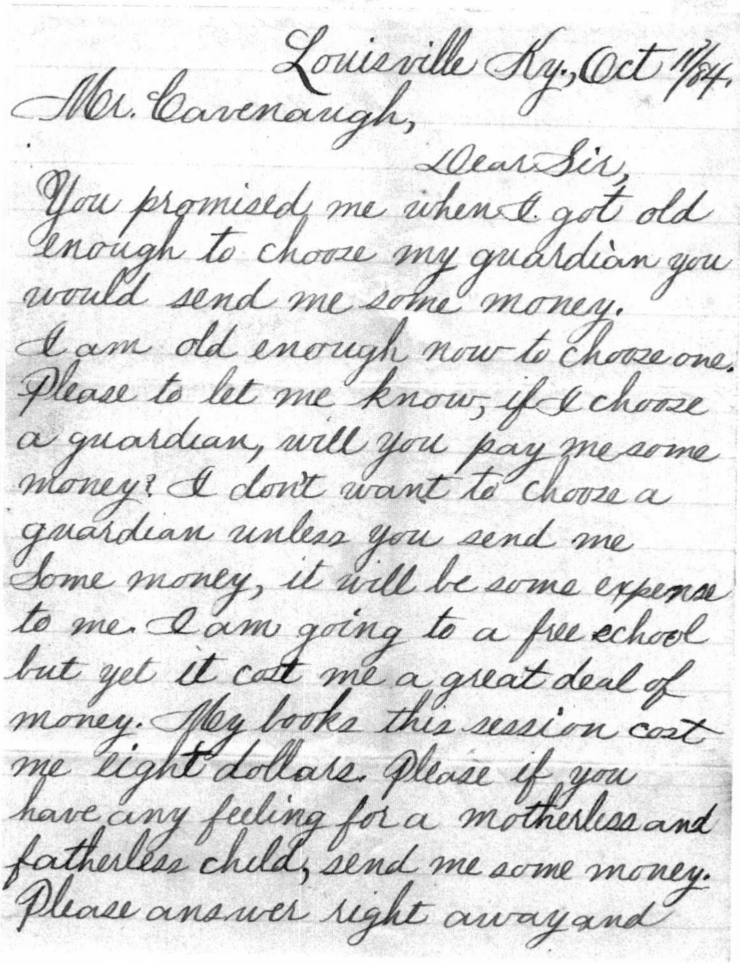

Louisville Ky., Oct 11/84.

Mr. Cavenaugh,

Dear Sir,

You promised me when I got old enough to choose my guardian you would send me some money. I am old enough now to choose one. Please to let me know, if I choose a guardian, will you pay me some money? I don't want to choose a guardian unless you send me some money, it will be some expense to me. I am going to a free school but yet it cost me a great deal of money. My books this session cost me eight dollars. Please if you have any feeling for a motherless and fatherless child, send me some money. Please answer right away and

FIGURE 19. Excerpt from Nettie Caldwell's October 11, 1884, letter to Septimus Cabaniss, the lawyer hired in the mid-1850s to manage the estate of Samuel Townsend. Caldwell was Townsend's granddaughter. MSS 252, Box 252.054, Folder 01, Septimus Douglas Cabaniss Papers, Special Collections, Stanley Hoole Library, University of Alabama.

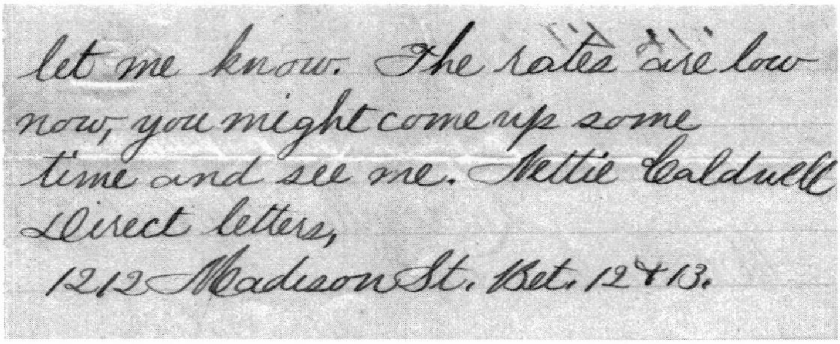

FIGURE 20. Second page from Nettie Caldwell's October 11, 1884, letter to Huntsville lawyer Septimus Cabaniss. MSS 252, Box 252.054, Folder 01, Septimus Douglas Cabaniss Papers, Special Collections, Stanley Hoole Library, University of Alabama.

a time when Jim Crow laws sought to separate white and black bodies, mixed-race characters in literature gestured toward long-established relations and intimacies between the same bodies.[161] Hopkins allows us to see, again, what nineteenth-century whites feared about racially ambiguous bodies like the Townsends, which disrupted notions about race and class. Suggesting the political possibilities of such unions, Hopkins replied to her angry reader by writing, "Amalgamation is an institution designed by God for some wise purpose, and mixed bloods have always exercised a great influence on the progress of human affairs."[162]

It is worth mulling over Hopkins's motives for making this statement. What was the "wise purpose" in question, and what influence did people of mixed race really have when they themselves were discriminated against, too? For possible answers we may return to the requests for a winter dress by Carrie and for money by Nettie. These Townsends represented progress in human affairs because they resisted racial ideology, which insisted they deserved neither a winter dress nor their inheritance.

But do their requests make them appear to be self-seeking young women of color or self-seeking young *American* women? In sorting through possible answers, the observations made decades earlier by Frances Trollope, the antebellum British travel writer, seem pertinent. Upon visiting New Orleans for the first time, the often haughty Trollope wrote:

> On first touching the soil of a new land, of a new continent, of a new world, it is impossible not to feel considerable excitement and deep interest in almost every object that meets us. New Orleans

presents very little that can gratify the eye of taste, but nevertheless there is much of novelty and interest for a newly arrived European. The large proportion of blacks seen in the streets, all labour being performed by them; the grace and beauty of the elegant Quadroons, the occasional groups of wild and savage Indians, the unwonted aspect of the vegetation, the huge and turbid river, with its low and slimy shore, all help to afford that species of amusement which proceeds from looking at what *we never saw before*.[163]

When Trollope arrived in New Orleans, she saw people of mixed race, females in particular, who were part of an American landscape about which she had much to say. She took note of such things in order to stress their novelty, but her biggest commentary seems to have been on the excess on display. New Orleans appeared brash and garish, even extravagant, as was suggested by Trollope's pointed reference to those elegantly dressed mixed-race women, many of whom were doubtless the mates of wealthy white men. Such excess troubled Trollope possibly because she believed that American greed and privilege was visible in women who had also been oppressed, though their oppression contrasted sharply with that of the downtrodden laborer. Such ironic conflict clashed with a more natural order of things like the land and the muddy river. The complicated hierarchies that Trollope saw were something that the Townsend siblings represented.

Though Osborne could condemn "loose Negroes" migrating to Colorado, he was well aware that local whites regarded him in the same manner, even if they could also see in his complexion evidence of his white ancestry and some earlier intimacy between a white man and a black woman. The latter failed to provide protection against ongoing hostility. Osborne subscribed to the *Huntsville Gazette*, which in the final decades of the century was filled with stories concerning both the triumphs and the escalating trials of people of color in the Jim Crow South. In one letter to Thomas, Osborne wrote, "I read gloomy reports of the condition of the colored man in the South." In another letter, this one bearing the self-description "C. O. Townsend [T]onsorial Artist," Osborne wrote, "I never expect to come South again until I can travel like other people."[164]

But Osborne had seen discrimination even outside the South. During a trip to Lawrence, Kansas, by train, he reportedly was denied first-class service even though he had purchased a first-class ticket. He was evidently sometimes well regarded by whites in Georgetown because the *Colorado Miner*, his local newspaper, was outraged about the incident, saying, "If corporations sell first-class tickets, the holders thereof are entitled to first-class fare."[165]

Osborne wrote this even as he, like his siblings and their children, was well aware of the advantages his family had. Many whites looked upon such advantages with regret even as some admitted that some if not all of the Townsends were respectable people. While writing her dissertation, Roberts, Cabaniss's great-granddaughter, conducted a personal interview with the elderly Thomas Townsend. Pleased by his accomplishments as a lawyer and his demeanor, she wrote the following in the closing pages of her dissertation: "In all of his public life he conducted himself in such a way as to command the respect of both white and colored citizens of Huntsville."[166] While complimentary, her comments stand in stark contrast to her refusal—as generally reflected in her dissertation—to acknowledge that the apparent failures of other family members were usually the outcome of systemic discrimination, beginning with whites' efforts to deny them their inheritance, rather than the result of individual failings or innate black "inferiority," an all but universal belief when Roberts was a graduate student. Thomas himself may have shared some of her sentiments because Osborne appears to have written him several times without receiving a reply. In one letter to Thomas, Osborne congratulated him on his marriage, which he learned about in the *Huntsville Gazette*.[167] Thomas may have intended no harm. Then again, he may have distanced himself from his half siblings' financial troubles or behavior that he felt was discreditable.

Ultimately, their actions and other factors, among them, their head start as freedpeople, where they settled, community attitudes, and even luck, determined the degree to which the Townsends prospered. Any success they achieved was surely the kind for which their mothers—Rainey, Hannah, Celia, Lucy, and Winney—hoped while acquiescing or being forced to share a bed with their white father years earlier.

Although we do not know what agreements were made between these women and Samuel Townsend, there can be no doubt that agreements existed, compelling him to act favorably on their behalf or those of their children. Yet when settling outside the South in cities like Cincinnati, these migrants of color had merely crossed a legal boundary. They would have to strive to attain that for which their mothers and father had hoped.[168]

From time to time, the Townsend children glimpsed or accessed a bit of white men's power and in doing so laid claim to the promise of freedom at that time intended for only a few African Americans. Sometimes such claims manifested as a sense of entitlement to something as practical as a bed, something as extravagant as a winter dress, or something of larger importance such being freed or the ability to marry someone of one's own choosing. Consider the experience of Susanna, one of Samuel Townsend's daughters. When Susanna and her siblings left Wilberforce following the outbreak of the Civil War, she relocated to New Richmond, where she resided with the family of her older brother, Wesley.[169] While there, she attended a school for free people of color and later Clermont Academy. Though still a teenager, she reportedly got pregnant with a child who died at birth, after having dated a young white man she desired to marry. "He is the nicest young man I ever did see," she told Cabaniss in a June 1868 letter.[170] She asked Cabaniss for permission to marry her beau because Wesley was apparently angered that she had disgraced herself and the family. "Wesley treats me like I was a dog or some kind of . . . animal[,] Mr Cabaniss," wrote Susanna of the brother she, probably because of their age difference, called "uncle." She was so angry at him that she renounced her family connection, stating she was Susanna "forever" but not a Townsend.[171]

Between her birth in 1853 and her death in 1869, Susanna experienced slavery, a momentous war, and the beginnings of Reconstruction. Along the way, she, like many other people who straddled racial boundaries, attempted to realize the dream of autonomy. In her case, she wished to marry the man of her choice. Her naïveté is not what is most striking—her beau might only have wanted her money—but rather her nerve. Her boldness must not have come as a shock to her father's lawyer, who had seen it in an earlier letter, one written when she was only thirteen years old. In it, she stated that she would not let anyone take her money.[172] In it, too, there were echoes of Elvira's assertiveness and that of other Townsend women and girls.

What encouraged free women and girls to make demands of Southern white men? Something intangible but unmistakable existed between themselves and such men, which made such utterances possible. It was an understanding born from an intimate relationship, not always a sexual one, although this dimension was rarely absent. It was something that even a former enslaved man like Wesley could not fully comprehend because he had not inhabited the complicated, always unequal, but often contradictory space between white men and black women and girls.

That space has been in the background of this study and frequently appears in the foreground, too, as in the case of Louisa Picquet's bargaining with Mr. Cook, her second owner, and her domestic arrangement

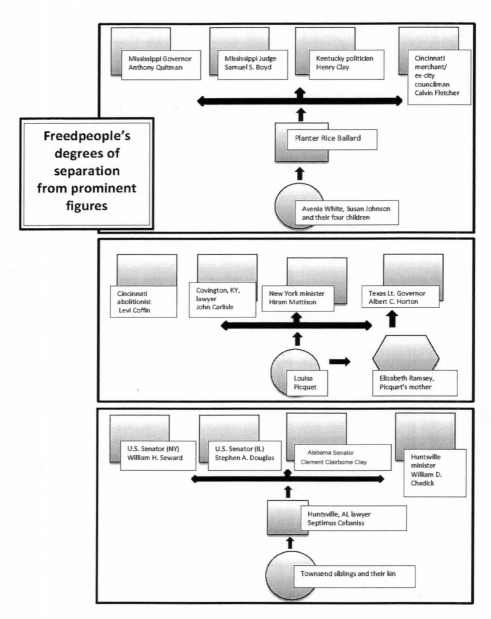

FIGURE 21. Degree of separation chart demonstrating ties between enslaved and freed people of color and prominent antebellum white men. Sharony Green.

with John Williams, in which companionship, housekeeping, and sex were exchanged for the promise of eventual freedom. In all likelihood Avenia White, Susan Johnson, and Samuel Townsend's sexual partners were also aware of and took advantage of the dynamic existing between themselves and white men, the sort that could and did reap benefits. Thomas Townsend's mother certainly never envisioned that he would one day want a buffalo robe, but she may well have foreseen as she shared Samuel Townsend's bed that he would be able to afford it.

The voices of the women and girls in the Townsend family point to their self-awareness of their status as the daughters and granddaughters of a wealthy white man and black women. Elvira Townsend, Susanna Townsend, Nettie Caldwell, even the women that Lakin felt compelled to reprimand sternly—all demonstrated both independence and assertiveness. And so did Nettie when she bluntly told Cabaniss that she would not choose a guardian "unless you send me some money." Nettie was not merely speaking her mind; she was laying bare the cracks and contradictions in the ideology of white patriarchy and America's race and class relations, foreshadowing the emergence of a new social order. That order has yet fully to materialize, but immense strides have been made since Nettie let Cabaniss know her wishes.

Samuel Townsend was aware of laws limiting the full promise of his children's lives and, seeing his imminent death, made determined attempts to secure their futures and those of their children and their surviving mothers. John Williams, Louisa Picquet's former master, did much the same, and so did Rice Ballard. These Southern white men endeavored to offer protection, however imperfectly, to enslaved bodies in which they had invested themselves financially and emotionally in hidden and not so hidden ways—as the reports of Cincinnatians like Levi Coffin and Eliza Potter reveal. Such relationships were as complex as they were numerous. Examining their complexity will help us achieve a better understanding of the contradictions in human behavior when racial divisions are all too present.

Epilogue

The act of talking through the past in search of understanding often begins with unexpected conversations like one I once had with an African American repairman in my home. As he worked on the project at hand, we talked about many things, including my research. He told me that he had a Southern white ancestor who had married not one, not two, but three African American women, and he had a white wife.

When I first heard this story, it seemed a bit far-fetched. Three black wives? The repairman also said some of his relatives still resided in the house once owned by this white man. They even have his papers and photographs. It is a big house "down a really long dirt road in the middle of nowhere," he said. I laughed when he said this because he seemed to want nothing to do with this property, although he admitted that his male kinfolk made a workshop of a building that once served as slave quarters.

Though his skin was as dark as mine, the curl in his hair affirmed that he, like most African Americans (and many white ones, too), was of mixed race. As he walked out the door, he said, as if he did not entirely believe it, "Not all white people are bad."

After he departed, I reflected on what he said about his white male ancestor and wondered whether those four marriages had been short ones because of public pressure or whether this man had just outlived the women he had married. The researcher in me longed to know more. It would have been good to have other accounts. While those in this book are better documented than most, they are still based on slim evidence. They do, however, give voice to many small details surrounding black-white intimacies of the past, among them, that Rice Ballard's ancestry can be traced to the English county in which Shakespeare was born, though the four children he freed in Cincinnati doubtless never knew this trivial fact.

As the repairman's truck left the driveway, I took comfort in having been made aware of another relationship that appears to resonate with my subject. While completing this book, I learned about a former coworker's ancestor who ran off with a freedwoman before the Civil War. This coworker mentioned as much in a memoir capturing his own life as the white husband of a black woman and father of an adopted African child.[1] As society's obsession with genealogy continues, other newly found records will doubtless reveal more individuals whose fears, self-interests, and triumphs tell us more about the "messiness" of black-white encounters.[2] Many of them will begin with stories like the one the repairman heard about his ancestors or the one my former coworker shared, stories researchers should take to heart especially because the general public readily sees traces of them in imagined works.

No matter our take on them, interracial relationships are a known legacy of American history. That they are might help explain the success of certain television shows and motion pictures.[3] Many such works are more willing to take up the subject of intimacy between African Americans and whites than are scholarly ones.[4] There are reasons for this, including the obvious lack of evidence. But the arrival of more and more evidence such as the letters, legal documents, and other sources presented here provide opportunities for scholars boldly to reimagine people of the past, even though stories have been told in certain ways for so long that it is hard to change the narratives.

I initially only wanted to explore the power of fancy girls after reading about them in Deborah Gray White's now-classic *Ar'n't I a Woman: Female Slaves in the Plantation South.*[5] While learning about these expensive women and girls, I also delved into the issue of kinship between them and their children, if they were mothers. After stepping back, I realized something difficult had gone unsaid: the degree to which Southern white men figured into these individuals' lives before and after they were freed. I did not know how to address this topic with the obvious horrors of slavery always in view. I learned how by teaching a class.

It is interesting to see that so much of what is learned goes back to the classroom, even for instructors. It was only after teaching the course African Americans in the City at the University of Alabama while on a graduate fellowship that I saw how changes in nineteenth-century

American society and culture, including how people scrutinized one another and how they demonstrated their awareness of what it means to be an individual in a modern and increasingly wealthy and urban society, factored into this project. These related developments helped me craft my central argument. Even if Southern white men were only a loan away from being penniless, they were capable of freeing instead of selling black women and children for whom they cared.

All of a sudden I could see a generational portrait of a particular kind of man—one who was married, had not married, or would never marry, or one who was aging or divorced—who might invest himself emotionally and financially in "relationships" with women and children of color. I struggled with how to name such investments. After looking at five letters from Avenia White to Rice Ballard, her former master, the most appropriate word seemed to be intimacy. This book explores one huge outcome for enslaved women like her, and their children: manumission, specifically, manumission that resulted in the relocation of African Americans who received some measure of white men's favor to, as I would soon discover, a particular place, Cincinnati.

Such favor existed in my own family. Years before I was born, my fair-skinned maternal great-grandmother was the mistress of a white man named Mister Ray. My mother told me she and her sister could charge whatever they wanted at the local general store in their Mississippi Delta town because Mister Ray paid the bill. And whenever my mother and my auntie passed the local dress shop, they were summoned by Miss Diamond, a Jewish shopkeeper, who would say, "Hello, girls! Tell Louella I got some pretty dresses. Mister Ray said y'all can have any you want. Just come on by." But my mom and auntie had been given strict orders to never enter this or any store without my great-grandma's permission. In their town, Jim Crow "whites only" signs served as a constant reminder that though my family had access to the white man's money, they were not white.[6]

Though I did not realize it consciously, my interest in fancy girls was a way to explore the particular pain of fair-skinned African Americans, including women like my great-grandmother.[7] She and the former enslaved individuals presented here and elsewhere, the women in particular, seemed to stand in a very complicated space. Being of mixed race could lead to ostracism by other blacks if it was believed they received material or financial advantages as a result of their fair complexion. Such ostracism occurred even though many fair-skinned blacks were themselves poor.

African Americans, even those in the scholarly community, often do not want to acknowledge, much less confront, such intragroup conflict.[8] Certainly the peculiar institution generated tensions even between people in the African American community. Such tensions manifests in "color struck" attitudes of those who buy into white Americans' normative standards of beauty and the accompanying myths that fair-skinned people are not only more beautiful (and have "better" hair) but are smarter, too. It was not simply the privileged access that some blacks had to powerful white men that other blacks found off-putting: it was the way in which such pairings, coerced or not, produced fair-skinned individuals who reinforced the caste system. Illustrative of this attitude is the disposition of Cora Gillam, a freedwoman from Arkansas. Gillam's half sister was sent to Ohio to attend Oberlin and her half brother to a school in Cincinnati. Gillam, whose white father was an overseer and presumably of more modest means than the fathers of her half siblings, attended neither. But as if to align herself with them in any manner she knew how, Gillam reportedly announced, "My father was not a slave. Can't you tell by me that he was white?"[9]

It should be emphasized that some black men certainly resented African American women's involvement with white men, some even blaming them for inviting white men's overtures. Robert Smalls, a former slave from South Carolina who became a boat pilot for the U.S. government and later a congressman, reportedly once charged that African American women were inherently immoral. He bemoaned that they seemed to want "principally" "white men with whom they would rather have intercourse than with their own color."[10] At least one woman of color similarly took a jaundiced view of women of color engaging in interracial sex, whether they had a choice or not. Said Sarah Fitzpatrick, a former bondswoman interviewed in Alabama, "The reason our race is so mixed up," she stated, "is by fooling with these white men."[11] All this as white Americans often do not want to be confronted with how the oppressive ideas of their ancestors were foundational to such conflict in the first place. Each act of favor black women and children received from white men seems to point to the hypocrisy in American life. Certainly after losing the Civil War, as a part of reconciling itself to the nation, white Southerners reasserted control over their region by means of Jim Crow laws and lynchings but also storytelling about black-white relationships. Annette Gordon-Reed argues that such rewriting was a necessary part of their healing process.[12] The imposition of white domination required that whites remain silent about "ubiquitous" interracial sex and illegitimate children with women of color.

Nowadays such conversations are especially difficult in this so-called postracial world.[13] With so much unspoken, it is hard to see the many little-discussed costs some fair-skinned African American women paid while sometimes accruing a bit of power from their intimate encounters with white men. Certainly my great-grandmother paid such costs while maintaining her ties to Mister Ray. It may have been worth it for she was driven by poverty. The gains were not just dresses and other material items, but really important items like food. Mister Ray provided things that she and other family members needed, even as the segregationist practices around them never permitted him fully to flaunt his African American woman. Their relationship occurred in an environment in which interracial unions were acknowledged at the community level, as they had been since the colonial era, but they were never sanctioned either socially or legally owing to the rules that elite white men themselves imposed on women, people of color, children, and poor whites.[14]

I believe that historical actors' ways of speaking and understanding their lives and tactics shift across time and must be contextualized and delineated according to the norms of the moment, but I also believe that in some ways my great-grandmother's life had parallels with the experiences of untold numbers of other women, even former enslaved women, with whom white men developed some form of intimacy. I carried on with my research, knowing the experiences of such women and their children are an understandably taboo subject for those who have conflicted feelings about the era of slavery.

The women to whom Smalls pointed forever carried with them traces of their particular past, isolated not only by whites, but other African Americans. Frederick Law Olmsted, the renowned landscape architect who traveled throughout the South to document the evils of slavery, once saw a coffle containing a woman who did not wear "the usual plantation apparel" worn by other slaves. This woman, he observed, also took "no part in the light chat" of the others. He noted, too, that she did not help them make a fire, nor did she later stand with them around it. Instead, she stood alone, like a statue, "bowed and gazing" into the flames.[15] This bondswoman's past is unknowable, but from Olmsted's description she appears to have been a female slave in whom whites, not just white men, had invested more time and interest than they had in others.

A growing number of scholars have urged those in the academic community to take seriously the African American oral history tradition, which "has long realized the significance of white men as fathers of mixed-race enslaved children providing a foundation for a pre-Civil

War black elite even though mainstream scholars are unwilling to do the same."[16] Again, that such African Americans have remained members of the black elite may have had some impact on how their lives are presented in academic writings. The black elite, some may have decided, needs little help.

To be sure, the favor some women of color had was manifested in the New World. Just months before the start of the Civil War, Mary Seacole, a Jamaican woman of mixed race, attempted to help a young man enlist in the Royal Navy. Having had much contact with British society because of her services as a nurse during the Crimean War, she sought an appointment with Alexander Milne, a senior naval officer, upon his arrival in Port Royal, Jamaica. What makes their meeting especially meaningful is that Milne took the time to record this event in a gossipy letter to one of his colleagues. "Mrs Seacole is on board in high Crinoline," he wrote. "She wants me to Enter a Boy but he is all head and no body."[17]

As did others of his day, Milne objectified Seacole. He noted her crinoline dress, which was standard attire for middle- and upper-class white British women. He probably did so because the dress was at odds with the naval uniforms on the men around him and possibly because it went against the grain of what was expected of a woman of color. In noting her attire, Milne was suggesting that she was no ordinary "Negro." She had a respectable occupation. She was of mixed race. She had good breeding. These three facts were intricately connected. Because she was all of these things, she had Milne's attention, even being allowed on his quarterdeck or into his office, both of them male, professional spaces.[18]

This meeting, one about which we have a few details, makes visible a level of intimacy between two people of very different social statuses in a private space. Although Milne refused to recruit the young boy for whom Seacole had lobbied, he granted her an audience, something both he and she understood as being a reasonable gesture despite his racial identity given her privileged position in society and her service. His failure to comply with her request was almost certainly based on sound professional reasons, not on racial or gender prejudices.

It has been far easier to explore the blatant oppression experienced by people of African descent than such intimacy, especially the kind that concerns fair-skinned women and girls who, in imagined works and surviving records, often appear larger than life. While some were people of real significance to white men, others were bodies exploited by lonely and sometimes vile individuals. Getting at both extremes and all of the grayer areas in the middle requires investigation. It is through such scrutiny that we can probe how black women emerged as both victors and victims, immoral and upright, enslaved and indeed free *with* white men's help. As if addressing the hurdles of such a task, a white woman, this one from the upper South, once told me, "It's easier for both blacks and whites to say it was only rape, because to say it was love or something approaching that is too difficult. We'd then have to explain how this happened alongside of everything else."[19]

Notes

Introduction

1. Avenia White to Ballard, October 25, 1838, Folder 25, Rice C. Ballard Papers (hereafter Ballard Papers), Southern Historical Collection, Wilson Library, University of North Carolina, Chapel Hill.

2. Kentucky Death Records, 1852–1953, at www.ancestry.com (accessed October 23, 2012); 1850 U.S. Census at www.ancestry.com (accessed June 12, 2013); *Mississippi State Gazette (Natchez)*, January 8, 1820, Vol. 7, Issue 2, p. 1; *John B. Jegli's Louisville Directory, 1845–46* (Louisville: Jeglis, 1845), 32; Lewis Collins, *History of Kentucky* (Covington: Collins & Co., 1882), 38–41; John E. Kleber, *The Encyclopedia of Louisville* (Lexington: University Press of Kentucky, 2000).

3. Isaac Franklin to Ballard, September 27, 1834, Folder, 15, Ballard Papers; "old woman, n.," OED Online, June 2013 (Oxford: Oxford University Press, 1989, 1993, 1997), www.oed.com/view/Entry/130999 (accessed June 24, 2013).

4. Rosemary Brana-Shute and Randy J. Sparks, eds., *Paths to Freedom: Manumission in the Atlantic World* (Columbia: University of South Carolina Press, 2009), vii.

5. Such women and even girls were highly valued typically because of their fair skin. Such bondswomen and girls, who were often found in Southern port cities through which men and money moved, could bring as much $5,000 on the auction block, far surpassing the $2,500 average price of an adult male slave with blacksmithing skills. But not all prospective customers were drawn to fancies, nor had they the money to pay for them. Some customers preferred dark-skinned bondswomen and girls, who were often assumed to be freer from disease than fair-skinned ones who were likewise believed to have been "handled" more. Still, the greater evidence of white men's ties to fair-skinned women before the war suggests a preference for them owing to attitudes that held that any individual—especially a woman—whose appearance approximated that of whites was more desirable. Frederic Bancroft, *Slave-Trading in the Old South* (Baltimore: J. H. Furst Company, 1931), 131; J. Winston Coleman,

Slavery Times in Kentucky (Chapel Hill: University of North Carolina Press, 1940), 137; John W. Blassingame, *The Slave Community: Plantation Life in the Antebellum South* (New York: Oxford University Press, 1972, 1979), 155; Eugene D. Genovese, *Roll, Jordan, Roll: The World the Slaves Made* (New York: Pantheon, 1974), 416–17, 423–24; Deborah Gray White, *Ar'n't I a Woman: Female Slaves in the Plantation South* (New York: W. W. Norton, [1985] 1999), 34–38; Edward E. Baptist, "'Cuffy,' 'Fancy Maids,' and 'One-Eyed Men': Commodification, and the Domestic Slave Trade in the United States," *American Historical Review*, 106.5 (December 2001): 1619–50; Walter Johnson, *Soul by Soul: Life inside the Antebellum Slave Market* (Cambridge, MA: Harvard University Press, 1999), 113; Michael Tadman, *Speculators and Slaves: Masters, Traders, and Slaves in the Old South* (Madison: University of Wisconsin Press, 1989), 125. For more on the sexual objectification of women of African descent as a racially gendered concept, see Anne McClintock, *Imperial Leather: Race, Gender, and Sexuality in the Colonial Contest* (New York: Routledge, 1995).

6. The birth of biracial people has escalated markedly in recent years. Susan Saulny, "Census Data Presents Rise in Multiracial Population of Youths," *New York Times*, March 24, 2011; Sharon Jayson, "Census Shows Big Jump in Interracial Couples," *USA Today*, April 26, 2012; U.S. Bureau of Statistics, 2010, Table 60, www.census.gov/compendia/statab/2011/tables/11s0060.pdf (accessed June 3, 2014); Jeffrey S. Passel, Wendy Wang, and Paul Taylor, "Marrying Out: One in Seven New U.S. Marriages is Interracial or Interethnic," PEW Research Center, A Social and Demographic Trends Report, June 15, 2010.

7. James Oliver Horton and Stacy Flaherty, "Black Leadership in Antebellum Cincinnati," in Henry Louis Taylor Jr., ed., *Race and the City: Work, Community, and Protest in Cincinnati, 1820–1970* (Urbana: University of Illinois Press, 1993), 81.

8. Ibid.

9. David Gerber, *Black Ohio and the Color Line, 1860–1915* (Urbana: University of Illinois Press, 1976), 17; Horton and Flaherty, "Black Leadership in Antebellum Cincinnati," 81; Joe William Trotter Jr., *River Jordan: African American Urban Life in the Ohio Valley* (Lexington: University of Kentucky Press, 1998).

10. Their brother Charles was also politically active in Ohio. William Cheek and Aimee Lee Cheek, "John Mercer Langston," in Taylor, *Race and the City*, 29–69.

11. Ibid.

12. Gerber, *Black Ohio*, 37; Darrel Bigham, *Jordan's Banks: Emancipation and Its Aftermath in the Ohio River Valley* (Lexington: University Press of Kentucky, 2006); Nikki M. Taylor, *Frontiers of Freedom: Cincinnati's Black Community, 1802–1868* (Athens: Ohio University Press, 2005); Taylor, *Race and the City*; Trotter, *River Jordan*.

13. Ira Berlin, *Slaves without Masters: The Free Negro in the Antebellum South* (New York: New Press, [1974] 2007); Michael P. Johnson and James Roark, *Black Masters: A Free Family of Color in the Old South* (New York: W. W. Norton, 1976); Larry Koger, *Black Slaveowners: Free Black Slave Masters in South Carolina, 1790–1860* (Columbia: University of South Carolina Press, 1995); Leonard P. Curry, *The Free Black in Urban America, 1800–1850: The Shadow of the Dream* (Chicago: University of Chicago Press, 1986).

14. *National Anti-Slavery Standard*, April 21, 1855, in Carter G. Woodson, ed., *The Mind of the Negro as Reflected in Letters during the Crisis, 1800–1860* (Eastford, CT: Martino Fine Books, 2010), 371.

15. Gerber, *Black Ohio*, 8, 22.

16. Ibid., 19; Frederick A. McGinnis, *History of Wilberforce* (Blanchester, OH: Brown Publishing Company, 1941); Wanda M. Davis, "First Foundations: An Enquiry into the Founding of Three Selected African American Institutions of Higher Learning" (EdD diss., Pennsylvania State University, 1994); Eric Metaxas, *Amazing Grace: William Wilberforce and the Heroic Campaign to End Slavery* (New York: HarperOne, 2007); William Wilberforce, Robert Isaac Wilberforce, and Samuel Wilberforce, eds., *The Life of William Wilberforce, Cambridge Library Collection—Slavery and Abolition (Volume 1)* (Cambridge: Cambridge University Press, 2011). Though its chief focus is Southern institutions of higher learning, for more on the history of higher education for African Americans during the bellum and postwar years, see James D. Anderson, *The Education of Blacks in the South, 1860–1935* (Chapel Hill: University of North Carolina Press, 1988).

17. Eliza Potter, *A Hairdresser's Experience in High Life* (1859; New York: Oxford University Press, 1991), 171.

18. Gerber, *Black Ohio*, 4–6; Taylor, *Frontiers of Freedom*, 2, 28–36; Curry, *Free Black in Urban America*, 245; Cheek and Cheek, "John Mercer Langston," 31–32.

19. Ibid.

20. Gunther Barth, *The Rise of Modern City Culture in Nineteenth-Century America* (Oxford: Oxford University Press, 1982), 3.

21. Taylor, *Frontiers of Freedom*, 11–13.

22. Ibid., 24; Horton and Flaherty, "Black Leadership in Antebellum Cincinnati," 74; Cheek and Cheek, "John Mercer Langston," 31.

23. Clark once stated that the American frontier explorer William Clark, younger brother of George Rogers Clark, the renowned northwestern frontier military leader, was his paternal grandfather but later recanted his story. Surviving documents suggest that John Clark, William and George's father, had an enslaved African American woman as a sexual partner. Nikki M. Taylor, *America's First Black Socialist: The Radical Life of Peter H. Clark* (Lexington: University Press of Kentucky, 2013), 61–86, 226–30.

24. Ibid., 85.

25. Ibid., 86.

26. Mary Niall Mitchell, *Raising Freedom's Child: Black Children and Visions of Freedom after Slavery,* (American History and Culture) (New York: New York University Press, 2011), 9. For more on the responses of newly freedpeople, see David Roediger, *Seizing Freedom: Slave Emancipation for All* (New York: Verso, 2014).

27. "Woman," "girl," "gal," and "wench" were habitually used to discuss women like White when they were enslaved. This study uses the words woman or girl, bondswomen or "bondsgirls, and even mate in the rare instance when it seems appropriate. "Concubine," the label some researchers have used to refer to such women and girls, is so closely associated with ancient societies that invoking it for the antebellum period introduces profound interpretational problems. If the purpose of language is to contextualize a specific era, concubine is not fitting here. The word mistress is one possible alternative. Certainly one cheeky visitor to Cincinnati noted the numerous "unmarried women who had been the mistresses of planters in Louisiana, Mississippi and Tennessee." But its use is also problematic because the term is firmly embedded in nineteenth-century notions of *white* womanhood, which assigned a place of honor to

them via the "cult of domesticity" and in doing so rendered women of African descent in far less favorable light. The terms bondsman, bondswoman, bondsboy, or bonds-girl dates to the biblical era and well into the nineteenth century to refer to enslaved people. See "bondsman, n.," OED Online, March 2014, Oxford University Press, www.oed.com/view/Entry/21290?rskey=pGY5jf&result=2&isAdvanced=false (accessed June 8, 2014); Taylor, *Frontiers of Freedom*, 135; Victoria Bynum, *Unruly Women: The Politics of Social and Sexual Control in the Old South* (Chapel Hill: University of North Carolina Press, 1992), 6–9; Thavolia Glymph, *Out of the House of Bondage: The Transformation of the Plantation Household* (Oxford: Cambridge University Press, 2008); Drew Gilpin Faust, *Mothers of Invention: Women of the Slaveholding South in the American Civil War* (Chapel Hill: University of North Carolina Press, 2004). For more on "the cult of domesticity," see Laura F. Edwards, *Gendered Strife and Confusion: The Political Culture of Reconstruction* (Urbana: University of Illinois Press, 1997); Anya Jabour, *Scarlett's Sisters: Young Women in the Old South* (Chapel Hill: University of North Carolina Press, 2007); Kathleen M. Brown, *Good Wives, Nasty Wenches, and Anxious Patriarchs* (Chapel Hill: University of North Carolina Press, 1996).

28. William H. Freehling, *The Reintegration of American History: Slavery and the Civil War* (New York: Oxford University Press, 1994).

29. Sara Ahmed, *Queer Phenomenology: Orientations, Objects, Others* (Durham, NC: Duke University Press, 2006); Rosalyn Terborg-Penn, "Migration and Trans-Racial/National Identity Re-Formation: Becoming African Diaspora Women," *Black Women, Gender and Families* 5.2 (Fall 2011):.4–24.

30. Patricia O'Brien, "Michel Foucault's History of Culture," in Lynn Hunt, ed., *The New Cultural History* (Berkeley: University of California Press, 1989); Michel Foucault *Power/Knowledge: Selected Interviews and Other Writings ,1972–1977, ed. Colin Gordon* (New York: Pantheon Books, [1972] 1980); Michel Foucault, *The History of Sexuality: An Introduction, Volume 1* (New York: Vintage, 1978); Joan Wallach Scott, *Gender and the Politics of Hi*story, rev. ed. (New York: Columbia University Press, [1988] 1999).

31. In acknowledging this flux in their social condition, this study cautiously addresses the work of power in Southern race and class relations. It does so by cautiously reflecting on the "psychology of power" in such relations, a task that requires ongoing study. Glymph, *Out of the House of Bondage*, 193.

32. Amy Dru Stanley, *From Bondage to Contract: Wage Labor, Marriage and the Market in the Age of Slave Emancipation* (New York: Cambridge University Press, 1998).

33. Ibid., xi.

34. Jennifer Morgan uses the word messiness as a way of describing the complexities of interracial relationships involving white men and black female slaves in the "New World." Jennifer L. Morgan, *Laboring Women: Reproduction and Gender in New World Slavery* (Philadelphia; University of Pennsylvania Press, 2004), 195.

35. New Orleans's reputation as a site for interracial relationships is well documented. As Carolyn Morrow Long has written in her study of Marie Laveau, the renowned voodou priestess, men and women there worked across the color line to form domestic partnerships and "employ strategies to circumvent the increasingly repressive laws against the amalgamation of African and European blood and the flow of white prosperity into black hands." Laveau descended from white French colonialists, Africans, and free mixed-race people of color and thus serves as a "paradigm for

race relations during the first two hundred years of Louisiana's history." Carolyn Morrow Long, *A New Orleans Voudou Priestess: The Legend and Reality of Marie Laveau* (Gainesville: University Press of Florida, 2006), 3.

36. But as the historian Stephanie M. H. Camp has written, we can still closely read archival documents and speculate about their broader significance as many incidents reflected wider practices. Stephanie M .H. Camp, *Closer to Freedom: Enslaved Women and Everyday Resistance in the Plantation South* (Chapel Hill: University of North Carolina Press, 2004), 95

37. See also Mark Scott, "Permira to Buy Ancestry.com for $1.6 billion," *New York Times*, October 22, 2012, http://dealbook.nytimes.com/2012/10/22/permira-said-to-buy-ancestry-com-for-1–6-billion/?_r=0 (accessed July 2, 2013).

38. See two contracts for partnership in the slave trade between Ballard, Franklin, and Franklin's nephews James Franklin and John Armfield dated 1833 and 1835, Folder 421, Ballard Papers. Franklin's elder brother, James Rawlings Franklin, was also a domestic slave trader. Robert H. Gudmestad, "The Troubled Legacy of Isaac Franklin: The Enterprise of Slave Trading," *Tennessee Historical Quarterly* 62 (Fall 2003): 193–217. For more, see Wendell Holmes Stephenson, *Isaac Franklin: Slave Trader and Planter of the Old South; With Plantation Records* (Baton Rouge: Louisiana State University Press; [1938] 1968), 89; Steven Deyle, *Carry Me Back: The Domestic Slave Trade in American Life* (New York: Oxford University Press, 2006), 12.

39. Receipt for clothing, November 27, 1837, Ballard Papers.

40. Levi Coffin, *Reminiscences of Levi Coffin, the Reputed President of the Underground Railroad: Being a Brief History of the Labors of a Lifetime in Behalf of the Slave, with the Stories of Numerous Fugitives, Who Gained Their Freedom through His Instrumentality, and Many Other Incidents* (Cincinnati: Robert Clark & Co., 1880), 287, 481. http://docsouth.unc.edu/nc (accessed September 5, 2012).

41. Illustrative of his callous side toward blacks are his actions during an 1832 cholera epidemic in Natchez. The disease threatened to wipe out the bondspeople Ballard shipped from Virginia. He urged Franklin to abandon them. "We had better loose [sic] them all and begin again than loose ourselves," Ballard wrote in one of the few letters he copied for his own records. Ballard to Isaac Franklin, December 2, 1832, Folder 8, Ballard Papers.

42. Ballard to Isaac Franklin, September 7, 1832, Folder 7, Ballard Papers.

43. For more, see Eric Foner, *Free Soil, Free Labor, Free Men: The Ideology of the Republican Party before the Civil War* (New York: Oxford University Press, 1970).

44. Genovese, *Roll, Jordan, Roll*; Robin D. G. Kelley, *Race Rebels: Culture, Politics, and the Black Working Class* (New York: Simon and Schuster, 1996); Johnson, *Soul by Soul*; Camp, *Closer to Freedom*.

45. Johnson, *Soul by Soul*, 111.

46. James C. Scott, *Weapons of the Weak: Everyday Forms of Peasant Resistance* (New Haven: Yale University Press, 1997).

47. One way of coping was to foster intimacy with such men who might eventually free them and contribute to their financial future. To say "intimate" is to say the white men and African Americans before us did things that allowed themselves to become "familiar" with one another in ways that *improved the condition and influence, however minor,* of the weaker party, namely black women and children. One aside: for labeling purposes, the terms black and African American are used in this

study while acknowledging that many of the people discussed were of mixed race. In fact, well into the nineteenth century, such individuals were often designated as either being of mixed race or otherwise—for example, some were called "black" if brown or dark-skinned—in many surviving documents, both private and public. However, in using the terms black and African American, this book ultimately acknowledges that individuals of mixed race have more often been characterized by the dominant culture as being of African descent to the exclusion of other ancestry.

48. Morgan, *Laboring Women*, 2.

49. Ibid.

50. Paul J. Lammermeier, "The Urban Black Family of the Nineteenth Century: A Study of Black Family Structure in the Ohio Valley, 1850–1880," *Journal of Marriage and the Family* 35.3 (August 1973): 441–43; E. Franklin Frazier, *The Negro Family in the United States* (Chicago: University of Chicago Press, 1939); Kenneth M. Stampp, *The Peculiar Institution: Slavery in the Ante-Bellum South* (New York: Vintage, 1956); Herbert G. Gutman, *The Black Family in Slavery and Freedom, 1750–1925* (New York: Vintage, 1976); *Angela Davis, Women, Race and Class* (New York: Vintage, 1983), 5.

51. Speaking partly to this point is the controversy involving the notes Thomas Jefferson made in the margins of a 1792 report, calculating the profits he planned to make on the birth of slave children. It has been suggested that these notes demonstrate that he cared only about his own wealth, not the enslaved, Sally Hemings included. Some have argued no genuine warmth can ever exist between two unequal bodies, for to be enslaved was to be forced into a legal arrangement that excluded the possibility for expressive moments. Such beliefs were and continue to be so widespread that Jefferson's "relationship" with Hemings is sometimes dismissed as fiction, a view that doubtlessly persists because Hemings was never freed. The experiences of certain freed women and children offer an opportunity to rethink this logic. Jennifer Schuessler, "Some Scholars Reject Dark Portrait of Jefferson," *New York Times*, November 26, 2012, www.nytimes.com/2012/11/27/books/henry-wienceks-master-of-the-mountain-irks-historians.html?pagewanted=all&_r=0 (accessed December 4, 2012); Annette Gordon-Reed, "Engaging Jefferson: Blacks and the Founding Father," *William and Mary Quarterly*, 3rd. ser., 57.1 (Jan. 2000): 178.

52. Patricia Hill Collins, *Black Feminist Thought: Knowledge, Consciousness and the Politics of Empowerment* (New York: Routledge, 1991), 11.

53. In the past decade, a growing body of literature has addressed the emotions of historical actors. Such research is a result of the scholarly community being fully attentive to its usage of the words emotion and emotional. Barbara H. Rosewein has argued that when emotions are referenced in historical writing, it is far too often an attempt to make one's writing livelier. She points out that sociologists now claim that the origins "of emotion, its governing laws, and its consequences are an inseparable part of the social process," something historians and others are only beginning to appreciate. While this study is attentive to the emotions of antebellum people of color and whites, it relies more on *the words and actions* of such individuals than on *exploring emotions as a part of their socialization*. What is at stake here is investigating how the words and behaviors of historical subjects permit us to learn more about certain freedpeople, and further, how their relations with white men can reveal more about black-white intimacies during the nineteenth century. This study, thus, assumes the emotional entanglements of such individuals were ever present, but the emotions

themselves—be they anger, fear, etc.,—are not the primary focus. Barbara H. Rose-
wein, *Emotional Communities in the Early Middle Ages* (Ithaca: Cornell University
Press, 2006), 1. For more on historical approaches to examining emotions, see Susan
Broomhall, *Emotions in the Household, 1200–1900* (New York: Palgrave Macmillan,
2008); and Nicole Eustace, *Passion Is the Gale: Emotion, Power, and the Coming of the
American Revolution* (Chapel Hill: University of North Carolina Press, 2008).

54. Some of slavery's most invasive forms of violation indeed occurred when
enslaved women willingly gave their bodies to ensure their safety and that of their
children. Saidiya Hartman, *Scenes of Subjection: Terror, Slavery, and Self-Making in
Nineteenth-Century America* (New York: Oxford University Press, 1997), 42.

55. Moreover, the favor the freedwomen and freed children under scrutiny received
was not the kind associated with the "cardinal rule" of slaveholding, which is to say the
sort that occurred when slaveholders indulged "well-behaved" enslaved men, women,
and children.Tadman, *Speculators and Slaves,* 203.

56. Evidently not only Southern white men did as much. In Southern port cities
where free people of color acquired wealth, male slaveholders of African descent may
have also done as much with women and children they owned. Though he may be
more representative of an extreme case of Old World concubinage than an example
of this particular phenomenon, Jean Montanee, an African-born New Orleans slaveholder and conjurer, also known as Dr. John, reportedly made at least fifteen enslaved
women his "concubines." These women "bore him children in great multitude." His
sexual partners also included a "white woman of the lowest class." In addition, cre-
ators of imagined works have presented him as a mentor, lover, and rival of the voodou
priestess Marie Laveau. Long, *New Orleans Voudou Priestess,* 137, 146.

57. Betty DeRamus and Emily West are among several researchers who have examined love, romantic and familial alike, involving enslaved or recently freed African
Americans. One example of such love involves Lear Green, a black Baltimore woman
who hid for eighteen hours in a sailor's chest in 1857 to travel to Philadelphia in order
to be with the black man she loved. There is also a case involving a white Mississippi
physician who sought to leave his rural community to start a practice in New Orleans.
In the process of moving, he hired out his bondsmen and bondswomen, requiring
them to work for others in Baton Rouge for a fee that the physician himself received.
His actions upset one enslaved man who understood that being hired out could desta-
bilize the black family. This man did not want to be separated from his wife and told
the agent orchestrating his master's move as much. In fact, the enslaved man said he
would rather die than be separated, even for a short period. Even though the slave
was eventually sent on to Baton Rouge, he was permitted to remain with his wife for
an additional six months. Betty DeRamus, *Forbidden Fruit: Loves Stories from the
Underground Railroad* (New York: Atria Books, 2005), 29–35; *Daily Evening Bulletin*
(San Francisco, CA), May 10, 1873, Issue 29, col. E; *Cleveland Morning Daily Herald*
(Cleveland, OH), May 3, 1873, Issue 106, col. G; Emily West, *Chains of Love: Slave
Couples in Antebellum South Carolina* (Urbana: University of Illinois Press, 2004);
Johnson, *Soul by Soul,* 34–35.

58. However, burdened by societal expectations, white women were condemned for
engaging in sex with black men, whose masculinity was so threatening to white men,
and such black-white unions were often surrounded by shame and misfortune. Speaking to this point, as Emily West has written, as an infant, John C. Brown, a former slave

from South Carolina, was found on a railroad track in "nice baby clothes," abandoned by his white mother. His father was reportedly enslaved on his white master's plantation. However, some white women, especially when wealth was involved, entered into marriage with men of African descent. For example, one Virginia white woman married a wealthy man whose mother was of mixed race and father was of French descent. Her husband had been sent to Paris to be educated. Many knew of his racial identity, but "on account of his millions and his father, nothing was said."

Homosexual unions across the color line, intimate and otherwise, also existed in the antebellum South, though limited evidence of them survives. One unfortunate case is strongly hinted at in the 1861 memoir of Harriet Jacobs, the pen name of Linda Brent, an enslaved woman. Jacobs recalled how Luke, a slave, was required to wait on a bedridden young white man, sometimes wearing only a shirt. Sometimes chained to a bed, Luke was forced to "submit" to his master's orders, which, according to Jacobs, were "too filthy to be repeated." West, *Chains of Love*, 120–26. See also chapter 7 of Brown, *Good Wives, Nasty Wenches, and Anxious Patriarchs;* Linda Brent, *Incidents in the Life of a Slave Girl* (New York: Oxford University Press, 1988), 288–89; Potter, *Hairdresser's Experience in High Life,* 155.

59. DoVeanna S. Fulton Minor and Reginald H. Pitts, *Speaking Lives, Authoring Texts: Three African American Women's Oral Slave Narratives* (Albany: SUNY Press, 2010), 3; White, *Ar'n't I a Woman,* 164.

60. That amount in today's currency is $5.5 million, http://futureboy.us/fsp/dollar.fsp?quantity=200000&currency=dollars&fromYear=1856 (accessed Sept. 20, 2012); Frances Cabaniss Roberts, "An Experiment in Emancipation of Slaves by an Alabama Planter" (Master's thesis, University of Alabama, 1940), 8–10, 108–9; Deposition of S. D. Cabaniss, MSS 252, Box Number 251.056, Folder 04, Septimus Douglas Cabaniss Papers, Special Collections, Stanley Hoole Library, University of Alabama (hereafter Cabaniss Papers).

1 / Probing a Planter's Hidden Life

1. Stampp, *The Peculiar Institution,* 31.

2. The occasion for this story was a portrait commissioned in Ballard's honor following his large donation to a Natchez orphanage. "Colonel R. C. Ballard," *Mississippi Free Trader and Natchez Gazette* (Natchez, MS), December 21, 1848, Issue 54, Col. D; John Wesley Monette, *Observations on the Epidemic Yellow Fever of Natchez, and of the South-west* (Louisville: Prentice and Weissinger, 1842).

3. 1860 U.S. Federal Census and New Orleans, Louisiana, Slave Manifests, 1807–60, www.ancestry.com (accessed June 12, 2013).

4. Bacon Tait to Ballard, August 16, 1839, Folder 28, Ballard Papers.

5. John F. Kasson, *Rudeness and Civility: Manners in Nineteenth-Century Urban America* (New York: Hill and Wang, 1990), 19.

6. While domestic slave traders have been considered unfavorably in Southern society, abolitionists' earliest antislavery efforts in the late 1830s publicized human cruelty, including rape and maiming at the hands of slaveholders on plantations, not by traders inside the slave market. Johnson, *Soul by Soul,* 24–25, 54–55, 217; Tadman, *Speculators and Slaves,* 3.

7. A letter Ballard received from Henry Clark, a Virginian, strongly hints at Fletcher's racial politics. Henry Clark to Ballard, October 10, 1838, Folder 18, Ballard Papers;

Calvin Fletcher to Ballard, January 28, 1839, Folder 26, Ballard Papers; David Henry Shaffer, *The Cincinnati, Covington, Newport and Fulton Directory for 1840* (Cincinnati: J. B. & R. P. Donogh, 1839), 181; Gayle Thornbrough and Dorothy L. Riker, eds., *Diary and Letters of Calvin Fletcher, Vol. I (1838–1843)* (Indianapolis: Indianapolis Historical Society, 1973), 210. See also a clipping of Fletcher's obituary in an unidentified newspaper, which was placed in a November 17, 1860, diary entry by his cousin Calvin Fletcher who lived in Indianapolis. Filson Historical Society, Special Collections. Arnold Lloyd and Herbert G. Wood eds., *Quaker Social History, 1669–1738* (London: Longmans, Green, 1950); William C. Braithwaite, *The Second Period of Quakerism*, 2nd ed. (Cambridge: Cambridge University Press, 1961); J. William Frost and John M. Moore, *Seeking the Light: Essays in Quaker History in Honor of Edwin B. Bronner* (Wallingford, PA: Pendle Hill Publications; Haverford, PA: Friends Historical Association, 1986); and Margaret Abruzzo, *Polemical Pain: Slavery, Cruelty, and the Rise of Humanitarianism* (Baltimore: Johns Hopkins University Press, 2011), 16–48.

8. Also: "A list of balances due James Ballard & Company, 1 Jany [sic] 1838," Folder 425a, and Folders 406 and 430 for business documents, Ballard Papers.

9. Thornbrough and Riker, *Diary and Letters of Calvin Fletcher,* 210.

10. The Indianapolis Fletcher described his cousin as being "a man of no pride who lives in a very ordinary house" and "far below his means." Ibid.

11. Bernie D. Jones, *Fathers of Conscience: Mixed Race Inheritance in the Antebellum South (Studies in the Legal History of the South)* (Athens: University of Georgia Press, 2009); Amrita Chakrabarti Myers, *Forging Freedom: Black Women and the Pursuit of Liberty in Antebellum Charleston* (Chapel Hill: The University of North Carolina Press, 2011).

12. Jones, *Fathers of Conscience,* 26–27.

13. Amrita Myers, "Public Rhetoric, Private Realities: Julia Chinn, Richard Johnson, and Debates over Interracial Sex in Antebellum America" (Paper presented at the 6th Biennial Conference of the Association for the Study of the Worldwide African Diaspora [ASWAD], Pittsburgh, PA, November 3–6, 2011); Leon Litwack, *Been in the Storm So Long: The Aftermath of Slavery* (New York: Alfred A. Knopf, 1979), 167–98; Cheryl Crowell, *Images of America: New Richmond* (Charleston: Arcadia Publishing, 2012), l, 8–9, 43; Charles S. Sydnor, "The Free Negro in Mississippi before the Civil War," *American Historical Review* 32.4 (July 1927): 767–77; Tiya Miles, *Ties That Bind: The Story of an Afro-Cherokee Family in Slavery and Freedom* (Berkeley: University of California Press, 2006), 57; Catherine Clinton, *The Plantation Mistress: Woman's World in the Old South* (New York: Pantheon, 1984), 215–17; Sterling Lecater Bland Jr., ed., *African American Slave Narratives, An Anthology , vol. 2* (Westport, CT: Greenwood Press, 2001), 310; Catherine Adams and Elizabeth Pleck, *Love of Freedom: Black Women in Colonial and Revolutionary England* (New York: Oxford University Press, 2010), 113.

14. Edmund Morgan, Oscar Handlin, Theodore Allen, Lerone Bennett, Nikhil Pal Singh, Kathleen M. Brown, and Claire Robertson are among the scholars who have examined race and gender as social constructions. Two important works that address these subjects are David R. Roediger, *The Wages of Whiteness: Race and the Making of the American Working Class* (Brooklyn: Verso, 1991); and Morgan, *Laboring Women.*

15. Morgan, *Laboring Women,* 191–95.

16. Ibid.

17. The first, passed in Maryland in 1661, prevented marriage between white women and enslaved people of color. After the American Revolution, a growing number of states passed miscegenation laws. Even after passage of the Fourteenth amendment, which theoretically gave African Americans "equal protection of the laws," many states that had repealed antimiscegenation laws reenacted them during the late nineteenth century. As late as 1944, thirty states had laws against interracial marriage, with the ban most often targeting black-white unions. Twelve southern states had miscegenation laws until 1967. Many of those laws remained on the books after 1967, although federal laws prohibited their enforcement. In 2007 interracial unions still accounted for just one percent of white marriages, 5 percent of African American marriages, but 14 percent of Asian marriages in the United States. These numbers reflect underreporting just has it had during the antebellum period because many consider interracial unions taboo. For more, see Thomas P. Monahan, "An Overview of Statistics on Interracial Marriage in the United States with Data on Its Extent from 1963–1970, " *Journal of Marriage and the Family* 38.2 (May 1976): 223–31; Irving G. Tragen, "Statutory Prohibitions against Interracial Marriage," *California Law Review* 32.3 (September 1944): 270; Roland G. Fryer Jr., "Guess Who's Coming to Dinner? Trends in Interracial Marriages over the Twentieth Century," *Journal of Economic Perspectives* 21.2 (Spring 2007): 72–73.

18. Jeanne Boydston, *Home & Work: Housework, Wages, and the Ideology of Labor in the Early Republic* (New York: Oxford University Press, 1990); John D'Emilio and Estelle B. Freedman, *Intimate Matters: A History of Sexuality in America* (Chicago: University of Chicago Press, 1988), 20.

19. D'Emilio and Freedman, *Intimate Matters*, 46–51.

20. For example, throughout the seventeenth century free white men outnumbered free white women in Jamestown, the first settlement in the United States, by three or four to one. Not until the end of the seventeenth century did these numbers begin to even out. As late as 1790 the sex ratio for free white Virginian men to women was 105.6 to 100, or 227,051 to 215,046. Herbert Moller, "Sex Composition and Correlated Culture Patterns of Colonial America," *William and Mary Quarterly* 2.2 (April 1945): 128. For more on sex ratios in early America, see Edmund Morgan, "The Puritans and Sex," *New England Quarterly* 15.4 (December 1942): 591–607; and D'Emilio and Freedman, *Intimate Matters*.

21. Philip D. Morgan, "Interracial Sex in the Chesapeake and the British Atlantic World," in Jan Ellen Lewis and Peter S. Onuf, eds., *Sally Hemings and Thomas Jefferson: History, Memory, and Civic Culture* (Charlottesville: University Press of Virginia, 1999), 42–84; Joshua Rothman, "James Callender and Social Knowledge of Interracial Sex in Antebellum Virginia," in Lewis and Onuf, eds., *Sally Hemings and Thomas Jefferson*, 96–97; Joshua D. Rothman, *Notorious in the Neighborhood: Sex and Families across the Color Line in Virginia, 1787–1861* (Chapel Hill: University of North Carolina Press, 2003).

22. Building on the work of the South African sociologist Pierre van den Berghe, George Fredrickson borrowed the term *Herrenvolk* to describe America's "peculiar" racism. For more, see George M. Fredrickson, *The Black Image in the White Mind: The Debate on Afro-American Character and Destiny, 1817–1914* (Middletown, CT: Wesleyan University Press, 1987); and C. Vann Woodward, *The Strange Career of Jim Crow*, 2nd ed. (New York: Oxford University Press, [1955] 1966).

23. Joshua D. Rothman, *Flush Times and Fever Dreams: A Story of Capitalism and Slavery in the Age of Jackson* (Athens: University of Georgia Press, 2012), 3. For more on slavery as an economic enterprise, see Edward E. Baptist, The Half Has Never Been Told: Slavery and the Making of American Capitalism (New York: Basic Books, 2014).

24. Well into the nineteenth century, this kind of imagery generally character-ized mixed-race women. Such characterizations figured into how such women were objectified in Brazilian urban music. "*I am a vain mulata/ Beautiful, coquettish, ador-able/ How many white women are not!,*" went one popular song that revealed the gen-dered undercurrents surrounding mixed-race women in postemancipation societies. Martha Abrue, translated from the Portuguese by Amy Chazkel and Junia Claudia Zaidan, "Mulatas, Crioulos, and Morenas: Racial Hierarchy, Gender Relations, and National Identity in Postabolition Popular Song (Southeastern Brazil, 1890–1920)," in Pamela Scully and Diana Paton, eds., *Gender and Slave Emancipation in the Atlantic World* (Durham, NC: Duke University Press, 2005), 272; Walter Johnson, "The Slave Trader, the White Slave, and the Politics of Racial Determinism in the 1850s," *Journal of American History* 87.1 (June 2000): 18; David R. Roediger and Elizabeth D. Esch, *The Production of the Difference: Race and the Management of Labor in U.S. History* (New York: Oxford University Press, 2012), 35.

25. Hilary McD. Beckles, *Centering Woman: Gender Discourses in Caribbean Slave Society* (Kingston: Ian Randle Publishers, 1999), 33.

26. The literature does not make clear exactly when and how such unions took place. *Placee* arrangements had origins in early American quadroon balls. Although such arrangements continued well into the 1850s, public toleration of the practice waned with the growing restrictions on people of color in the 1830s following the 1831 Nat Turner rebellion. Stephanie Li, "Resistance, Silence, and *Placees*: Charles Bon's Octoroon Mistress and Louisa Picquet," *American Literature* 79.1 (March 2007): 87.

27. Jennifer M. Spear, *Race, Sex and the Social Order in Early New Orleans* (Balti-more: Johns Hopkins University Press, 2009), 212.

28. Bynum, *Unruly Women*, 19.

29. Ibid., 6–9.

30. "fancy, n. and adj." OED Online, September 2012 (Oxford: Oxford University Press, 1989, 1993, 1997), www.oed.com/view/Entry/68025?redirectedFrom=fancy+g irl& (accessed October 08, 2012).

31. The view of women of color as being uninhibited sexually was a "ubiquitous part of Europe's critique of and encounter with Africa." In 1727 one surveyor's initial visit to the Gold Coast demonstrates this point. During his first view of the land-scape, he was intrigued by the African women he saw, calling them "hot constitution'd Ladies." Morgan, *Laboring Women*, 44–45.

32. Coleman, *Slavery Times in Kentucky*, 149.

33. Miles, *Ties That Bind*, 175.

34. Coffin, *Reminiscences of Levi Coffin*, 175–76.

35. Here I am building on the ideas of the poststructuralist philosopher Judith Butler who has argued that being "female" is not a biological fact but rather a cultural performance. Though she has not fully probed the racial implications of such a posi-tion, Butler's thoughts have special resonance with reference to the fancy girl, a term utilized to mark a particular mixed race being presumed to be in a "female" body, one intended for exploitation. For more, see Judith Butler, *Gender Trouble (Feminism and*

the Subversion of Identity) (New York: Routledge, 1990). Among the works addressing white men's fantasies of female slaves are Monique Guillory, "Some Enchanted Evening on the Auction Block: The Cultural Legacy of the New Orleans Quadroon Balls" (PhD diss., New York University, 1999); and Baptist, "'Cuffy,' 'Fancy Maids,' and 'One-Eyed Men.'"

36. John W. Blassingame, ed., *Slave Testimony: Two Centuries of Letters, Speeches, Interviews, and Autobiographies* (Baton Rouge: Louisiana State University Press, 1977), 400.

37. The "tragic mulatta/mulatto" as a cultural character can be traced to the mixed-race American actress and poet Adah Isaac Menken, who was born outside New Orleans in 1835. Inspired by a British muse "immortalized" in the works of Benjamin Disraeli and Honore de Balzac, among others, Menken appropriated this "marketable identity" on a New Orleans stage in 1857. Since then, the "tragic mulatto" as a symbolic figure has entered the public imagination through creative works. Whether male or female, such a figure manifests as suffering owing to his or her being a person of mixed race. An example is the character evoked in "Cross," a Langston Hughes poem: *"My old man's a white old man/And my old mother's black/If ever I cursed my white old man/I take my curses back/If ever I cursed my black old mother/And wish she were in hell/I am sorry for that evil wish/And now I wish her well/My old man died in a big fine house/My old mother died in a shack/I wonder where I'm gonna die/ Being neither white or black?"* Arthur P. Davis, "The Tragic Mulatto Theme in Six Works of Langston Hughes," *Phylon* 9 (1940–56), 16.2 (2nd Qtr. 1955): 196–97; and Kimberly Snyder Manganelli, *Transatlantic Spectacles of Race: The Tragic Mulatta and the Tragic Muse* (New Brunswick, NJ: Rutgers University Press, 2011), 1–6.

38. Bancroft, *Slave-Trading in the Old South,* 251.

39. Ibid.

40. James A. Ramage, *Rebel Raider: The Life of General John Hunt Morgan* (Lexington: University of Kentucky Press, 1986), 33.

41. Coleman, *Slavery Times in Kentucky,* 159.

42. Orville Hickman Browning, *The Diary of Orville Hickman Browning, vol. 1, 1850–1864* (1861: Springfield: Illinois State Historical Library, 2007), 139.

43. White, *Ar'n't I a Woman,* 46.

44. Bancroft, *Slave-Trading in the Old South,* 50.

45. Baptist, "'Cuffy,' 'Fancy Maids,' and 'One-Eyed Men,'" 1621; Adrienne Davis, "'Don't Let Nobody Bother Yo' Principle: The Sexual Economy of American Slavery," in Sharon Harley, ed., *Sister Circle: Black Women and Work* (New Brunswick, NJ: Rutgers University Press, 2002), 117.

46. *Alexandria (VA) Gazette,* August, 20, 1833. See two contracts for partnership in the slave trade between Ballard, Franklin, and Armfield dated 1833 and 1835, Folder 421, Ballard Papers; Deyle, *Carry Me Back,* 12; Tadman, *Speculators and Slaves,* 12, 16, 21; Baptist, "'Cuffy,' 'Fancy Maids,' and 'One-Eyed Men,'" 1628.

47. *Alexandria (VA) Gazette,* December 3, 1832.

48. Deyle, *Carry Me Back,* 100.

49. Baptist, "'Cuffy,' 'Fancy Maids,' and 'One-Eyed Men,'" 1628; Deyle, *Carry Me Back,* 100.

50. James Franklin to Ballard, March 27, 1832, Folder 5, Ballard Papers.

51. Other domestic slave traders wrote "fancy" larger than other words in their letters to indicate their possession of a fair-skinned enslaved woman or girl who could be potentially marketed as a fancy girl. See Philip Thomas to William Finney, July 26, 1859, William A. J. Finney Papers, Duke University.

52. Isaac Franklin to Ballard, September 27, 1834, Ballard Papers.

53. Walter Johnson has addressed how designations of a bondsperson's color were the slave trader's way of delineating their complexion and racial lineage. Walter Johnson, "The Slave Trader, the White Slave and the Politics of Racial Determination in the 1850s," 16–17; Stephenson, *Isaac Franklin*, 167–78; and Nell Irvin Painter, "Thinking about the Languages of Money and Race: A Response to Michael O'Malley, 'Specie and Species,'" *American Historical Review* 99.2 (April 1994): 398.

54. R.C. Ballard and Co. Expence [sic] Book, 1831, Box 11, Folder 425, Ballard Papers.

55. While his grave marker indicates that he was born in 1800, his date of birth is inconsistent in public records. He may have been born as early as 1798 and as late as 1803 in Fredericksburg, Virginia. His parents were Benjamin Ballard and Ann Heslop. The spelling of his mother's maiden name is also inconsistent in public records. Ballard had at least three siblings, two brothers and a sister. He would father twin daughters in 1847, one of which was named Ann. See 1850 U.S. Federal Census and 1860 U.S Federal Census, www.ancestry.com (accessed November 21, 2006); Virginia Land, Marriage and Probate Records, 1690–1850, www.ancestry.com (accessed June 26, 2013); Virginia, Compiled Census and Census Substitutes Index, 1607–1809, www.ancestry.com; Lyman Chalkley, *Chronicles of the Scotch-Irish Settlement in Virginia, 1745–1800* (Baltimore: Genealogical Publishing Co., 1965); William Armstrong Crozier, ed., *Virginia County Records—Spotsylvania County Records, 1721–1800* (New York: Fox, Duffield & Co., 1905) , www.ancestry.com (accessed June 24, 2013); U.S. Federal Census Reconstructed Records, 1660–1820, www.ancestry.com (accessed June 24, 2013); U.S. and International Marriage Records, 1560–1900, www.ancestry.com (accessed June 24, 2013). Also, again see "A list of balances due James Ballard & Company, 1 Jany [sic] 1838," Folder 425a and Folders 406 and 430, Ballard Papers; 1850 U.S. Federal Census, www.ancestry.com (accessed June 15, 2013). Also see baptismal record for Warwickshire County, England, www.ancestry.com (accessed June 15, 2013).

Marie Tyler McGraw, *At the Falls: Richmond, Virginia, and Its People* (Chapel Hill: University of North Carolina Press, 1994), 35–37.

56. Ibid.

57. Tadman, *Speculators and Slaves*, 7; McGraw, *At the Falls*, 108–9.

58. William G. Hewes to Ballard, November 27, 1832, Folder 8, Ballard Papers.

59. Creecy Smith to Ballard, March 7, 1838, Folder 22, Ballard Papers; and N. J. Duke to Ballard, March 17, 1838, Folder 22, Ballard Papers.

60. Johnson, *Soul by Soul*, 24–25.

61. Robert H. Gudmestad, *A Troublesome Commerce: The Transformation of the Interstate Slave Trade* (Baton Rouge: Louisiana State University Press, 2003), 157.

62. Catherine Prince to Ballard, May 14, 1839, Folder 27, Ballard Papers .

63. Such a transition reduced some of the uncertainty they had earlier faced, including rising restrictions on interregional slave trading in the lower South. Deyle, *Carry Me Back*, 100; Stephenson, *Isaac Franklin*, 76.

64. For his holdings, see certificates of ownership for the Big Black and Karnac plantations in Warren County, Mississippi, and the certificate of release for the Laurel Hill plantation, also in Warren. See Rice C. Ballard Papers, Natchez Small Manuscript Collection, Box 2E549, Briscoe Center for American History, University of Texas, Austin. See account books for six plantations in Folder 396, Ballard Papers. Finally, a representative sample of letters in his business correspondence related to his cotton interests may be found in Folder 61, Box 2; Folder 110, Box 3; Folder 113, Box 3; Folder 401, Box 11, and "Collection Overview," Ballard Papers; 1850 U.S. Federal Census; 1860 U.S. Federal Census.

65. Ballard hired Clay to advise him on legal matters concerning some of his slave sales in Mississippi. Ballard would later oppose Clay in a lawsuit. The Supreme Court decided in favor of Clay and ordered Ballard to pay him $4,000. Henry Clay to Ballard, June 23, 1841, Folder 42, Ballard Papers; Henry Clay to Ballard, July 4, 1844, Folder 75, Ballard Papers; John Anthony Quitman to Ballard, February 1, 1851, Folder 165, Ballard Papers; A. G. Nalle to Ballard, February 2, 1852, Folder 173, Ballard Papers.

66. Bacon Tait to Ballard, May 1, 1838, Folder 24, Ballard Papers.

67. Bacon Tait to Ballard, November 25, 1838, Folder 25, Ballard Papers.

68. Ann Redd, Ballard's niece who was attending a boarding school for which Ballard paid the fees, wrote him a letter confirming as much when she asked Ballard to send a hello to Franklin and "Mrs. Franklin." The circumstances under which he became a quasi-guardian of this child are unclear. Ann Redd to Ballard, September 24, 1839, Folder 28, Ballard Papers. See also Redd to Ballard, May 14, 1839, Folder 27, Ballard Papers.

69. Stephenson, *Isaac Franklin*, 18.

70. Ibid., 19.

71. Ibid., 21.

72. Ibid., 21.

73. U.S. 1850 Census (accessed June 11, 2013); Jesse Cage to William Cotton, August 27, 1839, Folder 28, Ballard Papers; "Slave Records 1719–1820," www.ancestry. com (accessed June 18, 2014).

74. Jesse Cage to William Cotton, August 27, 1839, Folder 28, Ballard Papers.

75. Stephenson, *Isaac Franklin*, 19.

76. *Slave Narratives: A Folk History of Slavery in the United States from Interviews with Former Slaves*, Washington, DC: Library of Congress, 2006), 23, 25.

77. 1860 U.S. Federal Census.

78. Thomas C. Buchanan, *Black Life on the Mississippi: Slaves, Free Blacks, and the Western Steamboat World* (Chapel Hill: University of North Carolina Press, 2004), 88.

79. Virginia to Ballard, May 6, 1853, Folder 192, Ballard Papers. For more, see Philip Troutman, "Correspondences in Black and White: Sentiment and the Slave Market Revolution," *New Studies in the History of American Slavery*, ed. Edward T. Baptist and Stephanie M. H. Camp (Athens: University of Georgia Press, 2006), 222–23; William Kauffman Scarborough, *Masters of the Big House: Elite Slaveholders of the Mid-Nineteenth-Century South* (Baton Rouge: Louisiana State University Press, 2006), 213–16.

80. Virginia to Ballard, May 6, 1853, Folder 192, Ballard Papers.

81. Ibid.

82. C. M. Rutherford to Ballard, August 8, 1853, Folder 196, Ballard Papers.

83. Ibid.

84. Maria may have been a relative of Avenia White as a black woman named "Maria White" is listed on one of Ballard's 1838 slave ledgers. If not, she may be a woman of "yellow complexion" that Ballard purchased in Natchez in 1840; 1850 U.S. Federal Census and 1841 Adams County, Natchez and Washington, Census, www. ancestry.com (accessed June 14, 2014); J. M. Duffield to Ballard, May 29, 1848, Folder 127, Ballard Papers; Magnolia Journal 1838–1840, vol. 11, Folder 429; Receipt, Folder 351, Ballard Papers.

85. J. M. Duffield to Ballard, May 29, 1848, Folder 127, Ballard Papers.

86. Ibid.

87. James was the cousin of the African American physician Edward C. Mazique. Florence Ridion, *A Black Physician's Struggle for Equal Rights, Edward C. Mazique* (Albuquerque: University of New Mexico Press, 2005), 33.

88. Ibid., 33–34.

89. Ibid., 34.

90. Ibid.

91. Schafer, *Becoming Free*, 25.

92. Potter, *Hairdresser's Experience in High Life*, 176.

93. Taylor, *Frontiers of Freedom*, 3, 6, 186–202.

94. In today's currency, their personal holdings range from approximately $138,711.96 to $646,736.56. See 1860 U.S. Federal Census; Taylor, Frontiers of Freedom, 222–26. Also see http://futureboy.us/fsp/dollar.fsp?quantity=50000&currency=dollars&fromYear=1860; and http://futureboy.us/fsp/dollar.fsp?quantity=25300&currency=dollars&fromYear=1860 (accessed June 20, 2014).

95. To be clear, any sighting of power in the African Americans in question here requires us to never overemphasize their influence. Speaking to this point, Ann Douglas has studied the influence that Victorian Era clergy and middle-class female writers had on American readers' tastes. As Douglas has written, to state that these individuals had "power" over the readers and listeners of one of the world's most influential industrializing societies would be overstating their impact. It is more accurate to state that they had a hand in making a leisure activity like reading a counterpoint to an increasingly busy society. While the influence of the antebellum black women in question was similarly situated, any guess on our part is informed speculation. Ann Douglas, *The Feminization of American Culture* (New York: Alfred A. Knopf, 1977), 9–10. For more, see Walter Johnson, "On Agency," *Journal of Social History* 37.1 (Fall 2003): 113–24, Special Issue.

96. Elizabeth H. Pleck, "The Two-Parent Household: Black Family Structure in Late Nineteenth-Century Boston," *Journal of Social History* 6.1 (Fall 1972): 17.

97. See petition in Folder 411, Ballard Papers.

98. Ballard was a member of the Whig party, possibly explaining his initial ties to the Kentucky politician and Whig leader Henry Clay. By midcentury ideology was the center of the nation's political system. Economic differences between the parties were significant, subtle, and varied by region. As sectional conflict escalated, efforts to find agreement on the issue of territorial expansion and slavery resulted in, among other things, Clay and Stephen Douglas, an Illinois Democrat, drafting the Compromise of 1850, which required Northerners to participate in the enforcement of the Fugitive Slave Act. The record offers no answers about the fugitives' presence in Ballard's home. If they arrived after passage of the 1850 Fugitive Slave Act, the Ballards were

legally required to aid in their return. Notably, a letter from Joseph Alsop, the Virginia farmer who emerges as a confidant of Ballard's allows us to see that even Ballard's contemporaries were not always sure of his true political stance. In this letter Alsop stated, "What [do] you think of Mr. Polk and his Mexican war? Has it not cooled your Democracy a little?" Alsop was almost certainly speaking about U.S. President James Polk's high-handed role in the Mexican-American War. Polk, who served from 1845 to 1849, was a prominent Democrat. James M. McPherson, *Battle Cry of Freedom: The Civil War Era* (New York: Oxford University Press, 1988), 80. For more, see Sean Wilentz, *The Rise of American Democracy: Jefferson to Lincoln* (New York: Norton, 2005), Michael F. Holt, *The Fate of Their Country: Politicians, Slavery Extension and the Coming of the Civil War* (New York: Hill and Wang, 2004); Eric Foner, *Free Soil*; Eric Foner, *Politics and Ideology in the Age of the Civil War* (New York: Oxford University Press, 1980); Harry L. Watson, *Liberty and Power: The Politics of Jacksonian America* (New York: Hill and Wang, 1990); Joseph Alsop to Ballard, August 31, 1848, Folder131, Rice Ballard Papers.

99. Delia to Ballard, October 22, 1854, Folder 217, Ballard Papers.

100. Bray Hammond, *Banks and Politics in America: From the Revolution to the Civil War* (Princeton: Princeton University Press, 1957), 4.

101. Joseph Alsop to Ballard, January 30, 1838, Folder 25, Ballard Papers.

102. Joseph F. Pierce to Ballard, October 7, 1838, Folder 25, Ballard Papers.

103. Bacon Tait to Ballard, November 1838, Folder 25, Ballard Papers.

104. Bacon Tait to Ballard, August 16, 1839, Folder 28, Ballard Papers.

105. Samuel Alsop to Ballard, September 20, 1839, Folder 24, Ballard Papers.

106. 1850 and 1860 U.S. Federal Census, www.ancestry.com (accessed June 12, 2013).

107. Joseph Alsop to Ballard, May 8, 1840, Folder 34, Ballard Papers.

108. *U.S. City Directories, 1821–1989* (South Jordan, UT: Genealogy Research Associates, 2005); New Orleans Passenger List Quarterly Abstracts, 1820–1875, ancestry. com (both accessed June 12, 2013).

109. W. R. Glover to Ballard, March 24, 1840, Folder 32, Ballard Papers.

110. Ibid.

111. Receipt for room and board, August, 1840, Folder 351, Ballard Papers.

112. 1870 U.S. Federal Census, www.ancestry.com (accessed June 12, 2013).

113. Joseph Alsop to Ballard, May 12, 1841, Folder 41, Ballard Papers.

2 / The Wife and the "Old Lady" Speak

1. Kentucky Death Records, 1852–1953, www.ancestry.com (accessed October 23, 2012). See also 1850 U.S. Federal Census, www.ancestry.com (accessed June 12, 2013).

2. John F. Sears, *Sacred Places: American Tourist Attractions in the Nineteenth Century* (Amherst: University of Massachusetts Press, 1999), 51.

3. Having relatives who were early settlers of a territory was a shared attribute with her husband. Ballard's original attraction to Kentucky was possibly also due in part to the presence of his cousin Bland Ballard, a Revolutionary War sergeant, who was among the Virginians relocating to Kentucky in the late 1780s. Ballard County and the city of Blandville, both in Kentucky, were named in honor of this relative. However, few documents from Ballard's kin survive in his papers, suggesting possibly strained relations in his birth family. Kentucky Land Grants, 1782–1924; and

U.S. Sons of the American Revolution Membership Applications, 1889–1970, www. ancestry.com (accessed June 14, 2014).

4. Louise's mother first married Armstrong Ellis in 1811. The circumstances under which they parted are unclear. Ellis owned 82 acres in Yazoo County, Mississippi, in 1840, the year Louise married Ballard. Jordon Dodd, *Early American Marriages: Mississippi to 1825* (Bountiful, UT: Precision Indexing, 1991); and Marriages to 1825, www.ancestry.com (accessed July 28, 2013); U.S. General Land Office Records, 1796–1907, www.ancestry.com (accessed July 28, 2013).

5. *Mississippi State Gazette (Natchez)*, January 8, 1820; February 2, 1820; April 29, 1820.

6. See advertisement in *Mississippi State Gazette*, February 2, 1820.

7. 1860 U.S. Federal Census, www.ancestry.com (accessed July 28, 2013).

8. Her husband secured the house she lived in prior to their 1840 marriage. Based on the contents of a letter Louise and an unidentified man, probably a realtor, sent Ballard in 1848, the Ballards were within eight years looking to rent temporary lodgings while building a bigger home. On at least one occasion, Louise complained about living far from the center of town. Louise Ballard to Ballard, November 22, 1847, Folder 120; Louise Ballard to Ballard, February 17, 1848, Folder 123; Adams to Ballard, April 1, 1848, Folder 125, Ballard Papers; 1850 U.S. Federal Census and 1860 Census.

9. See Kentucky Land Grants, 1782–1924, and U.S. Sons of the American Revolution Membership Applications, 1889–1970, www.ancestry.com (accessed June 14, 2014).

10. Kleber, *Encyclopedia of Louisville*, xvi.

11. Lowell Harrison and James C. Klotter, *A New History of Kentucky* (Lexington: University Press of Kentucky, 1997), 103.

12. Ibid.

13. Kleber, *Encyclopedia of Louisville*, 731.

14. Ibid.,105.

15. Ibid.

16. Receipt from Henderson and Gaines, New Orleans, January 9, 1841, Folder 352, Ballard Papers.

17. Receipt from Darwin Wordlief Co., New Orleans, May, 1841, Folder 352, Ballard Papers.

18. Receipt for wagon, February 24, 1841, Folder 352, Ballard Papers.

19. Receipt for Kentucky toll road, October 1, 1841, Folder 352, Ballard Papers.

20. *The Daily Picayune (New Orleans)*, April 1840, 3.

21. A representative sample of business correspondence for these properties may be found in Folder 61, Box 2; Folder 110, Box 3; Folder 113, Box 3; Folder 401, Box 11, Ballard Papers. Also see, "Collection Overview," Ballard Papers.

22. 1860 U.S. Federal Census at www.ancestry.com (accessed June 13, 2013).

23. Her name does not appear in the Louisiana property census entry. On the Arkansas property, the census taker wrote her husband's name and her name, as well as that of her firstborn, but used quotation marks for her younger children, adding, "from best information cou[n]ted." These words suggest the census taker received the information secondhand, perhaps from a plantation manager, not Ballard and certainly not Louise. 1860 U.S. Federal Census, www.ancestry.com (accessed June 13, 2013).

24. 1850 U.S. Federal Census, www.ancestry.com (accessed June 12, 2013).

25. Louise Ballard to Ballard, November 18, 1847, Folder 120, Ballard Papers.

26. Louise's fears were characteristic of her day. At this time child mortality rates, even for white Americans of means, remained high—one in ten children died—which may have been a factor in the delay in giving her children names. Grateful to see healthy offspring, wealthy whites invested themselves in every aspect of their children's lives even as moralists warned against indulging the young. Jacques Gelis, "The Child: From Anonymity to Individuality" in Roger Chartier, ed., *A History of Private Life: Passions of the Renaissance* (Cambridge, MA: Belknap Press, 1989), 309, 320; Marie Jenkins Schwartz, *Birthing a Slave: Motherhood and Medicine in the Antebellum South* (Cambridge, MA: Harvard University Press, 2006), 207; Steven M. Stowe, *Doctoring the South: Southern Physicians and Everyday Medicine in the Mid-Nineteenth Century* (Chapel Hill: University of North Carolina Press, 2004), 211; Louise Ballard to Ballard, November 18, 1847, Folder 120, Ballard Papers.

27. Louise Ballard to Ballard, November 18, 1847, Folder 120, Ballard Papers.

28. Ibid.

29. Glymph, *Out of the House of Bondage*, 89.

30. Jabour, *Scarlett's Sisters*, 86.

31. Ibid., 87.

32. Ibid.

33. Louise Ballard to Ballard, November 22, 1847, Folder 120, Ballard Papers.

34. Lucile Tucker to R.C. Ballard, June 25, 1847, Folder 113, Ballard Papers.

35. Ballard had apparently left Tucker in the care of a man named R. W. Hanson, who had left for Mexico. Georgia, like other slave states, required enslaved people working independently to have guardians. The 1830 U.S. Census lists a Reubin Hanson in Coweta County, Georgia. The 1840 census lists a Reubin Hanson in Carroll County, Georgia. The 1850 census lists a Robert Hanson in Morgan County, Georgia. 1830, 1840, and 1850 U.S Census; Lucile Tucker to R. C. Ballard, June 25, 1847, Folder 113, Ballard Papers.

36. 1870 U.S. Federal Census, www.ancestry.com (accessed June 26, 2013).

37. Frank S. Jones, *History of Decatur County, Georgia* (Spartanburg: Reprint Company, 1996), 210.

38. Commercial sex was readily available in port cities and river communities throughout the United States in the nineteenth century, even amid midcentury moral reform campaigns. Beginning in the 1820s, it was especially visible in New York City, where black- and white-run establishments could be found even as many city residents frowned on interracial sex. In the South, enslaved women were generally not independent contractors when employed as prostitutes. One account from a former bondsman, Henry Bibb, illustrates this point: he stated that a Louisville slave trader forced his wife into prostitution. Henry Bibb, *Narrative of the Life and Adventures of Henry Bibb, an American Slave* (New York: The Author, 1849), 98–99.

While the institution of slavery was integral to the South's economy and fiercely defended, sex work was regarded as a carnal and intolerable profession in the religious climate of the antebellum period. Northern white ministers and abolitionists condemned slaveholders who prostituted enslaved women. Reverend Hiram Mattison, a white Methodist minister and abolitionist in Buffalo, deplored "the moral atmosphere [of the South] in which such monsters can live and breathe." Mattison was obviously aware of the enslaved women and girls who were put to work in brothels in Southern port cities. Philo Tower, another abolitionist, once reported seeing a slave broker keep "whole barracoons of beautiful slave women" for use by "gentlemen" as "sleeping companions."

As the century matured, the sex trade in the lower South blossomed. In the years surrounding the Civil War, Chattanooga, Knoxville, Nashville, and Memphis experienced an increase in prostitution. After the war, Chattanooga, in particular, witnessed the arrival of "sporting" white women eager to cater to railroad workers.

During the postbellum period, iron ore deposits in Birmingham, Alabama, and newly built rail lines drew wealthy men desiring to open businesses and poor ones looking for work. Many of them were doubtless patrons of Louise Wooster, a local madam whose "great love" was John Wilkes Booth, the actor who assassinated Abraham Lincoln.

The most well known red light district in the nation was inarguably New Orleans's Storyville, whose existence between 1898 and 1917 continues to fascinate writers and readers alike. The city's origins as a site for prostitution can be traced to the French kings Louis XIV and Louis XV, who were said to have transported to Louisiana, their new colony, hundreds of "disreputable" women. By the first decade of the twentieth century, arriving single men were handed tiny guidebooks directing them to local prostitutes. Both in and outside New Orleans, however, lax or nonenforcement or the outright legalization of prostitution during the postbellum years created favorable conditions that allowed madams to earn enough money to purchase homes until 1920, when the "Golden Age of the Brothel in America," as researchers have called it, ended. DoVeanna S. Fulton Minor and Reginald H. Pitts, *Speaking Lives, Authoring Texts,* 84; Philo Tower, *Slavery Unmasked* (New York: Negro Universities Press, 1969), 316; Beckles, *Centering Woman,* 31; Henry Bibb, *Narrative of the Life and Adventures of Henry Bibb, an American Slave* (New York, 1849), 98–99, 112–16; Timothy J. Gilfoyle, *City of Eros: New York City, Prostitution, and the Commercialization of Sex, 1790–1920* (New York: Norton, 1992), 29–30, 41–4; J. Winston Coleman, *Belle Breezing: A Famous Lexington Bawd* (Lexington, KY: Winburn Press, 1966, 1980), 8–9, 112–20; James L. Baggett, *The Autobiography of a Magdalen* (1911; Birmingham: Birmingham Public Library Press, 2005), 11–12; Ellin Sterne, "Prostitution in Birmingham, Alabama, 1890–1925" (MA thesis, Samford University, Birmingham, 1977); Al Rose, *Storyville, New Orleans: Being an Authentic, Illustrated Account of the Notorious Red-Light District* (Tuscaloosa: University of Alabama Press, 1974), ix, 5, 135.

39. Virginia to Ballard, May 6, 1853, Folder 192, Ballard Papers.

40. Troutman, "Correspondences in Black and White," 222.

41. Ibid., 212.

42. Louise Ballard to Ballard, December 5, 1847, Folder 120, Ballard Papers.

43. Ibid.

44. Ibid.

45. Financial concerns related to his plantations had overwhelmed Franklin, who considered selling his home in Tennessee. As late as 1856, Ballard and Armfield were still discussing how to settle receipts related to their slave trading. Outstanding debts related to the firm did not make the liquidation an easy matter. The 1837 panic, which did not show signs of easing until the mid-1840s, doubtless had much to do with Armfield's and Ballard's worries. John Armfield to Ballard, December 9, 1847, Folder 121,

Ballard Papers; John Armfield to Ballard, January 4, 1856, Folder 238, Ballard Papers; Stephenson, *Isaac Franklin*, 106, 116, 293.

46. This letter writer addressed Ballard as "Col" (Colonel). Beginning in the 1840s, a great deal of the correspondence he received addressed him in this manner. This title suggests that many of Mississippi's adult white male population was involved in the state militia, whose chief purposes were to put down slave revolts or insurrections. Landowners like Ballard were fitting officers. But also indicating the light-hearted attitudes some took regarding such titles is an 1841 letter in Ballard's papers addressed to "Col John Armfield of the Bloody 4th Regiment of Mississippi Militia and the Hill at Natchez." C.A. Moore to Ballard, May 12, 1847, Folder 111; Armfield to Ballard, May 25, 1841, Folder 41.

47. Louise Ballard to Ballard, December 11, 1848, Folder 135, Ballard Papers.

48. The Ballards paid a wage to at least one black servant in their Louisville home, which may not have been unusual given that slavery was not as pervasive in Kentucky as it was in the lower South. Perhaps Delia was the woman in question.

49. Glymph, *Out of the House of Bondage*, 89.

50. Woodson, ed., *The Mind of the Negro as Reflected in Letters*, 371.

51. Delphine was put on trial in an attempt to prove that she did not deserve to be free. Witnesses characterized her as a woman who frequented one apothecary so often that men patronizing this shop were well acquainted with her. Some of the male patrons teased her, and her resistance via threats and even laughter proved such an affront that the proprietor threatened to report her behavior to local authorities. Her master reminded the proprietor of his patrons' participation her ordeal. This story was retold in court. Delphine lost the case. Schafer, *Becoming Free*, 67–68.

52. Eliza Potter, the hairdresser of mixed race who observed up close the lives of wealthy antebellum white Americans, recalls a situation in which a woman was distanced from others for this very reason. Potter, *Hairdresser's Experience in High Life*, 184.

53. Ibid., 121.

54. Brown, *Good Wives, Nasty Wenches, and Anxious Patriarchs*, 339.

55. Mary Boykin Miller Chesnut, *The Private Mary Chesnut: The Unpublished Civil War Diaries*, ed. C. Vann Woodward and Elizabeth Muhlenfeld (New York: Oxford University Press, 1984); Mary Chesnut, *Mary Chesnut's Civil War*, ed. C. Vann Woodward (New Haven: Yale University Press, 1983).

56. Chesnut and Woodward, ed., *Mary Chesnut's Civil War*, 15; Elizabeth Fox-Genovese, *Within the Plantation Household: Black and White Women of the Old South* (Chapel Hill: University of North Carolina Press, 1988), 348–49.

57. Glymph, *Out of the House of Bondage*, 92.

58. Ibid., 3.

59. Johnson, *Soul by Soul*, 28.

60. Ibid.

61. Louise Ballard to Ballard, February 17, 1848, Folder 123, Ballard Papers.

62. J. T. F. Cox to Ballard, April 14, 1847, Folder 110, Ballard Papers.

63. A letter confirms that Ballard had been seeking china. He did so via a commission merchant, men who served as both creditors and transporters of a planter's cotton. Because fluctuations in the weather and the marketplace could lead to a good or bad year, men like Ballard relied on such merchants to purchase household luxuries

and food staples on credit when money was not plentiful. A. G. Nalle to Ballard, May 25, 1847, Folder 111, Ballard Papers.

64. Ibid.

65. List of Purchases for the Year 1832, Box 11, Folder 420, Ballard Papers.

66. For an example of how slave dealers listed children in this manner, see Stephenson, *Isaac Franklin*, 166–67.

67. Expence [sic] Book, January 23, 1833, Box 11, Folder 425, Ballard Papers.

68. Ballard paid $237 for Avenia White, $425 for Susan Johnson, and $425 for Preston. The purchase price for Avenia was curiously low, suggesting Nathaniel White gave Ballard a deal that was recouped, perhaps, on the purchase price of other slaves. List of Purchases for the Year 1832, Box 11, Folder 420, Ballard Papers.

69. R. C. Ballard and Co. Expence Book, 1831, Box 11, Folder 425, Ballard Papers.

70. Isaac Franklin to Ballard, September 27, 1834, Folder, 15, Ballard Papers.

71. Stephenson, *Isaac Franklin*, 35–36, 44; and Shipment record, Franklin and Ballard Company, Box 11, Folder 421, Ballard Papers.

72. Such a transition from slave trader to planter was not typical, nor was it was unusual, for the 1830s witnessed a wave of land speculation unseen since the years immediately following the War of 1812. Pers. comm., Harold D. Woodman, July 5, 2010. For more on cotton production, see Harold D. Woodman's *King Cotton & His Retainers: Financing & Marketing the Cotton Crop of the South, 1800–1925* (Columbia: University of South Carolina Press, 1968).

73. This observation was made in 1901 by Felix Houston Hadsell, a Natchez resident. See *Fork of the Roads: A Major Southwest Hub of America's Domestic Slave Trade* (Natchez, MS: Friends of the Fork of the Roads Society). 7. See also the public history exhibit on Fork of the Roads Site at Washington Natchez Trace (now D'Evereaux) and Old Courthouse Roads (now Liberty and St. Catherine Streets, one mile east of downtown Natchez).

74. *Fork of the Roads*, 6.

75. Coffin, *Reminiscences*, 519–520.

76. Sterling Lecater Bland Jr., ed., *African American Slave Narratives, An Anthology, vol. 2* (Westport, CT: Greenwood Press, 2001), 310.

77. Taylor, *Frontiers of Freedom*, 11–13.

78. Ibid., 2; Curry, *The Free Black in Urban America*, 245.

79. Clarence Lang, *Grassroots at the Gateway Class Politics and Black Freedom Struggle in St. Louis, 1936–75* (Ann Arbor: University of Michigan Press, 2009); Tracy E. K'Meyer, *Civil Rights in the Gateway to the South: Louisville, KY, 1945–1990* (Lexington: University Press of Kentucky, 2009).

80. Chesnut, *The Private Mary Chestnut*, 42.

81. For more on the geographic distribution of urban African Americans in the North during the nineteenth century, see Henry Louis Taylor Jr., "City Building, Public Policy, the Rise of the Industrial City, and Black Ghetto-Slum Formation in Cincinnati, 1850–1940," in Taylor, ed., *Race and the City*; David Katzman, *Before the Ghetto: Black Detroit in the Nineteenth Century* (Urbana: University of Illinois Press, 1975); Taylor and Dula, "Black Residential Experience," in Taylor, ed., *Race and the City*, 102–19.

82. Gerber, *Black Ohio*, 100–104; Taylor, *Frontiers of Freedom*, 186; Taylor. and Dula, "Black Residential Experience," , 100, 115.

83. Taylor and Dula, "Black Residential Experience," 104.

84. Gerber, *Black Ohio*, 100–102; Taylor, *Frontiers of Freedom*, 196.

85. In White's September 13, 1838, letter to Ballard, she describes having paid rent and board to Bruster, establishing that she and Susan and their four children lived in this house. Avenia White to Ballard, September 13, 1838, Folder 24, Ballard Papers.

86. The 1840 U.S. Federal Census spells Bruster's name "Brewster." Bruster, who was born in Virginia, may have been married to Thomas Brewster, an African American barber and hairdresser in Cincinnati. 1840 U.S. Federal Census; David Henry Shaffer, *The Cincinnati, Covington, Newport and Fulton Directory for 1840* (Cincinnati: J. B. & R. P. Donogh, 1839), 468; *Cincinnati Directory Advertiser for the Years 1836–7* (Cincinnati: J. H. Woodruff, 1836), 25.

87. This is confirmed in a May 1838 letter that Bruster wrote Ballard in Natchez. In the letter she mentioned that when they first met in New Orleans, he said he wished to make a friend of her. He almost certainly said as much because he wanted the women and children to reside in her home. Frances M. Bruster to Ballard, May 14, 1838, Folder 24, Ballard Papers.

88. Avenia White to Ballard, September 13, 1838, Folder 24, Ballard Papers.

89. Ballard may have wanted to move them sooner, but he was stricken with yellow fever in early 1838. Joseph Alsop to Ballard, January 30, 1838, Folder 20, Ballard Papers.

90. The low-water season on the Ohio typically began in late June and continued through late September, although the "fall rise" was dependent on arrival of heavy rains, which varied from year to year. Even then, unrestricted movement lasted just a few weeks because of either low water or ice between late November and early January. Five to six feet of water was necessary if a steamboat captain wanted to carry a full load. Hunter, *Steamboats on the Western Rivers*, 219–23, 251, 255.

91. *Cincinnati Republican*, September 19, 1838.

92. Taylor and Dula, "Black Residential Experience," 115.

93. D. J. Kenny, *Illustrated Cincinnati Pictorial Handbook of the Queen City* (Cincinnati: Robert Clarke & Co., 1875), 295.

94. *Cincinnati Republican*, December 11, 1838.

95. Avenia White to Ballard, October 25, 1838, Folder 25, Ballard Papers.

96. Shaffer, *The Cincinnati, Covington, Newport and Fulton Directory for 1840*, 181; Thornbrough and Riker, *Diary and Letters of Calvin Fletcher*, 210; Frances M. Bruster to Ballard, November 29, 1838, Folder 25, Ballard Papers.

97. Ibid.

98. See a letter Ballard received in October 1838. Henry Clark to Ballard, October 10, 1835, Folder 18, Ballard Papers.

99. Avenia White to Ballard, December 30, 1838, Folder 25, Ballard Papers.

100. Calvin Fletcher to Ballard, January 28, 1839, Folder 26, Ballard Papers.

101. In the postscript, she stated that her landlord was waiting on money, presumably for the mortgage that was being sent via Fletcher. "When you write you can mention it to him," White said. Avenia White to Ballard, January 20, 1839, Folder 26, Ballard Papers.

102. He also inquired about the African American man to whom the $100 draft should be written. He was William Stewart, a local pattern maker of mixed race. Fletcher told Ballard that Stewart appeared to be reliable. The reasons for Stewart's

presence in Bruster's life are unclear. Maybe Bruster was purchasing her boarding-house with Stewart's assistance and that of other local African Americans. Given the degree to which black Cincinnatians during this era needed and depended on each other, Stewart might have been furnishing such help.

103. Avenia White to Ballard, February 2, 1840, Folder 31, Ballard Papers.

104. A letter Ballard received nearly fifteen years later suggests that Mary January was a woman of color. A man named P. B. January wrote him to request information on a "yellow woman" earlier purchased from Ballard by his uncle. A court determined that this woman was born free, kidnapped, and sold into slavery and should thus be manumitted. The letter writer may have been the former owner—or may have known the former owner—of Mary January, who likewise might have been or was related to the woman. The census offers no clear answers on January's identity. There were several women named Mary January alive during the nineteenth century but none listed as living in Cincinnati in 1840. A sixty-year-old Virginia-born white house-keeper bearing this name lived in Greene, Ohio, about 60 miles north of Cincinnati, in 1880; a Virginia-born black woman bearing this name lived in Claiborne County, MS, in 1870; a widowed sixty-year-old Tennessee-born white woman with this name lived in Saint Mary, LA, in 1901; U.S. Federal Censuses 1870, 1880, and 1901, www.ancestry.com (accessed June 8, 2014); P. B. January to Ballard, November 29, 1854, Folder 207, Ballard Papers.

105. Avenia White to Ballard, February 2, 1840, Folder 31, Ballard Papers.

106. Isaac Franklin to Ballard, September 27, 1834, Folder, 15, Ballard Papers.

107. Bigham, *Jordan's Banks,* 23.

108. List of Purchases for the Year 1832, Box 11, Folder 420, Ballard Papers. Also see "Negroes Shipped," Box 11, Folder 417, Ballard Papers.

109. Though laws were passed in 1804 and 1907 to limit black settlement, the city's black population grew from 700 in 1826 to more than 2,000 in 1829. By 1840 the growth of the city's black population was stunted. In that year, blacks numbered 2,240, or 4.8 percent of the total population. Taylor, *Frontiers of Freedom,* 2–3, 9; *The WPA Guide to Cincinnati,* 30.

110. Potter, *Hairdresser's Experience in High Life,* 11.

111. James Oliver Horton and Hartmut Keil, "African Americans and Germans in Mid-Nineteenth Century Buffalo," in Horton, ed., *Free People of Color,* 170; Steven J. Ross, *Workers on the Edge: Work, Leisure, and Politics in Industrializing Cincinnati, 1788–1890* (New York: Columbia University Press, 1985), 72; Amy Hill Shevitz, *Jewish Communities on the Ohio River: A History* (Lexington: University Press of Kentucky, 2007), 24, 35.

112. *The WPA Guide to Cincinnati* (Cincinnati: Cincinnati Historical Society, 1987), 59; Taylor, *Frontiers of Freedom,* 4.

113. Frances Trollope, *Domestic Manners of the Americans,* ed. Donald Smalley (1832; Gloucester, MA: Peter Smith, 1974), 36.

114. Buchanan, *Black Life on the Mississippi,* 6, 20, 97; Taylor and Dula, "Black Residential Experience," 115.

115. Horton and Keil have made this argument using antebellum Buffalo as a case study, though their findings can be applied to other areas with German immigrants, including Cincinnati. James Oliver Horton and Hartmut Keil, "African Americans and Germans in Mid-Nineteenth Century Buffalo," in James Oliver Horton, ed., *Free*

People of Color: Inside the African American Community (Washington, DC: Smithsonian Institution Press, 1993), 170–71.

116. Coffin, *Reminiscences*, 528; *Daily Cincinnati Enquirer*, September 4, 1841; Taylor, *Frontiers of Freedom*, 117–25; *Cincinnati Daily Gazette*, September 6, 1841; Bigham, *Jordan's Banks*, 41; Trotter, *River Jordan*, 36.

117. *The Cincinnati Directory, for the Year 1842* (Cincinnati: E. Morgan and Company, 1842).

118. Woodson, ed., *The Mind of the Negro as Reflected in Letters*, 241.

119. In 1830, 52,317 people lived in Hamilton County, OH, which included Cincinnati, almost double the 28,797 population of Henrico County, VA, which included Richmond, and more than three times the 14, 937 population of Adams County, MS, which included Natchez. Even more telling of how different these cities' populations were is that 6,055 people lived in Richmond proper and just 2,789 in Natchez, compared to almost 25,000 in Cincinnati. The last was home to 46,338 people by 1840. Bigham, *Jordan's Banks*, 7, 299; U.S. 1830 Census, www.census.gov/prod2/decennial/documents/1830a-01.pdf (accessed October 24, 2012); Historical, Demographic, Economic, and Social Data: The United States, 1790–1970 (Inter-university Consortium for Political and Social Research, Ann Arbor, MI), www.virginiaplaces.org/population/pop1830numbers.html (accessed October 24, 2012); Taylor, *Frontiers of Freedom*, 19–20.

120. Louis Leonard Tucker, *Cincinnati: A Student's Guide to Localized History* (New York: Teachers College Press, 1969), 10–11; Trollope, *Domestic Manners of the Americans*, 36, 39–40.

121. *Cincinnati Republican*, June 15, 1838; October 19, 1838.

122. Barth, *The Rise of Modern City Culture*, 3.

123. *Cincinnati Republican*, September 29, 1838.

124. For more on the colonial origins of this hierarchy, see Spear, *Race, Sex and the Social Order in Early New Orleans*.

125. Morgan, *Laboring Women*, 44–45.

126. A growing number of scholars have addressed intragroup conflict in the African American community on a range of topics, among them, the different approaches of black radicals and conservatives during the black freedom movement. Some see this recognition as the "old American tradition of seizing on black people's disputes with each other to put down blacks as a people." In his study of how kinship and property claims figure into African Americans' survival tactics during the nineteenth century, Dylan C. Penningroth has addressed this issue, cautiously noting how blacks have argued among themselves. Here I do something similar as I acknowledge the ways in which African Americans often tiptoe around conflict in their own community because it is not easy to discuss how "we" oppress one another. Wesley C. Hogan, *Many Minds, One Heart: SNCC's Dream for a New America* (Chapel Hill: University of North Carolina Press, 2007); Yohuru Williams and Jama Lazerow, eds., *Liberated Territory: Untold Local Perspectives on the Black Panther Party* (Durham, NC: Duke University Press, 2009). See also Dylan C. Penningroth, *The Claims of Kinfolk: African American Property and Community in the Nineteenth-Century South* (Chapel Hill: University of North Carolina Press, 2003), 12.

127. Virginia to Ballard, May 6, 1853, Folder 192, Ballard Papers; Troutman, "Correspondences in Black and White," 222.

128. *Cincinnati Directory Advertiser for the Years 1836–7*, 82; Shaffer, *Cincinnati, Covington, Newport and Fulton Directory for 1840*, 182, 472.

129. Taylor, *Frontiers of Freedom*, 101.

130. Gerber, *Black Ohio*, 19; Taylor, *Race in the City*, 6; Taylor, *Frontiers of Freedom*, 101–3.

131. Hill's presence at this juncture of White's life and, for that matter, White's connection with Bruster is noteworthy because the boardinghouse on Elm Street was between Fifth and Sixth Streets, a neighborhood associated with abolitionist activity. Bruster might have been in the forefront of the city's antislavery community. Certainly other black-owned boardinghouses in the city often provided refuge for escaped slaves. Perhaps hers did too. Taylor, *Frontiers of Freedom*, 152.

132. For more on the hegemonic function of powerful men's emotion-based actions, see R. W. Connell, *Masculinities* (Berkeley: University of California Press, 1995).

133. White may have married, taking her husband's last name as her surname. She may have been widowed or divorced. Notably, "Avenia," a then-uncommon given name, appears so infrequently in nineteenth-century census records that it invites speculation that Ballard preferred to address her by her unusual middle name rather than her common first name, in order to distinguish her from the many enslaved women and girls, Susan Johnson's daughter among them, named Elizabeth. Also worth noting, while living in Greene County, Elizabeth Ward's eldest child was a boy, apparently born in 1841. If this woman was Avenia White, she was pregnant with him in 1840, the year Mary January slandered her. Perhaps January told Ballard that she was having sex with this child's father, who married her and also fathered the other three.

After the Civil War, this woman seems to have relocated to Lincoln, KS. The 1870 census for Lincoln lists a white woman named Avenia Ward, who within five years had relocated to Atchison, KS, more than 200 miles away, where, now listed as a "black" woman, she was one of two servants in a merchant's home. The other servant was white. That the age of this "A. Ward" was off by just one or two years from the white Elizabeth A. Ward listed in the 1850 census is noteworthy, but so are more significant details about her. If Elizabeth A. Ward and Avenia Ward were the same person, why did she appear under two different given names? One possibility is that the census takers were simply inconsistent, one recording her first given name and middle initial, the other two the name by which she preferred to be called. Finally, though Elizabeth A. Ward and Avenia Ward are at least six years older than the eldest possible age of Avenia White listed in the 1840 U.S. Census, this is not entirely problematic given that the actual age of enslaved people is difficult to ascertain given the lack of formal documents about their birth. 1850 U.S. Federal Census, 1870 U.S. Federal Census, and 1875 Kansas Census, www.ancestry.com (accessed June 16, 2014).

134. For currency conversion, see www.futureboy.us./fsp/dollar.fsp?quantity+50&currency=dollars&fromYear=1850 (accessed June 17, 2014).

135. Preston, who appears to have been Avenia White's son when she first arrived in Cincinnati, would have by now been in his late teens or early twenties and thus old enough to reside away from her. There are two Preston Whites in the 1860 U.S. Federal Census. Both are listed as white men. One, a schoolteacher, boarded with a Kentucky family; the other, a laborer, boarded with a family in Virginia. The former was born in 1836, the latter in 1838. Unless these men were unaware of their true

age, neither was the boy whose name appeared beneath Avenia's on Ballard's 1832 slave invoice. Both lived, however, in states to which Ballard and Avenia had ties. The fate of Susan Johnson and her children is more vague. An African American woman bearing this name resided in Cincinnati in 1860. She had three children whose names are different from the ones in White's surviving letters. This mother was unemployed but possessed $50—$1,386.12 today—given to her in all likelihood by her adult sons. One was a blacksmith, and the other was a "daily" laborer. 1860 U.S. Federal Census; www.futureboy.us./fsp/dollar.fsp?quantity+50&currency=dollars&fromYear=1860 (accessed June 20, 2014).

136. R. F. Morgan to Ballard, May 19, 1852, Folder 177, Ballard Papers.

137. Receipt for passage of Negro girl, January 29, 1841, Folder 352, Ballard Papers; Receipt for passage of Negro girl, freight charges, and passage for Ballard and servant, May, 19, 1841, Folder 41, Ballard Papers.

138. Coffin, *Reminiscences*, 479.

139. L. Virginia Gould, "Urban Slavery, Urban Freedom: The Manumission of Jacqueline Lemelle," in David Barry Gaspar and Darlene Clark Hine, eds., *More than Chattel: Black Women and Slavery in the Americas* (Bloomington: Indiana University Press, 1996), 298–310.

140. Brent, *Incidents in the Life of a Slave Girl*, Stephanie Li, "Resistance, Silence, and Placees: Charles Bon's Octoroon Mistress and Louisa Picquet," American Literature 79.1 (March 2007): 4, 6.

141. Emily West, *Family or Freedom: People of Color in the Antebellum South* (Lexington: University Press of Kentucky, 2012).

142. Ibid., 130.

143. Ibid., 134.

144. One of Louise's half siblings was named William Ellis. The letter writer may have been her relative and his presence in Kentucky might have been another reason Ballard settled her and their children in this city. Ellis might have decided that he would be able to look after them in his absence. W. A. Ellis to Ballard, March 1, 1857, Folder 254, Ballard Papers.

145. Ellis added that he was aware that Louise's father would soon be visiting, but he did not think it would help. In fact, it would make things worse. Charlotte, one of the Ballard's twins, once mentioned an unspecified illness from which her mother was suffering in a letter to their father. W. A. Ellis to Ballard, May 18, 1857, Folder 177, Ballard Papers; Charlotte and Ann Ballard to Ballard, March 1, 1857, Folder 166, Ballard Papers.

146. Ella Ballard to Ballard, March 5, 1857, Folder 254, Ballard Papers.

147. Ella Ballard to Ballard, March 25, 1857, Folder 255, Ballard Papers.

148. This advertisement can be found in Folder 411, Ballard Papers.

149. Isabel Howell, *John Armfield of Beersheeba Springs* (Beersheeba Springs, TN: Beersheeba Springs Historical Society, 1983).

150. S. P. Johnson to Ballard, June 9, 1858, Folder 281, Ballard Papers.

151. For the date of his death, see lawsuit filed by Louise and her second husband, James Purdy, in the wake of losses caused by Union troops on the Ballards' Outpost plantation in Carroll Parish, LA. *James Purdy and Wife, Administrators v. United States*, p. 2, Rice C. Ballard Papers, Natchez Small Manuscript Collection, Box 2E549, Briscoe Center for American History, University of Texas, Austin.

152. Elizabeth Fox-Genovese and Eugene D. Genovese, *The Mind of the Master Class: History of Faith in the Southern Slaveholders' Worldview* (Cambridge: Cambridge University Press, 2005), 98.

153. His accumulated wealth enabled his daughters to marry well. Two months after his death, Ella married William Fontaine Bullock, a Kentucky circuit court judge. Ann and Charlotte eventually married two brothers, one a banker, the other a merchant. U.S. and International Marriage Records, 1560–1900; 1850 U.S. Federal Census, 1880 U.S. Federal Census, 1920 U.S. Federal Census, www.ancestry.com (accessed June 13, 2013).

154. "Generous Donation of Col. Rice C. Ballard of This City to the 'Sisters of Charity'—the Notes Given for the Asylum, to the Amount of Three Thousand Two Hundred and Twenty-seven Dollars, Taken up," *Mississippi Free Trader and Natchez Gazette*, April 20, 1848, issue 48, col. A.

155. "Colonel R.C. Ballard," *Mississippi Free Trader and Natchez Gazette*, December 21, 1848, issue 54.

156. Ibid.

157. *Mississippi Free Trader*, January 26, 1848, 1; *New York Spectator*, August 7, 1848, vol. 1, p. 4.

158. At the time of the suit, she was living in Memphis with Purdy. See *James Purdy and Wife, Administrators v. United States*, p. 2, Ballard Papers, University of Texas, Austin.

159. Ibid., 1. For the age difference between Louise and James Purdy, see 1870 U.S. Federal Census, www.ancestry.com (accessed June 26, 2013).

160. By the time of his death, Louise lived on Broadway, five blocks from the house in which she had raised her children. By then, there were several Ballards in town, among them Charles, her first husband's brother, who ran a mill in Louisville. See Louisville, Kentucky, City Directory 1886, in U.S. City Directories, 1821–1989, http://search.ancestrylibrary.com/cgi-bin/sse.dll?rank=1&new=1&M SAV=0&msT=1&gss=angs-g&gsfn=Louise&gsln=Ballard&mswpn__ftp=Louis ville%2c+Jefferson%2c+Kentucky%2c+USA&mswpn=32672&mswpn_PInfo=8- |0|1652393|0|2|3246|20|0|1508|32672|0|&msbdy=1820&msbpn__ftp=Mississippi& uidh=20x&pcat=ROOT_CATEGORY&h=868291961&db=USDirectories&indiv=1 (accessed June 13, 2013).

3 / "The stain on it"

1. Reverend Hiram Mattison, a Buffalo minister, took credit as the author of *Louisa Picquet, The Octoroon: A Tale of Southern Slave Life* (New York: The Author, 1861), which chronicles the experiences of Picquet. This study relies on the edited version of her memoir in Fulton Minor and Pitts, *Speaking Lives, Authoring Texts*. See also 1840 U.S. Federal Census, www.ancestry.com (accessed June 26, 2013).

2. Mattison, in Minor and Pitts, *Speaking Lives, Authoring Texts*, 54.

3. Ibid., 55.

4. Horton had earlier served in the Alabama legislature. See /www.tshaonline. org/handbook/online/articles/fho62 (accessed August 11, 2012); Matthew Ellenberger, "Illuminating the Lesser Lights: Notes on the Life of Albert Clinton Horton," *Southwestern Historical Quarterly* 88 (April 1985); and Ralph A. Wooster, "Early Texas Politics: The Henderson Administration," *Southwestern Historical Quarterly* 73 (October 1969).

5. Mattison, in Minor and Pitts, *Speaking Lives, Authoring Texts*, 55.

6. Ibid.

7. Ibid., 56.

8. Ibid.

9. Ibid, 59.

10. Ibid., 60.

11. Ibid., 59.

12. Ibid., 61.

13. Ibid., 60.

14. Ibid.

15. Ibid., 61.

16. M. Jacqui Alexander, *Pedagogies of Crossing: Meditations on Feminism, Sexual Politics, and the Sacred* (Durham: Duke University Press, 2005), 7.

17. David Brion Davis, *The Problem of Slavery in the Age of Emancipation* (New York: Knopf, 2014).

18. So great was the hatred some enslaved women and girls felt, they resorted to violent measures to get back at their masters. One of them, a teenager named Celia, was tried and hanged in 1855 in Missouri for striking her master twice with a large stick, killing him, and burning his body in a fireplace. Melton A. McLaurin, *Celia, a Slave: A True Story* (Athens: University of Georgia Press, 1991). Mattison, in Minor and Pitts, *Speaking Lives, Authoring Texts*, 59.

19. Such consideration did not extend to fieldhands on a large plantation, who probably had no direct contact with a master. An overseer might treat such a slave in brutal ways without the owner's knowledge, much less his intervention. Still, those with whom a slaveholder was in regular contact—house servants and, above all, bed partners—were also likely to suffer because they were under constant monitoring. However, slaveholders, if they wanted to get their money's worth from a purchase, were compelled to show a measure of concern for their slaves, no matter the degree of physical proximity they had with them. Consider an enslaved pregnant woman who toiled in the fields like an enslaved man. Though there were many cruel exceptions, especially during the seventeenth century elsewhere in the Caribbean, a reasonable amount of care had to be shown to such a woman if a slaveholder was thinking about his or her financial outcomes. Following westward expansion and the creation of a cotton region from the 1820s on, slaveholders were usually attentive to enslaved women's pregnancies. It was a matter of arithmetic. A successful birth ensured the eventual replacement of aging bodies that could no longer work or be a source of profit if sold. Some women who had recently given birth sometimes received lighter work assignments. Richard Dunn, *Sugar and Slaves: The Rise of the Planter Class in the British-West Indies, 1624–1713* (Chapel Hill: University of North Carolina Press, 2000); Schwartz, *Birthing a Slave*, 13, 189.

20. Stephanie Li, "Resistance, Silence, and *Placees*: Charles Bon's Octoroon Mistress and Louisa Picquet," *American Literature* 79.1 (March 2007): 87.

21. Scott, *Weapons of the Weak*.

22. Mattison, in Minor and Pitts, *Speaking Lives, Authoring Texts*, 54–55.

23. Ibid., 3; Glymph, *Out of the House of Bondage*, 191.

24. White, *Ar'n't I a Woman*, 164.

25. Bancroft, *Slave-Trading in the Old South*, 57.

26. Ibid., 57.

27. Hunter, *To 'Joy My Freedom*, 2.

28. Edwards, *Gendered Strife and Confusion*, 59.

29. Mattison, in Minor and Pitts, *Speaking Lives, Authoring Texts*, 71.

30. Ibid., 46.

31. Ibid., 39, 46.

32. Ibid., 46.

33. Ibid., 58.

34. Richard F. Brown, *Coastal Encounters: The Transformation of the Gulf South in the Eighteenth Century* (Lincoln: University of Nebraska Press, 2008), 4.

35. Mattison, in Minor and Pitts, *Speaking Lives, Authoring Texts*, 47, 80.

36. To Picquet, the male head of household where she worked as a servant was a "real good man," one she would not have minded being her master, as he and his wife never whipped her. Ibid., 45–47, 54.

37. Ibid., 48.

38. Ibid.

39. Ibid.

40. Picquet's experiences have resonance with those of Harriet Jacobs. Like Picquet, Jacobs relied on a white woman, in her case, her master's wife, to protect her. Pretending to provide help, her mistress instructed Jacobs to sleep in a room "adjoining her own." Strangely, once there her mistress sometimes approached a sleeping Jacobs and whispered in her ear, pretending to be her master. She then "listened to hear what I would answer," Jacobs said. Overwhelmed, she became "fearful" for her life. Mattison, in Minor and Pitts, *Speaking Lives, Authoring Texts*, 48–49; Brent, *Incidents in the Life of a Slave Girl*, 54.

41. Mattison, in Minor and Pitts, *Speaking Lives, Authoring Texts*, 51.

42. Ibid., 52.

43. Ibid., 53.

44. Ibid., 55.

45. Lucy's relatives did not need her sister's owner to purchase her as they were apparently members of the small mulatto slaveholding class of South Carolina. They were free people of color who owned slaves, some as capital investments. Others were purchased and then freed because they were relatives. Mattison, in Minor and Pitts, *Speaking Lives, Authoring Texts*, 58.

46. Whether these purchases were ways of reclaiming bodies to be used for labor on these men's land, or whether there was a bond of emotion or kinship, we cannot know. Ibid., 47.

47. Mattison, in Minor and Pitts, *Speaking Lives, Authoring Texts*, 56.

48. Ibid., 59.

49. *Mississippi State Gazette*, May 13, 1820, Vol. III, Issue 20, p. 4.

50. Mattison, in Minor and Pitts, *Speaking Lives, Authoring Texts*, 57.

51. Ibid., 60.

52. Ibid., 61.

53. For more on the rise of the tea trade and its impact on global culture, see John Keay, *The Honourable Company: A History of the English East India Company* (New York: Scribner, 1994); and Sarah Rose, *For All the Tea in China: How England Stole the World's Favorite Drink and Changed History* (New York: Penguin, 2011).

54. Neil MacGregor, *A History of the World in 100 Objects* (New York: Penguin Books, 2008), 510–11.

55. Mattison, in Minor and Pitts, *Speaking Lives, Authoring Texts*, 61.

56. Sella Martin, house servant and boatman, in Blassingame, ed., *Slave Testimony*, 703.

57. Mattison, in Minor and Pitts, *Speaking Lives, Authoring Texts*, 58.

58. Ibid., 61.

59. Picquet was lucky in this regard. Ann Marie Barclay, a mulatta who had lived with her slave-dealer master for seventeen years, almost lost her furniture. In the wake of crackdowns on people of color after the 1831 Nat Turner rebellion, her master freed her in 1839 and sent her to Cincinnati. They lived apart for years, perhaps seeing each other only when he traveled north. When he finally died in 1856, he left her his piano and furniture. But she encountered difficulties claiming them. When she returned to the South, Barclay found not only her inheritance in jeopardy but also her freedom. Some questioned whether she was really free. In the end, a judge decided she should have the items and that she should remain free. Schafer, *Becoming Free, Remaining Free*, 111.

60. Francis J. Mastrogiovanni, "Cincinnati's Black Community, 1840–1850" (Master's thesis, University of Cincinnati, 1972).

61. Bigham, *Jordan's Banks*, 37–38. For more, see Thomas Paul Kessen, "Segregation in Cincinnati Public Education: The Nineteenth Century Experience" (PhD diss., University of Cincinnati, 1973).

62. Bigham, *Jordan's Banks*, 38; Kessen, "Segregation in Cincinnati Public Education."

63. Horton and Flaherty, "Black Leadership in Antebellum Cincinnati," 84.

64. Mattison, in Minor and Pitts, *Speaking Lives, Authoring Texts*, 40; and National Archives and Records Administration (NARA), Washington, DC; Compiled Military Service Records of Volunteer Union Soldiers who Served with the United States Colored Troops: Infantry Organizations, 41st through 46th, Microfilm Serial M1994, Microfilm Roll 27.

65. Woodson, ed., *The Mind of the Negro as Reflected in Letters*, 156. For more see, Edwin S. Redkey, *Black Exodus: Black Nationalist and Back-to-Africa Movements, 1890–1910* (New Haven: Yale University Press, 1969); Claude A. Clegg, *The Price of Liberty: African Americans and the Making of Liberia* (Chapel Hill: University of North Carolina Press, 2004); Eric Burin, *Slavery and the Peculiar Solution: A History of the American Colonization Society* (Gainesville: University Press of Florida, 2005).

66. 1850 U.S. Federal Census.

67. Mattison, in Minor and Pitts, *Speaking Lives, Authoring Texts*, 62–63.

68. Ibid., 62.

69. Ibid.

70. For more, see Larry Koger, *Black Slaveowners*; Ira Berlin, *Slaves without Masters: The Free Negro in the Antebellum South* (New York: New Press, 2007).

71. Gould, "Urban Slavery, Urban Freedom," 208.

72. Ludwig von Reizenstein, *The Mysteries of New Orleans*, trans. and ed. Steven Rowan (Baltimore: Johns Hopkins University Press, 2002); Emil Klauprecht, *Cincinnati, or The Mysteries of the West*, trans. Steven Rowan, ed. Don Heinrich Tolzmann

(New York: Peter Lang, 2006); Henry Boernstein, *The Mysteries of St. Louis: A Novel*, trans. Friedrich Munch, ed. Elizabeth Sims (Chicago: Charles H. Kerr, 1990).

73. Reizenstein, *The Mysteries of New Orleans*, xxv; Klauprecht, *Cincinnati, or The Mysteries of the West*.

74. Reizenstein, *The Mysteries of New Orleans*, xxvii, 11.

75. Mayne Reid, *The Quadroon: A Lover's Adventures in Louisiana* (New York: G. W. Dillingham Co., 1856, 1897), 47.

76. Mattison, in Minor and Pitts, *Speaking Lives, Authoring Texts*, 40, 65, 71; *Cincinnati Daily Gazette*, October 15, 1860.

77. Taylor, *Frontiers of Freedom*, 13, 51.

78. Mattison, in Minor and Pitts, *Speaking Lives, Authoring Texts*, 65.

79. Ibid., 65–66.

80. Ibid., 40; 1860 U.S. Federal Census.

81. Mattison, in Minor and Pitts, *Speaking Lives, Authoring Texts*, 67.

82. Mattison noted as much to the reader but only in order to allege that the image was Horton's attempt to demonstrate to Northerners the supposed "superior condition of the slave." Ibid., 70.

83. Ibid., 72.

84. Ibid., 73–74.

85. Ibid., 75–76.

86. Ibid., 86; and *Cincinnati Daily Gazette*, October 15, 1860.

87. Her mother also left behind her husband, the coachman who had been sold with her years earlier in Mobile. In 1860, unworried by the ongoing sectional tensions between the North and South, Horton went on to buy 58 slaves in Columbia, SC. Mattison, in Minor and Pitts, *Speaking Lives, Authoring Texts*, 79–80. See receipt for 58 slaves, Albert Clinton Horton Papers, Box Number 2E249, Dolph Briscoe Center for American History, University of Texas, Austin.

88. Mattison, in Minor and Pitts, *Speaking Lives, Authoring Texts*, 41; and NARA, Washington, DC; Compiled Military Service Records of Volunteer Union Soldiers who Served with the United States Colored Troops: Infantry Organizations, 41st through 46th, Microfilm Serial M1994; Microfilm Roll 27; www.ancestry.com (accessed June 9, 2014).

89. Lyle Koehler, *Cincinnati's Black Peoples: A Chronology and Bibliography, 1787–1982* (Cincinnati: University of Cincinnati, 1986), 52; and U.S. Federal Census, 1860, www.ancestry.com (accessed June 9, 2014).

90. Williston H. Lofton, "Northern Labor and the Negro during the Civil War," *Journal of Negro History* 32 (1949): 251–73.

91. Bigham, *Jordan's Banks*, 8; Crowell, *Images of America*, 31.

92. That amount in today's currency is $107.24. 1870 U.S. Federal Census; 1890 Veterans Schedule; www.futureboy.us./fsp/dollar.fsp?quantity+6&currency=dollars&fromYear=1870 (accessed June 22, 2014).

Faust has stressed that although the war was an "instrument of liberation" for many African American men, veterans and their survivors struggled during the pension claim process. Drew Gilpin Faust, *The Republic of Suffering: Death and the American Civil War* (New York: Alfred A. Knopf, 2008), 55, 255–60. For more on African American soldiers during the Civil War, see Chandra Manning, *What This Cruel War Was Over: Soldiers, Slavery, and the Civil War* (New York: Alfred A. Knopf, 2007).

93. U.S. Federal Census, 1880; Special Schedule for Surviving Soldiers, Sailors, Marines, Widows, Etc. Minor Civil Division, New Richmond, OH, www.ancestry.com (accessed June 9, 2014); Mattison, in Minor and Pitts, *Speaking Lives, Authoring Texts*, 41; Crowell, *Images of America*, 42.

94. Stanley, *From Bondage to Contract*, 33.

95. Potter, *Hairdresser's Experience in High Life*, 17–18.

96. Ibid., 159.

97. Ibid., 176.

98. This phenomenon has a long history. The success of Rachel Polgreen, a mixed-race hotelier who lived in late eighteenth-century Bridgetown, Barbados, came at great cost to other black women. The cost for one woman in Polgreen's care was merciless beatings. For more, see Marisa J. Fuentes, "Power and Historical Figuring: Rachel Pringle Polgreen's Troubled Archive," *Gender and History* 22.3 (November 2010): 564–84.

99. Chesnut, *Mary Chesnut's Civil War*, 15; Elizabeth Fox-Genovese, *Within the Plantation Household: Black and White Women of the Old South* (Chapel Hill: University of North Carolina Press, 1988), 348–49.

100. Potter, *Hairdresser's Experience in High Life*, 183.

4 / "Has anyone heard from Willis?"

1. Biographical and other details about individuals discussed in this chapter are drawn from letters and documents consulted by the late Frances Cabaniss Roberts for her 1940 dissertation on the nine children of Samuel Townsend, an antebellum cotton planter in Huntsville, Alabama, and their cousins and other relatives. Roberts was the great-granddaughter of Septimus Cabaniss, Townsend's lawyer. She donated her great-grandfather's papers to the University of Alabama in 1952. In the intervening years since her dissertation's completion, many of the letters and documents she quoted were recataloged. As a result, they are no longer easily traced in the collection. I will thus occasionally quote them from her thesis but also from the accessible recataloged documents. See Cabaniss Roberts, "An Experiment in Emancipation of Slaves by an Alabama Planter," 8–10, 108–9; Osborne Townsend to Thomas Townsend, December 12, 1882, MSS 252, Box 252.054, Folder 01, Cabaniss Papers.

2. Mitchell, *Raising Freedom's Child*, 12.

3. Gelis, "The Child," 312.

4. The letter discussing a child who jumped over a fence is undated and unsigned, though mailed to Thomas Townsend. Osborne likely wrote it. Osborne Townsend to Wesley and Thomas Townsend, December 3, 1872, Georgetown CO, MSS 252, Box 252.05, Folder 01, Cabaniss Papers.

5. Susanna's name is also spelled "Susannah" and "Susan" in drafts of Samuel Townsend's will and other documents in the Cabaniss Papers. See Deposition of S. D. Cabaniss, MSS 252, Box 251.056, Folder 04, Cabaniss Papers.

6. That amount in today's currency terms is worth about $5.5 million. See http://futureboy.us/fsp/dollar.fsp?quantity=200000&currency=dollars&fromYear=1856 (accessed September 20, 2012); Cabaniss Roberts, "An Experiment in Emancipation of Slaves by an Alabama Planter," 105.

7. Gutman, *The Black Family in Slavery and Freedom*, 463.

8. Osborne Townsend to Thomas Townsend, December 12, 1882, MSS 252, Box 252.054, Folder 01, Cabaniss Papers.

9. Their brother Parks S. Townsend also relocated to Huntsville and became a planter. Cabaniss Roberts, "An Experiment in Emancipation of Slaves by an Alabama Planter," 5. See also Joseph C. Kiger, *Some Social and Economic Factors Relative to the Alabama Large Planter*, Masters thesis, University of Alabama, 1947, 64; 1830 U.S. Federal Census and 1840 U.S. Federal Census, www.ancestry.com (accessed June 20, 2014); and MSS 252, Box 252.048, Cabaniss Papers.

10. *Williams' Huntsville Directory, City Guide, and Business Mirror, Vol. 1—1859-60* (Huntsville: Coltart & Sons, No. 10 Commercial Row, 1859) 1-2, 10; and Victor B. Haagen, *The Pictorial History of Huntsville, 1805-1865* (Huntsville, AL: Victor B. Haagen, 1963), 37.

11. Thomas W. Owen, *History of Alabama and Dictionary of Alabama Biography* (Chicago: S. J. Clarke, 1921), vol. 2, 926.

12. Cabaniss Roberts, "An Experiment in Emancipation of Slaves by an Alabama Planter," 4.

13. Ibid. 5.

14. The children's mothers were Hannah, Rainey and Lucy, Winney and Celia. The last two died before being freed. The other freedpeople included other relatives, among them, half siblings. Samuel Townsend Will, MSS 252, Box 0252.0050, Folder 5, Cabaniss Papers; and Cabaniss Roberts, "An Experiment in Emancipation of Slaves by an Alabama Planter," 24–25.

15. Foner, *Free Soil, Free Labor*, ix, xxvi.

16. Ibid., xxvi.

17. The 1857 Dred Scott decision, which was first argued in early 1856 and involved an enslaved man who unsuccessfully sued for his freedom, also reflected ongoing tensions surrounding the future of slavery. Foner, *Free Soil, Free Labor*, 28. See also McPherson, *Battle Cry*, 170–82.

18. In today's currency, $6,930,598,020.60. See http://futureboy.us/fsp/dollar.fsp?quantity=250000&currency=dollars&fromYear=1854, (accessed June 20, 2014); Cabaniss Roberts, "An Experiment in Emancipation of Slaves by an Alabama Planter," 9.

19. Ibid. 9.

20. Deposition of S. D. Cabaniss, MSS 252, Box 251.056, Folder 04, Cabaniss Papers.

21. Spear, *Race, Sex and the Social Order*, 210.

22. Cabaniss Roberts, "An Experiment in Emancipation of Slaves by an Alabama Planter," 38; S. D. Cabaniss to Thomas Townsend, September 14, 1865, S. D. Cabaniss Letterbook, Outgoing Legal Correspondence, 1845–1865, MSS 252, Box 0252.022, Folder 13, Cabaniss Papers.

23. Cabaniss died in 1889 before the Townsend case was fully settled. Cabaniss Roberts, "An Experiment in Emancipation of Slaves by an Alabama Planter," 11, 102, 105–6; and Septimus Cabaniss Biography, http://acumen.lib.ua.edu/u0003_0000252/ (accessed October 8, 2012).

24. Cabaniss Roberts, "An Experiment in Emancipation of Slaves by an Alabama Planter," 6.

25. Ibid., 7.

26. Horton and Flaherty in Taylor Jr., ed., *Race and the City*, 87.

27. For more on these developments, see H. Roger Grant, *The Railroad: The Life of a Technology* (Westport, CT: Greenwood Publishing Group, 2005), 82–83; Robert C. Post, *Urban Mass Transit: The Life Story of a Technology* (Baltimore: John Hopkins Press, 2010).

28. Ibid., 81, 87.

29. The letter writer was Mary Townsend. She lived in San Pedro, an agricultural colony founded in thirty years earlier in northeast Mexico. This area was a refuge for African Americans, among them railroad workers, agricultural laborers, farmers, businessmen and professionals, who had been dismayed by the hardening color line and outraged over the growing number lynchings in the United States. Mary Townsend, February 20, 1901, MSS 252, Box 252.054, Folder 01, Cabaniss Papers; William Schell Jr., *Integral Outsiders: The American Colony in Mexico City, 1876–1911* (Wilmington: Scholarly Resources, 2000), 24.

30. Mary Townsend, February 20, 1901, MSS 252, Box 252.054, Folder 01, Cabaniss Papers.

31. Osborne Townsend, possibly to his brother Thomas, August 5, 1890, MSS 252, Box 252.054, Folder 01, Cabaniss Papers.

32. Blassingame, ed., *Slave Testimony: Two Centuries of Letters*, 361.

33. Osborne Townsend to Thomas Townsend, December 12, 1882, MSS 252, Box 252.054, Folder 01, Cabaniss Papers.

34. Cabaniss Roberts, "An Experiment in Emancipation of Slaves by an Alabama Planter," 8.

35. W. E. B. Du Bois, *Black Reconstruction* (New York: Harcourt Brace, [1935] 1976), 352–53, 531.

36. For more on antebellum understandings of race on the basis of one's environment, see Ariela J. Gross, *Double Character: Slavery and Mastery in the Antebellum Southern Courtroom* (Princeton: Princeton University Press, 2000).

37. Freedmen's Bureau statement on behalf of Milcha Townsend, April 17, 1867, MSS 252, Box 252.054, Folder 01, Cabaniss Papers.

38. Mitchell, *Raising Freedom's Child*, 3.

39. This was also true for white children in urban areas as a historical work in progress on the role of young people in nineteenth-century American democracy makes clear. See Jon Grinspan, "The Wild Children of Yesteryear," *New York Times*, May 31, 2014, SR4, www.nytimes.com/2014/06/01/opinion/sunday/the-wild-children-of-yesteryear.html?_r=1 (accessed June 1, 2014).

40. Mitchell, *Raising Freedom's Child*, 55.

41. Jennifer Morgan credits Hazel Carby with such an assessment. Morgan, *Laboring Women*, 6.

42. Jones, *Fathers of Conscience*, 23.

43. Kent Anderson Leslie, *Woman of Color, Daughter of Privilege: Amanda America Dickson, 1849–1893* (Athens: University of Georgia Press, 1996).

44. Her husband was Nathan Toomer, the novelist Jean Toomer's father. Leslie, *Woman of Color, Daughter of Privilege*, 64, 119.

45. Coffin, *Reminiscences of Levi Coffin*, 477.

46. Ibid., 481.

47. Ibid., 475.

48. Ibid.

49. Ibid.

50. Ibid., 476.

51. Ibid.

52. Ibid.

53. Ibid., 479.

54. Ibid.

55. Ibid., 480–81.

56. "Report of Mission to Ohio, 1858," MSS 252, Box 0252.0050, Folder 6, Cabaniss Papers.

57. Drew Gilpin Faust, *James Henry Hammond and the Old South: A Design for Mastery* (Baton Rouge: Louisiana State University Press, 1983), 87; Leslie, *Woman of Color, Daughter of Privilege,* 8.

58. Cabaniss Roberts, "An Experiment in Emancipation of Slaves by an Alabama Planter," 15.

59. Ibid., 16.

60. Ibid., 7, 10, 19–24.

61. The amount quoted is quite high, suggesting that Wesley may have mistakenly added an extra zero. To add perspective, White located a house for $13 a month in cramped Cincinnati. Cabaniss Roberts's review of her great grandfather's records reveals that the Townsends were in fact paying $96.44 for rent. The amount of their stipend is unknown. Wesley Townsend to Chadick, January 27, 1860, MSS 252, Box 252.054 Folder 01, Cabaniss Papers; and Cabaniss Roberts, "An Experiment in Emancipation of Slaves by an Alabama Planter," 21–22.

62. The executors of the Townsend estate decided to send Elvira and Jane to Kansas to join the Townsend childrens' mothers and other relatives. Cabaniss Roberts, "An Experiment in Emancipation of Slaves by an Alabama Planter," 24, 84.

63. Wesley might have been particularly displeased with Willis because he had lost his clothes on the train during their trip to Ohio, and $21.20 had been spent on replacing his wardrobe. Cabaniss Roberts, "An Experiment in Emancipation of Slaves by an Alabama Planter," 22–23.

64. Willis Townsend to Cabaniss, February 8, 1860, MSS 252, Box 256.009, Folder 6, Cabaniss Papers.

65. Wesley Townsend to Chadick, January 27, 1860, MSS 252, Box 252.054 Folder 01, Cabaniss Papers.

66. Again, these former bondspeople included the three mothers of Townsend's nine children. Two of the mothers had earlier died. The number of freedpeople exceeded those mentioned in Townsend's will owing to the arrival of newborn children. Samuel Townsend Will, MSS 252, Box 0252.0050, Folder 5, Cabaniss Papers; and Cabaniss Roberts, "An Experiment in Emancipation of Slaves by an Alabama Planter," 24–25.

67. The "Exodusters," as these free people called themselves, were the "first, massive repudiation" of Southern racism. In connecting their struggles to those of the Jews during biblical times, these migrants' relocation was the beginning of a social, if not economic, "reordering of Southern life." The loss of these laborers was so worrying that white landholders often begged steamboat captains not to pick up black migrants. Nell Irvin Painter, *Exodusters: Black Migration to Kansas after Reconstruction,* (New York: Alfred A. Knopf, 1977), 4; Buchanan, *Black Life on the Mississippi,* 177–78.

68. Brewer and Pierce Realty Company possibly to S. D. Cabaniss, November 5, 1860, MSS 252, Box 252.054, Folder 01, Cabaniss Papers.

69. Elizabeth Townsend to unknown recipient, possibly her half brother Wesley, May 18, 1861, MSS 252, Box 252.054, Folder 01, Cabaniss Papers.

70. Paul Boyer, *Urban Masses and Moral Order in America, 1820–1920* (Cambridge, MA: Harvard University Press, 1978), 12.

71. Patricia Hill Collins, *Black Feminist Thought: Knowledge, Consciousness, and the Politics of Empowerment* (New York: Routledge, 1991), 11.

72. Dickson reportedly was "free to leave the Dickson home place, free to leave her position as 'housekeeper,' and free to terminate her sexual relationship with Dickson." She probably stayed because her child was enslaved. Leslie, *Woman of Color, Daughter of Privilege,* 57.

73. The women in question were Hannah, Rainey, and Lucy, three of the five mothers of the freed ten children. The other freedpeople included their relatives. D. L. Lakin to S. D. Cabaniss, February 29, 1860, MSS 252, Box 251.056, Folder 03, Cabaniss Papers; Samuel Townsend Will, MSS 252, Box 0252.0050, Folder 5, Cabaniss Papers; and Cabaniss Roberts, "An Experiment in Emancipation of Slaves by an Alabama Planter," 24–25.

74. John Duer to Wesley Townsend, May 22, 1861, MSS 252, Box 252.054, Folder 01, Cabaniss Papers.

75. Ibid.

76. J. K. Parker to R. S. Rust, January 5, 1865, MSS 252, Box 252.054, Folder 01, Cabaniss Papers.

77. Ibid.

78. Ibid.

79. Ibid.

80. A WPA interviewer speculated that Davis remained because Kentucky, unlike most other Southern states, did not secede from the Union. The interviewer also suggested that Davis remained because Kentucky was in the upper South, where enslaved people were reputedly better treated than in the Deep South. This belief was so widespread that some whites in lower South states looked at Kentucky with alarm. It and Arkansas were the only Southern states not to prohibit teaching slaves to read and write. Moreover, although Kentucky was a slave state, juries could not convict African Americans for crimes without a trial. Bigham, *Jordan's Banks,* 14; Library of Congress, Washington, DC, *Slave Narratives: A Folk History of Slavery in the United States from Interviews with Former Slaves,* vol. 7, State: Kentucky, 70.

81. *Slave Narratives: A Folk History of Slavery in the United States from Interviews with Former Slaves,* vol. 7, State: Kentucky, 23.

82. This phenomenon has an ongoing history, as suggested by South Carolina senator Strom Thurmond's attachment to the mixed-race child he fathered with a family servant in the early 1920s whose existence was only publicly revealed after his death in 2003. Meg Kinnard, "Strom Thurmond's Mixed Race Daughter Dies," *Washington Post,* February 4, 2013, www.washingtonpost.com (accessed June 15, 2014).

83. Elvira Townsend to Cabaniss, September 10, 1865, MSS 252, Box 252.009, Folder 5, Cabaniss Papers.

84. She possibly shared a bed with him—like her mother. For more, see R. Isabel Morales, "The Townsends: Reconstructing the Lives of Seven Enslaved Women,

1830–1856," unpublished paper, www.acumen.lib.ua.edu/content/u0015/ . . . / u0015_0000002_0000006.pdf (accessed August 20, 2013).

85. Willis Townsend to Cabaniss, September 7, 1866, MSS 252, Box 252.009, Folder 6, Cabaniss Papers.

86. Woodson Townsend to Cabaniss, February 16, year unknown, MSS 252, Box 252.009, Folder 5, Cabaniss Papers.

87. Ibid.

88. Elvira Townsend to Cabaniss, November 8, 1866, MSS 252, Box 252.009, Folder 5, Cabaniss Papers.

89. Cabaniss Roberts, "An Experiment in Emancipation of Slaves by an Alabama Planter," 58, 75.

90. Sandweiss writes that King "seemed most attracted to those women whose race and class and educational background rendered them most unlike" his "needy" white mother. Remarking on the indifference one white male acquaintance displayed toward women of color during a trip to Tahiti and Samoa, King half-joked, "I love primal women so madly." Speaking further of his attraction for women of color, perhaps for fair-skinned ones in particular (even though Ada was dark-skinned), King mentioned the woman as "lovely as mulatto lilies" he saw in Santiago de Cuba. Martha A. Sandweiss, *Passing Strange: A Gilded Age Tale of Love and Deception across the Color Line* (New York: Penguin, 2009), 2, 125, 128, 173, 196.

91. To marry, he had to pass as black. He hid this marriage from his white associates.

92. Sandweiss, *Passing Strange*, 156–57.

93. Ibid., 288.

94. Ibid., 241, 278.

95. Ibid., 297.

96. Ibid., 215.

97. Ibid., 214.

98. Ibid., 215.

99. Ibid., 222.

100. *Historic Georgetown: Centennial Gazette, 1866–1968* (Georgetown, CO: Georgetown Society, 1968), 3, 9, 21.

101. Osborne Townsend to Thomas Townsend, December 12, 1882, MSS 252, Box 252.054, Folder 01, Cabaniss Papers. For more on Osborne's experience in Georgetown, see Liston E. Leyendecker, Christine A. Bradley, and Duane A. Smith, *The Rise of the Silver Queen: Georgetown, Colorado, 1859–1896* (Boulder: University Press of Colorado, 2005), 88–90, 211.

102. Osborne Townsend to Thomas Townsend, August 5, 1890, MSS 252, Box 252.054, Folder 01, Cabaniss Papers.

103. Osborne Townsend to Wesley and Thomas Townsend, December 3, 1872, Georgetown, CO, MSS 252, Box 252.05, Folder 01, Cabaniss Papers; Deposition of S. D. Cabaniss, MSS 252, Box 251.056, Folder 04, Cabaniss Papers.

104. Osborne's yearning to learn more about Willis might have been an outcome of Osborne recently losing his wife in childbirth. He described himself as being "distraught." His wife appears to have been the niece of "Aunt Clara" Brown, a former enslaved woman and Georgetown resident who invested in a black-owned mining company. Although he faced discrimination, Osborne appeared to have left an impression on local whites who were among the guests at his wedding, which received

coverage in th local newspaper. Osborne Townsend to Thomas and Wesley Townsend, January 19, 1876, Georgetown, CO, MSS 252, Box 252.054, Folder 01, Cabaniss Papers; Cabaniss Roberts, "An Experiment in Emancipation of Slaves by an Alabama Planter," 97; Leyendeck, Bradley, and Smith, *The Rise of the Silver Queen*, 88–89, 211; *Colorado Miner*, February 28, 1873.

105. Willis's eldest child was named Alice. 1880 U.S. Federal Census; Carrie Leonteen Townsend to Thomas Townsend, August 19, 1870, MSS 252, Box 252.054, Folder 01, Cabaniss Papers.

106. Cabaniss Roberts, "An Experiment in Emancipation of Slaves by an Alabama Planter," 39, 82.

107. The term "butternut" originates from a dye made from the oil of butternuts and walnuts that was used in homespun clothing by this population, and also in Confederate army uniforms. Hence, in the case of the latter, the term was a synonym for a Confederate soldier. Cabaniss Roberts, "An Experiment in Emancipation of Slaves by an Alabama Planter," 51–52; McPherson, *Battle Cry*, 31; James M. McPherson and James K. Hogue, *Ordeal by Fire: The Civil War and Reconstruction,* 4th ed. (New York: McGraw-Hill, 2010), 19, 101.

108. Cabaniss Roberts, "An Experiment in Emancipation of Slaves by an Alabama Planter," 94; 1880 U.S. Federal Census, www.ancestry.com (accessed June 20, 2014).

109. Ibid.; 1900 U.S. Federal Census, www.ancestry.com (accessed June 20, 2014).

110. Cabaniss Roberts, "An Experiment in Emancipation of Slaves by an Alabama Planter," 95.

111. Carrie Leontee Townsend to Thomas Townsend, August 19, 1870, MSS 252, Box 252.054, Folder 01, Cabaniss Papers.

112. Ibid.; Alan Tractenberg, *The Incorporation of America: Culture and Society in the Gilded Age* (New York: Hill and Wang, 1982), 9.

113. Thomas Townsend handled pension applications for himself and Wesley. Active in the Republican Party, Thomas also worked as a teacher, a journalist, and was a Huntsville city alderman. Wesley Townsend to Thomas Townsend, July 5, 1888, MSS 252, Box 252.054, Folder 01, Cabaniss Papers; Cabaniss Roberts, "An Experiment in Emancipation of Slaves by an Alabama Planter," 99, 101; Bernice Fearn Young, "Howard Weeden, A Rose of Yesterday," n.d.. Copy can be found in the A. S. Williams III Americana Collection, Gorgas Library, University of Alabama.

114. See "John David Weeden, 1840–1908," www.rootsweb.ancestry.com/~allauder/bio-weeden.htm (accessed April 27, 2014); and Thomas Townsend, *Huntsville, Alabama, City Directory, 1908,* 31, www.ancestry.com (accessed April 27, 2014).

115. For more, see Osborne Townsend, possibly to his brother Thomas, December 29, 1908, Item 46, Box 252.054, Folder 01, Cabaniss Papers.

116. Osborne Townsend to Thomas Townsend, August 5, 1890, MSS 252, Box 252.054, Folder 01, Cabaniss Papers.

117. Ibid.

118. Hunter, *Steamboats on the Western Rivers,* 484–85.

119. Ibid., 484–85, 494.

120. However, between 1860 and 1870, African Americans were the preferred crewmembers on boats traveling on the upper Mississippi, owing to a belief that blacks were more "obedient" than Irishmen. Hunter, *Steamboats on the Western Rivers,* 450–51; Nancy Bertaux, "Structural Economic Change and Occupational Decline

among Black Workers in Nineteenth Century Cincinnati," in Taylor, ed., *Race and the City*, 142.

121. By 1850, there were 29, 401 workers in the city's shops and factories, almost as many as the 30,147 individuals working in St. Louis, Pittsburgh, Louisville, and Chicago combined. In fact, not until the late 1860s did Chicago strip Cincinnati of its title as the biggest midwestern employer in the industrial sector. Ross, *Workers on the Edge*, 72–73.

122. Bertaux, "Structural Economic Change and Occupational Decline," 127, 142–43.

123. While African Americans appeared to have more jobs than whites (54.8 percent were employed, compared to 47.2 percent of white Americans), these statistics reflected the growing number of black women in menial positions. In 1890 African American women made up as much as 28 percent of the city's labor force. Bertaux, "Structural Economic Change and Occupational Decline," 127–40.

124. Between 1870 and 1910 Cincinnati's foreign immigrant population declined as it did in other midwestern cities. Only New York City, Boston, and San Francisco continued to draw large numbers of new immigrants. However, despite the immigrant population decline in Cincinnati, white immigrants and their native-born descendants continued to make up more than half of Cincinnati's population in the 1850s. Taylor, "City Building, Public Policy, and the Rise of the Industrial City"; David Ward, *Cities and Immigrants: A Geography of Change in Nineteenth Century America* (New York: Oxford University Press, 1971), 20, 77; Ross, *Workers on the Edge*, 72.

125. In 1860, 11,428 African Americans lived in Indiana. There were just under 40,000 in 1880. Bigham, *Jordan's Banks*, 140.

126. Ross, *Workers on the Edge*, 212.

127. Ibid., 262.

128. Willis's employment on the river may have always been tenuous. The 1880 census lists his occupation as a porter. Cabaniss Roberts, "An Experiment in Emancipation of Slaves by an Alabama Planter," 55; 1880 U.S. Federal Census; Ross, *Workers on the Edge*, 241.

129. Ross, *Workers on the Edge*, 241.

130. Bigham, *Jordan's Banks*, 299–300.

131. Osborne Townsend to Thomas Townsend, March 21, 1884, MSS 252, Box 252.054 Folder 01, Cabaniss Papers.

132. As early as the 1850s, the country was becoming a more structured society with "new hierarchies of control." Such change accelerated in the 1870s with westward expansion, the birth of industrial corporations, the rise of the metropolis, and revolutions in transportation, communications, and bureaucracy. Few areas of American life went untouched. Tractenberg, *The Incorporation of America*, 4–6.

133. Osborne Townsend to Willis Townsend, July 8, 1889, MSS 252, Box 252.054, Folder 01, Cabaniss Papers.

134. Osborne Townsend to Thomas Townsend, August 5, 1890, MSS 252, Box 252.054 Folder 01, Cabaniss Papers.

135. Cabaniss Roberts, "An Experiment in Emancipation of Slaves by an Alabama Planter," 91–92.

136. For more, see W. Sherman Savage, *Blacks in the West* (Contributions in Afro-American and African Studies (New York: Greenwood, 1977); John W. Savage, *Black*

Pioneers: Images of the Black Experience on the Northern Frontier (Salt Lake City: University of Utah Press, 1997); Tomás Almaguer, *Racial Fault Lines: The Historical Origins of White Supremacy in California* (Berkeley: University of California Press, 2008).

137. Savage, *Black Pioneers*, 3.

138. Gross, *Double Character*, 129.

139. In this instance, he went by his first name, Charles. See National Archives Pacific Alaska Region (Seattle), Seattle, WA, Fourth Registration Draft Cards (WW II), www.ancestry.com (accessed August 11, 2013); 1885 Colorado State Census (accessed August 11, 2013); 1880 U.S. Federal Census, www.ancestry.com (accessed August 11, 2013).

140. 1910 U.S. Federal Census.

141. Mark. E. Hill, "Skin Color and the Perception of Attractiveness among African Americans: Does Gender Make a Difference?," *Social Psychology Quarterly* 65.1 (March 2002): 71–91; Trina Jones, "Shades of Brown: The Law of Skin Color," *Duke Law Journal* 49.6 (April 2000), 1487–1557.

142. Thomas also had a brother named Willis who was surely named for their uncle who resided in New Richmond. 1880 U.S. Federal Census, www.ancestry.com (accessed August 11, 2013).

143. For more on the challenges African Americans faced while "passing," see Allyson Hobbs, *A Chosen Exile: A History of Racial Passing in American Life* (Cambridge, MA: Harvard University Press, 2014).

144. 1920 U.S. Federal Census.

145. Ibid.

146. Arthur Meier Schlesinger Sr., *The Rise of the City, 1878–1898* (Columbus: Ohio State University Press, 1933, 1999), xxxvi.

147. Raymond A. Mohl, *The New City: Urban America in the Industrial Age, 1860–1920* (Arlington Heights, IL: Harlan Davidson, 1985), 9.

148. John Putman, "Racism and Temperance: The Politics of Class and Gender in Late 19th-Century Seattle," *Pacific Northwest Quarterly* 95.2 (Spring 2004): 70.

149. Dana Frank, "Race Relations and the Seattle Labor Movement, 1915–1929," *Pacific Northwest Quarterly*, 86.1 (Winter 1994–95): 35–44.

150. He was now employed by a firm used by the U.S. Army to store and distribute supplies for military posts. Thomas had evidently stretched the truth to get this position and in this way figured into an ongoing string of untruths made involving race mixing. Alma Fries, a white woman from Illinois who resided in a boarding house near his Seattle home was listed on his draft card as the person who "will always know" his address. He died in 1959 at age 76 in Seattle. A woman named Gertrude Townsend appears to have died in 1972. If she was his wife, they had parted ways. U.S. Social Security Death Index, www.ancestry.com (accessed August 11, 2013); National Archives Pacific Alaska Region (Seattle), Seattle, WA, Fourth Registration Draft Cards (WW II), http://search.ancestrylibrary.com/cgi-bin/sse.dll?db=WWIIdraft&h=10684930&indiv=try&o_vc=Record:OtherRecord&rhSource=6837 (accessed August 11, 2013); Washington, Deaths, 1883–1960, www.ancestry.com (accessed August 11, 2013).

151. William often went by his middle name, Bolden. William Bolden Townsend to Cabaniss, August 15, 1874, MSS 252, Box 252.009, Folder 5, Cabaniss Papers.

152. Brent M. S. Campney, "W. B. Townsend and the Struggle against Racist Violence in Leavenworth," *Kansas History: A Journal of the Central Plains* 31 (Winter

2008–9): 260–73; "William Bolden Townsend,: Kansas Memory," www.kansasmemory.org/item/213465 (accessed August 15, 2013); P. Clay Smith Jr., *Emancipation: The Making of the Black Lawyer, 1844–1944* (Philadelphia: University of Pennsylvania Press, 1999).

153. He may be the lawyer to whom Frances Cabaniss Roberts referred when she stated that Thomas Townsend told her that one of Osborne's sons was a lawyer practicing in Wyoming. *U.S. City Directories, 1821–1989*, www.ancestry.com (accessed August 11, 2013); Cabaniss Roberts, "An Experiment in Emancipation of Slaves by an Alabama Planter," 99.

154. Nettie Caldwell to S. D. Cabaniss, October 11, 1884, Louisville, KY, MSS 252, Box 252.054, Folder 01, Cabaniss Papers.

155. In 1865, Milcha Townsend married John Caldwell, a carpenter she called a "sober [and] industrious" husband. She gave birth to Nettie, whose father was the older brother of a Louisville woman named Nellie Bibb. Following Caldwell's death in 1872 and the death of another child, Milcha struggled financially and gave Nettie to her mother, Lucy, who, unable to take care of her, gave her to Bibb. At the time of this letter, she was living with Bibb. "If you ever come to this city call me and see Nettie," Bibb told Cabaniss in a letter four years before Nettie's appeal to him. See Milcha Townsend Caldwell statement, April 17, 1867, Topeka, KS, MSS 252, Box 252.054, Folder 01, Cabaniss Papers; Cabaniss Roberts, "An Experiment in Emancipation of Slaves by an Alabama Planter," 87; Nellie Bibb to S. D. Cabaniss, August 3, 1880, Louisville, KY, MSS 252, Box 252.054, Folder 01, Cabaniss Papers.

156. Bancroft, *Slave-Trading in the Old South*, 57.

157. Fulton Minor and Pitts, *Speaking Lives, Authoring Texts*, 3.

158. Cabaniss Roberts, "An Experiment in Emancipation of Slaves by an Alabama Planter," 87.

159. Ibid., 96–97.

160. Quoted in Siobhan B. Somerville, *Queering the Color Line: Race and the Invention of Homosexuality in American Culture* (Durham, NC: Duke University Press, 2000), 78–79.

161. Ibid., 80.

162. Ibid., 79.

163. Trollope, *Domestic Manners of the Americans*, 7; emphasis added.

164. Osborne Townsend to Thomas Townsend, February 14, 1888, MSS 252, Box 252.054, Folder 01, Cabaniss Papers and Osborne Townsend to Thomas Townsend, July 27, 1889, MSS 252, Box 252.054, Folder 01, Cabaniss Papers.

165. For more, see Leyendecker, Bradley, and Smith, *The Rise of the Silver Queen*, 88–89. See also *Colorado Miner*, September 28, 1871, 4.

166. Cabaniss Roberts, "An Experiment in Emancipation of Slaves by an Alabama Planter," 101.

167. Osborne Townsend to Thomas Townsend, February 14, 1888, MSS 252, Box 252.054, Folder 01, Cabaniss Papers.

168. Scott Hancock, "'From No Country?' to 'Our Country!' Living Out Manumission and the Boundaries of Rights and Citizenship, 1773–1855," in Brana-Shute and Sparks, *Paths to Freedom*, 265–66.

169. Wesley Townsend's second wife, Adelaide, revealed as much in a letter to Cabaniss. Her request to marry was in vain for she apparently died at age sixteen the following

year. Cabaniss Roberts, "An Experiment in Emancipation of Slaves by an Alabama Planter," 48–50; Adelaide Townsend to Cabaniss, May 10, 1869, MSS 252, Box 252.009, Folder 05, Cabaniss Papers. For more, see R. Isabela Morales, "Letters from a Planter's Daughter: Understanding Freedom and Independence in the Life of Susanna Townsend (1853–1869)" (BA thesis, University of Alabama); and "Letters from a Planter's Daughter: Understanding Freedom and Independence in the Life of Susanna Townsend (1853–1869)," University of Alabama McNair Journal 12 (March 2012).

170. Susanna Townsend to Cabaniss, June 4, 1868, MSS 252, Box 252.009, Folder 5, Cabaniss Papers; Adelaide M. Townsend to Cabaniss, May 10, 1869, MSS 252, Box 252.009, Folder 5, Cabaniss Papers.

171. Susanna Townsend to Cabaniss, June 4, 1868, MSS 252, Box 252.009, Folder 5, Cabaniss Papers.

172. Susanna Townsend to Cabaniss, January 1, 1866, MSS 252, Box 252.009, Folder 5, Cabaniss Papers.

Epilogue

1. Neely Tucker, *Love in the Driest Season* (New York: Three Rivers, 2004).

2. Genealogical records help fill in the silences, but not entirely. The same is true of other documents, among them archival newspapers that leave more questions than answers. For example, an undergraduate research assistant working on a newspaper advertisement database project with my colleague Joshua Rothman was intrigued to discover that one Alabama slaveholder ran numerous advertisements in several newspapers over one year asking for the return of a "small Negro boy, about two-years-old, of yellow complexion," who was allegedly stolen. He offered a $100 reward for the child and a $200 reward for the thief. Was this a matter of property only, or also paternity? The archival record does not tell us. Courtnee Cook to Sharony Green, May 3, 2015; *Huntsville Democrat*, June 4, 1824.

3. One such television show is the 1980 drama *In the Heat of the Night*, inspired by a 1960s movie involving a black Philadelphia policeman and his encounters in a racist Southern town. During the "color-blind" moment when the subsequent television series was made, the town's police chief (Carroll O'Connor) eventually married a black woman, something unthinkable when the movie was made. Equally unthinkable, the chief and his wife, Harriet, were married as Catholics, and ended up enforcing the law and running much of the city of Sparta, Mississippi. In one episode, a white man arrested for a crime sneeringly mentions the "pillow talk," or intimate conversations, between Chief Gillespie and his "ole lady." *In the Heat of the Night* (dir. Norman Jewison), 1967, www.imdb.com/title/tt0061811/ (accessed October 17, 2012) and *In the Heat of the Night* (television series), 1988–95, www.imdb.com/title/tt0094484/ (accessed October 17, 2012). The episode cited aired April 16, 2011, on WGN America, a Chicago-based cable channel.

4. This is almost certainly because, as Steven Spielberg once said, "one of the jobs of art is to go to the impossible places that history must avoid." When Hollywood plays with the truth, audiences receive only glimpses of what really happened, but some of those glimpses are insightful. For example, in Quentin Tarantino's 2012 film *Django Unchained*, the viewer cannot miss the favor that Broomhilda, an African American bondswoman destined to be a sex worker, had with the German bounty hunter to whom she has been given for the night by her master. The opening for such

an arrangement is her ability to speak German, something that situates her and this man in a more intimate space, a hidden one, one in which they had a shared understanding about something intangible, owing to their familiarity with the German language, if nothing else. That they inhabit this space is intriguing for us but not for those of another age. Many nineteenth-century Germans arrived in the United States during a period when they and African Americans were mutually inspired by the other's struggle and when antislavery campaigns in the United States converged with the upheaval in revolutionary Germany. As James Horton and Hartman Keil uncover, Germans in antebellum Buffalo lived beside and with people of color, some even marrying them. *Lincoln* (dir. Steven Spielberg), 2012, www.imdb.com (accessed September 26, 2013); Thavolia Glymph, "Untellable Human Suffering," *Chronicle of Higher Education*, www.chronicle.com/blogs/conversation.author.tglymph/ (accessed January 2, 2013); *Django Unchained* (dir. Quentin Tarantino), 2012, www.imdb.com/title/tt1853728/, (accessed January 21, 2013); James Oliver Horton and Hartmut Keil, "African Americans and Germans in Mid-Nineteenth-Century Buffalo."

5. Sharony Green, "'Mr Ballard I am compelled to write again': Beyond Bedrooms and Brothels, a Fancy Girl Speaks," *Black Women, Gender and Families* 5.1 (Spring 2011): 17–40.

6. Estella Andrews Myers to Sharony Green, May 15, 2012.

7. I was deeply interested in doing as much while being aware that I might reveal details about the lives of others that were intended to stay hidden. I continued my research because I wanted to join other scholars who mine archival material with the hope of making new discoveries about people of the past in order better to understand ongoing attitudes and behavior. As I completed this project, I was pleased to discover that other scholars are having conversations about the ethics of our research and the risks involved in exposing information historical actors may have desired to remain private. I look forward to future conversations on this subject. For more on this issue, see Jessica Marie Johnson, "My OAH Tribute to: Stephanie M. H. Camp and Deborah Gray White," *Diaspora Hypertext* blog, April 18, 2014, diasporahypertext.com/2014/18/my-oah-tribute-stephanie-m-h-camp-deborah-gray-white/ (accessed June 15, 2014).

8. As I put this book to bed, a nationwide outcry is raging about the treatment of African Americans in police custody in Baltimore, suggesting opportunities to discuss the complexities surrounding this and other subjects.

9. Cora's husband, Isaac, a former bondsman, was politically active in Arkansas during Reconstruction. Her son Isaac Jr. studied at Yale University and the University of Cincinnati and her granddaughter Dorothy Gillam taught French in Cincinnati. George P. Rawick, ed., *The American Slave: A Composite Autobiography, vol. 1* (Westport, CT: Greenwood, 1972), 68; Fay A. Yarbrough, "Power, Perception and Interracial Sex: Former Slaves Recall Multiracial South," *Journal of Southern History* 71.3 (August 2005): 584; Tom Dillard, *Statesmen, Scoundrels, and Eccentrics: A Gallery of Amazing Arkansans* (Little Rock: University of Arkansas Press, 2010), 70.

10. Robert Smalls, freedman and native of Beaufort, South Carolina; American Freedmen's Inquiry Commission Interview, 1863, Blassingame, ed., *Slave Testimony: Two Centuries of Letters*, 373.

11. Sarah Fitzpatrick, former enslaved servant in Alabama, interviewed in 1938, in Blassingame, ed., *Slave Testimony: Two Centuries of Letters*, 639.

12. Annette Gordon-Reed, "Engaging Jefferson: Blacks and the Founding Father," *William and Mary Quarterly*, 3rd ser., 57.1 (January 2000): 171–82.

13. Thomas J. Sugrue, *Not Even Past: Barack Obama and the Burden of Race* (Princeton: Princeton University Press, 2010).

14. Rothman, *Notorious in the Neighborhood*.

15. Frederick Law Olmsted, *The Cotton Kingdom: A Traveller's Observations on Cotton and Slavery in the American Slave States based upon three former volumes of journeys and investigations by the same author, vol. 1, ed.* Arthur M. Schlesinger Sr. (New York: Alfred A. Knopf, 1953), 60.

16. Jones, *Fathers of Conscience*, 185; Rothman, *Notorious in the Neighborhood*.

17. Milne's use of "Enter" meant "recruit" or "enlist." Alexander Milne to Charles Eden, April 21, 1860, National Maritime Museum, UK, Milne MSS MLN/116/3 [2].

18. Ibid.

19. If there was any remaining doubt about the extent of the inconsistencies in American slave society, they are present in the following words from Alabama lawyer and slaveholder, and later Confederate politician, Septimus Cabaniss on the subject of freeing his client's enslaved children and their immediate kinfolk: "He expresses a preference for their settlement on the N.[orth] American continent, and desires that in making a selection of the country, his Executors will act with a view to the ultimate improvement and *happiness* of his servants. Emphasis added. S.D. Cabaniss to Stephen A. Douglas, Box 13, Folder 26, Stephen A. Douglas Papers 1764–1908, Special Collections Research Center, University of Chicago.

BIBLIOGRAPHY

Primary Sources

Rice C. Ballard Papers. Natchez Trace Collection, University of Texas, Austin.

Rice C. Ballard Papers. Southern Historical Collection, Wilson Library, University of North Carolina, Chapel Hill.

Bland, Sterling Lecater, Jr., ed. *African American Slave Narratives: An Anthology. Vol. 2.* Westport, CT: Greenwood Press, 2001.

Blassingame, John W., ed. *Slave Testimony: Two Centuries of Letters, Speeches, Interviews, and Autobiographies.* Baton Rouge: Louisiana State University Press, 1977.

Browning, Orville Hickman. *The Diary of Orville Hickman Browning, vol. 1, 1850–1864.* Springfield: Illinois State Historical Library, 1850.

Septimus Douglas Cabaniss Papers. Special Collections, Stanley Hoole Library, University of Alabama.

Federal Writer's Project, 1936–38. Works Progress Administration (WPA), Manuscript Division, Library of Congress.

William A. J. Finney Papers, David M. Rubenstein Rare Book & Manuscript Library, Duke University.

Albert Clinton Horton Papers. Dolph Briscoe Center for American History, University of Texas, Austin.

Mattison, Hiram. *Louisa Picquet, the Octoroon, or, Inside Views of Southern Domestic Life.* New York: The Author, 1861.

National Maritime Museum. London.

Oakes Papers. Boston Public Library.

Silas and R. H. Omohundra Ledger, 1857–64. Manuscripts Department, University of Virginia Library, Richmond.

Slave Narratives: A Folk History of Slavery in the United States from Interviews with Former Slaves. Library of Congress, Washington, DC, 2006.

U.S. Bureau of Statistics.

U.S. Census.

U.S. Social Security Death Index.

DIARIES

Chesnut, Mary. *Mary Chesnut's Civil War.* Ed. C. Vann Woodward. New Haven: Yale University Press, 1983.

Chesnut, Mary Boykin Miller. *The Private Mary Chestnut: The Unpublished Civil War Diaries.* Ed. C. Vann Woodward and Elizabeth Muhlenfeld. New York: Oxford University Press, 1984.

Thornbrough, Gayle, and Dorothy L. Riker, eds. *Diary and Letters of Calvin Fletcher, vol. 1, 1838–1843.* Indianapolis: Indianapolis Historical Society, 1973.

NEWSPAPERS

Alexandria Gazette, December 3, 1832; August, 20, 1833

Bainbridge Argus

Cincinnati Republican

Cleveland Morning Daily Herald

Daily Evening Bulletin

Daily Picayune

Mississippi Free Trader and Natchez Gazette

Mississippi State Gazette

DIRECTORIES

Cincinnati Directory Advertiser for the Years 1836–7. Cincinnati: J. H. Woodruff, 1836.

Cincinnati Directory, for the Year 1842. Cincinnati: E. Morgan and Company, 1842.

The Louisville Directory and Annual Business Advertiser for 1855–6. Louisville: W. Lee White & Co., 1855.

Shaffer, David Henry. *The Cincinnati, Covington, Newport and Fulton Directory for 1840.* Cincinnati: J. B. & R. P. Donogh, 1839.

Tucker, Louis Leonard. *Cincinnati: A Student's Guide to Localized History.* New York: Teachers College Press, 1969.

Williams' Huntsville Directory, City Guide, and Business Mirror, vol. 1, 1859–60. Huntsville: Coltart & Sons, No. 10 Commercial Row, 1859.

The WPA Guide to Cincinnati. Cincinnati, OH: Cincinnati Historical Society, 1987.

GUIDES

Haagen, Victor B. *The Pictorial History of Huntsville, 1805–1865.* Huntsville, AL: Victor B. Haagen, 1963.

Historic Georgetown: Centennial Gazette, 1866–1968. Georgetown, CO: Georgetown Society, 1968.

Kenny, D. J. *Illustrated Cincinnati Pictorial Handbook of the Queen City.* Cincinnati, OH: Robert Clarke & Co., 1875.

The WPA Guide to Cincinnati. Cincinnati, OH: Cincinnati Historical Society, 1987.

MOTION PICTURES AND TELEVISION

Django Unchained. Dir. Quentin Tarantino. 2012. www.imdb.com/title/ tt1853728/ (accessed January 21, 2013).

In the Heat of the Night. Dir. Norman Jewison. 1967. www.imdb.com/title/ tt0061811/ (accessed October 17, 2012).

In the Heat of the Night (television series). 1988–95. www.imdb.com/title/ tt0094484/ (accessed October 17, 2012).

Websites

www.Ancestry.com.

Secondary Sources

Abruzzo, Margaret. *Polemical Pain: Slavery, Cruelty, and the Rise of Humanitarianism.* Baltimore: Johns Hopkins University Press, 2011.

Adams, Catherine, and Elizabeth Pleck. *Love of Freedom: Black Women in Colonial and Revolutionary England.* New York: Oxford University Press, 2010.

Ahmed, Sara. *Queer Phenomenology: Orientations, Objects, Others.* Durham, NC: Duke University Press 2006.

Alexander, M. Jacqui. *Pedagogies of Crossing: Meditations on Feminism, Sexual Politics, and the Sacred.* Durham, NC: Duke University Press, 2005.

Almaguer, Tomás. *Racial Fault Lines: The Historical Origins of White Supremacy in California.* Berkeley: University of California Press, 2008.

Anderson, James D. *The Education of Blacks in the South, 1860–1935.* Chapel Hill: University of North Carolina Press, 1988.

Anderson Leslie, Kent. *Woman of Color, Daughter of Privilege: Amanda America Dickson, 1849–1893.* Athens: University of Georgia Press, 1996.

Baggett, James L. *The Autobiography of a Magdalen.* 1911; Birmingham, AL: Birmingham Public Library Press, 2005.

Bancroft, Frederic. *Slave-Trading in the Old South.* Baltimore: J. H. Furst Co., 1931.

Baptist, Edward E. "'Cuffy,' 'Fancy Maids,' and 'One-Eyed Men': Rape, Commodification, and the Domestic Slave Trade in the United States." *American Historical Review* 106.5 (December 2001): 1619–650.

———. *The Half Has Never Been Told: Slavery and the Making of American Capitalism*. New York: Basic Books, 2014.

Barth, Gunther. *The Rise of Modern City Culture in Nineteenth-Century America*. Oxford: Oxford University Press, 1982.

Beckles, Hilary McD. *Centering Woman: Gender Discourses in Caribbean Slave Society*. Kingston: Ian Randle Publishers, 1999.

Berlin, Ira. *Slaves without Masters: The Free Negro in the Antebellum South*. New York: New Press, 2007.

Bernstein, Henry. *The Mysteries of St. Louis: A Novel*. Trans. Friedrich Munch. Ed. Elizabeth Sims. Chicago: Charles H. Kerr, 1990.

Bibb, Henry. *Narrative of the Life and Adventures of Henry Bibb, an American Slave*. New York, 1849.

Bigham, Darrel. *Jordan's Banks: Emancipation and Its Aftermath in the Ohio River Valley*. Lexington: University Press of Kentucky, 2006.

Blassingame, John W. *The Slave Community: Plantation Life in the Antebellum South*. New York: Oxford University Press, 1972, 1979.

Boydston, Jeanne. *Home & Work: Housework, Wages, and the Ideology of Labor in the Early Republic*. New York: Oxford University Press, 1990.

Boyer, Paul. *Urban Masses and Moral Order in America, 1820–1920*. Cambridge, MA: Harvard University Press, 1978.

Braithwaite, William C. *The Second Period of Quakerism*. 2nd ed. Cambridge: Cambridge University Press, 1961.

Brana-Shute, Rosemary, and Randy J. Sparks, eds. *Paths to Freedom: Manumission in the Atlantic World*. Columbia: University of South Carolina Press, 2009.

Brent, Linda. *Incidents in the Life of a Slave Girl*. New York: Oxford University Press, 1988.

Broomhall, Susan. *Emotions in the Household, 1200–1900*. New York: Palgrave Macmillan, 2008.

Brown, Kathleen M. *Good Wives, Nasty Wenches, and Anxious Patriarchs*. Chapel Hill: University of North Carolina Press, 1996.

Brown, Richard F. *Coastal Encounters: The Transformation of the Gulf South in the Eighteenth Century*. Lincoln: University of Nebraska Press, 2008

Buchanan, Thomas C. *Black Life on the Mississippi: Slaves, Free Blacks, and the Western Steamboat World*. Chapel Hill: University of North Carolina Press, 2004.

Burin, Eric. *Slavery and the Peculiar Solution: A History of the American Colonization Society*. Gainesville: University Press of Florida, 2005.

Butler, Judith. *Gender Trouble: Feminism and the Subversion of Identity*. New York: Routledge, 1990.

Bynum, Victoria. *Unruly Women: The Politics of Social and Sexual Control in the Old South*. Chapel Hill: University of North Carolina, 1992.

Camp, Stephanie M. H. *Closer to Freedom: Enslaved Women and Everyday Resistance in the Plantation South*. Chapel Hill: University of North Carolina Press. 2004.

Campney, Brent M. S. "W. B. Townsend and the Struggle against Racist Violence in Leavenworth." *Kansas History: A Journal of the Central Plains* 31 (Winter 2008–9): 260–73.

Carby, Hazel V. "Policing the Black Woman's Body in an Urban Context." *Critical Inquiry* 18 (Summer 1992): 733–755.

Chalkley, Lyman. *Chronicles of the Scotch-Irish Settlement in Virginia, 1745–1800*. Baltimore: Genealogical Publishing Co., 1965.

Chazkel, Amy, and Junia Claudia Zaidan. "Mulatas, Crioulos, and Morenas: Racial Hierarchy, Gender Relations, and National Identity in Postabolition Popular Song (Southeastern Brazil, 1890–1920)." In Pamela Scully and Diana Paton, eds., *Gender and Slave Emancipation in the Atlantic World*. Durham, NC: Duke University Press, 2005. 267–88.

Clegg, Claude A. *The Price of Liberty: African Americans and the Making of Liberia*. Chapel Hill: University of North Carolina Press, 2004.

Clinton, Catherine. *The Plantation Mistress: Woman's World in the Old South*. New York: Pantheon, 1984

Coffin, Levi. *Reminiscences of Levi Coffin, the Reputed President of the Underground Railroad: Being a Brief History of the Labors of a Lifetime in Behalf of the Slave, with the Stories of Numerous Fugitives, Who Gained Their Freedom through His Instrumentality, and Many Other Incidents*. Cincinnati, OH: Robert Clark & Co., 1880. http://docsouth.unc.edu/nc/coffin/illustr.html.

Collins, Lewis. *History of Kentucky*. Covington: Collins & Co., 1882, 1966, 1980.

Collins, Patricia Hill. *Black Feminist Thought: Knowledge, Consciousness, and the Politics of Empowerment*. New York: Routledge, 1991.

Coleman, J. Winston. *Belle Breezing: A Famous Lexington Bawd*. Lexington: Winburn Press, 1980.

———. *Slavery Times in Kentucky*, Chapel Hill: University of North Carolina Press, 1940.

Connell, R. W. *Masculinities*. Berkeley: University of California Press, 1995.

Crowell, Cheryl. *Images of America: New Richmond*. Charleston: Arcadia Publishing, 2012.

Crozier, William Armstrong, ed. *Virginia County Records—Spotsylvania County Records, 1721–1800*. New York: Fox, Duffield & Co., 1905.

Curry, Leonard P. *The Free Black in Urban America, 1800–1850: The Shadow of the Dream*. Chicago: University of Chicago Press, 1986.

Davis, Adrienne. "Don't Let Nobody Bother Yo' Principle: The Sexual Economy of American Slavery." In Sharon Harley, ed., *Sister Circle: Black Women and Work*. New Brunswick: Rutgers University Press, 2002. 103–27.

Dabney, William P. *Cincinnati's Colored Citizens: Historical, Sociological, and Biographical*. New York: Negro Universities Press, 1926.

Davis, Angela. *Women, Race, and Class*. New York: Vintage Books, 1983.

Davis, Arthur P. "The Tragic Mulatto Theme in Six Works of Langston Hughes." *Phylon 9* (1940–56), 16.2 (2nd Qtr. 1955): 195–204.

Davis, David Brion. *The Problem of Slavery in the Age of Emancipation*. New York: Knopf, 2014.

Davis, Wanda M. "First Foundations: An Enquiry into the Founding of Three Selected African American Institutions of Higher Learning." EdD diss., Pennsylvania State University, 1994.

D'Emilio, John, and Estelle B. Freedman. *Intimate Matters: A History of Sexuality in America*. Chicago: University of Chicago Press, 1988.

Deyle, Steven. *Carry Me Back: The Domestic Slave Trade in American Life*. New York: Oxford University Press, 2006.

Dillard, Tom. *Statesmen, Scoundrels, and Eccentrics: A Gallery of Amazing Arkansans*. Little Rock: University of Arkansas Press, 2010.

Douglas, Ann. *The Feminization of American Culture*. New York: Knopf, 1977.

Dunn, Richard. *Sugar and Slaves: The Rise of the Planter Class in the British West Indies, 1624–1713*. Chapel Hill: University of North Carolina Press, 2000.

Edwards, Laura F. *Gendered Strife and Confusion: The Political Culture of Reconstruction*. Urbana: University of Illinois Press, 1997.

Ellenberger, Matthew. "Illuminating the Lesser Lights: Notes on the Life of Albert Clinton Horton," *Southwestern Historical Quarterly* 88 (April 1985): 363–86.

Eustace, Nicole. *Passion Is the Gale: Emotion, Power, and the Coming of the American Revolution*. Chapel Hill: University of North Carolina Press, 2008.

Faust, Drew Gilpin. *James Henry Hammond and the Old South: A Design for Mastery*. Baton Rouge: Louisiana State University Press, 1983.

———. *Mothers of Invention: Women of the Slaveholding South in the American Civil War*. Chapel Hill: University of North Carolina Press, 2004.

———. *This Republic of Suffering: Death and the American Civil War*. New York: Knopf, 2008.

Foner, Eric. *Free Soil, Free Labor, Free Men: The Ideology of the Republican Party before the Civil War*. New York: Oxford University Press, [1970] 1995.

———. *Politics and Ideology in the Age of the Civil War*. New York: Oxford University Press, 1980.

Fork of the Roads: A Major Southwest Hub of America's Domestic Slave Trade. Natchez, MS: Friends of the Fork of the Roads Society.

Foucault, Michel. *The History of Sexuality: An Introduction, Volume 1*. New York: Vintage, 1978.

———. *Power/Knowledge: Selected Interviews and Other Writings, 1972–1977*. Ed. Colin Gordon. New York: Pantheon Books, 1972, 1980.

Fox-Genovese, Elizabeth. *Within the Plantation Household: Black and White Women of the Old South*. Chapel Hill: University of North Carolina Press, 1988.

Fox-Genovese, Elizabeth, and Eugene D. Genovese. *The Mind of the Master Class: History of Faith in the Southern Slaveholders' Worldview.* Cambridge: Cambridge University Press, 2005.

Frank, Dana. "Race Relations and the Seattle Labor Movement, 1915–1929." *Pacific Northwest Quarterly* 86.1 (Winter 1994–95): 35–44.

Frazier, E. Franklin. *The Negro Family in the United States.* Chicago: University of Chicago Press, 1939.

Fredrickson, George M. *The Black Image in the White Mind: The Debate on Afro-American Character and Destiny, 1817–1914.* Middletown, CT: Wesleyan University Press, 1987.

Freehling, William H. *The Reintegration of American History: Slavery and the Civil War.* New York: Oxford University Press, 1994.

Frost, J. William, and John M. Moore. *Seeking the Light: Essays in Quaker History in Honor of Edwin B. Bronner.* Wallingford, PA: Pendle Hill Publications; Haverford, PA: Friends Historical Association, 1986.

Fryer, Roland G., Jr. "Guess Who's Coming to Dinner? Trends in Interracial Marriages over the Twentieth Century." *Journal of Economic Perspectives* 21.2 (2007): 71–90.

Fuentes, Marisa J. "Power and Historical Figuring: Rachel Pringle Polgreen's Troubled Archive." *Gender and History* 22.3 (November 2010): 564–84.

Fulton Minor, DoVeanna S., and Reginald H. Pitts. *Speaking Lives, Authoring Texts: Three African American Women's Oral Slave Narratives.* Albany: SUNY Press, 2010.

Gelis, Jacques. "The Child: From Anonymity to Individuality." In Roger Chartier, ed., *A History of Private Life: Passions of the Renaissance.* Cambridge, MA: Belknap Press, 1989. 309–20.

Genovese, Eugene G. *Roll, Jordan, Roll: The World Slaves Made.* New York: Vintage, 1972.

Gerber, David. *Black Ohio and the Color Line, 1860–1915.* Urbana: University of Illinois Press, 1976.

Gilfoyle, Timothy J. *City of Eros: New York City, Prostitution, and the Commercialization of Sex, 1790–1920.* New York: Norton, 1992.

Glymph, Thavolia. *Out of the House of Bondage: The Transformation of the Plantation Household.* New York: Cambridge University Press, 2008.

———. "Untellable Human Suffering." *Chronicle of Higher Education,* www.chronicle.com/blogs/conversation.author.tglymph/ (accessed January 2, 2013).

Gordon-Reed, Annette. "Engaging Jefferson: Blacks and the Founding Father." *William and Mary Quarterly,* 3rd. ser., 57.1 (January 2000): 171–82.

Gould, L. Virginia. "Urban Slavery, Urban Freedom: The Manumission of Jacqueline Lemelle." In David Barry Gaspar and Darlene Clark Hine, eds., *More than Chattel: Black Women and Slavery in the Americas.* Bloomington: Indiana University Press, 1996. 298–310.

Grant, H. Roger. *The Railroad: The Life of a Technology.* Westport, CT: Greenwood, 2005.

Green, Sharony. "'Mr Ballard I am compelled to write again': Beyond Bedrooms and Brothels, a Fancy Girl Speaks." *Black Women, Gender and Families* 5.1 (Spring 2011): 17–40.

Grinspan, Jon. "The Wild Children of Yesteryear." *New York Times,* May 31, 2014.

Gross, Ariela J. *Double Character: Slavery and Mastery in the Antebellum Southern Courtroom.* Princeton, NJ: Princeton University Press, 2000.

Gudmestad, Robert H. "The Troubled Legacy of Isaac Franklin: The Enterprise of Slave Trading." *Tennessee Historical Quarterly* (Fall 2003): 193–217.

Guillory, Monique. "Some Enchanted Evening on the Auction Block: The Cultural Legacy of the New Orleans Quadroon Balls." PhD diss., New York University, 1999.

Gutman, Herbert. *The Black Family in Slavery and Freedom.* New York: Vintage, 1977.

Hammond, Bray. *Banks and Politics in America: From the Revolution to the Civil War.* Princeton, NJ: Princeton University Press, 1957.

Harris, Cheryl. "Finding Sojourner's Truth: Race, Gender, and the Institution of Property." *Cardozo Law Review* 18 (1996): 309–409.

Harrison, Lowell, and James C. Klotter. *A New History of Kentucky.* Lexington: University Press of Kentucky, 1997.

Hartman, Saidiya. *Scenes of Subjection: Terror, Slavery, and Self-Making in Nineteenth-Century America. Race and American Culture.* New York: Oxford University Press, 1997.

Hill, Mark. E. "Skin Color and the Perception of Attractiveness among African Americans: Does Gender Make a Difference?" *Social Psychology Quarterly* 65.1 (March 2002): 77–91.

Hogan, Wesley C. *Many Minds, One Heart: SNCC's Dream for a New America.* Chapel Hill: University of North Carolina Press, 2007.

Hogue, James K. *Ordeal by Fire: The Civil War and Reconstruction.* 4th ed. New York: McGraw-Hill, 2010.

Holt, Michael F. *The Fate of Their Country: Politicians, Slavery Extension and the Coming of the Civil War.* New York: Hill and Wang, 2004.

Horton, James Oliver, and Stacy Flaherty. "Black Leadership in Antebellum Cincinnati." In Henry Louis Taylor Jr., ed., *Race and the City: Work, Community, and Protest in Cincinnati, 1820–1970.* Urbana: University of Illinois Press, 1993. 70–95.

Horton, James Oliver, and Hartmut Keil. "African Americans and Germans in Mid-Nineteenth Century Buffalo." In James Oliver Horton, ed., *Free People of Color: Inside the African American Community.* Washington, DC: Smithsonian Institution Press, 1993. 170–83.

Howell, Isabel. *John Armfield of Beersheeba Springs.* Beersheeba Springs, TN: Beersheeba Springs Historical Society, 1983.

Hunter, Tera W. *To 'Joy My Freedom: Southern Black Women's Lives and Labors after the Civil War.* Cambridge, MA: Harvard University Press, 1997.

Jason, Sharon. "Census Shows Big Jump in Interracial Couples." *USA Today,* April 26, 2012.

Johnson, Jessica Marie. "My OAH Tribute to: Stephanie M. H. Camp and Deborah Gray White." *Diaspora Hypertext* blog, April 18, 2014, diaspora-hypertext.com/2014/18/my-oah-tribute-stephanie-m-h-camp-deborah-gray-white/ (accessed June 15, 2014).

Johnson, Walter. "On Agency." *Journal of Social History* 37.1 (Fall 2003): 113–24. Special Issue.

———. "The Slave Trader, the White Slave and the Politics of Racial Determination in the 1850s." *Journal of American History* 87.1 (June 2000): 13–38.

———. *Soul by Soul: Life Inside the Antebellum Slave Market.* Cambridge, MA: Harvard University Press, 1999.

Jones, Bernie D. *Fathers of Conscience: Mixed Race Inheritance in the Antebellum South. Studies in the Legal History of the South.* Athens: University of Georgia Press, 2009.

Jones, Frank S. *History of Decatur County, Georgia.* Spartanburg: Reprint Company, 1996.

Jones, Trina. "Shades of Brown: The Law of Skin Color." *Duke Law Journal* 49.6 (April 2000): 1501–18.

Kasson, John F. *Rudeness and Civility: Manners in Nineteenth-Century Urban America.* New York: Hill and Wang, 1990.

Katzman, David. *Before the Ghetto: Black Detroit in the Nineteenth Century.* Urbana: University of Illinois Press, 1975.

Keay, John. *The Honourable Company: A History of the English East India Company.* New York: Scribner, 1994.

Kelley, Robin D. G. *Race Rebels: Culture, Politics, and the Black Working Class.* New York: Simon and Schuster, 1996.

Kessen, Thomas Paul. "Segregation in Cincinnati Public Education: The Nineteenth Century Experience," PhD diss., University of Cincinnati, 1973.

Kiger, Joseph C. "*Some Social and Economic Factors Relative to the Alabama Large Planter.*" Master's thesis, University of Alabama, 1947.

Kinnard, Meg. "Strom Thurmond's Mixed Race Daughter Dies." *Washington Post*, February 4, 2013.

Klauprecht, Emil. *Cincinnati, or The Mysteries of the West.* Trans. Steven Rowan. Ed. Don Heinrich Tollzmann. New York: Peter Lang, 2006.

Kleber, John E., ed. *The Encyclopedia of Louisville.* Lexington: University Press of Kentucky, 2000.

K'Meyer, Tracy E. *Civil Rights in the Gateway to the South: Louisville, KY, 1945–1990.* Lexington: University Press of Kentucky, 2009.

Koehler, Lyle. *Cincinnati's Black Peoples: A Chronology and Bibliography, 1787–1982.* Cincinnati, OH: University of Cincinnati, 1986.

Koger, Larry. *Black Slaveowners: Free Black Slave Masters in South Carolina, 1790–1860*. Columbia: University of South Carolina Press, 1995.

Lammermeier, Paul J. "The Urban Black Family of the Nineteenth Century: A Study of Black Family Structure in the Ohio Valley, 1850–1880." *Journal of Marriage and the Family* 35.3 (August 1973): 441–43.

Lang, Clarence. *Grassroots at the Gateway: Class Politics and Black Freedom Struggle in St. Louis, 1936–75*. Ann Arbor: University of Michigan Press, 2009.

Leyendecker, Liston E., Christine A. Bradley, and Duane A. Smith. *The Rise of the Silver Queen: Georgetown, Colorado, 1859–1896*. Boulder: University Press of Colorado, 2005.

Li, Stephanie. "Resistance, Silence, and *Placees*: Charles Bon's Octoroon Mistress and Louisa Picquet." *American Literature* 79.1 (March 2007): 85–112.

———. *Something Akin to Freedom: The Choice of Bondage in Narratives by African American Women*. Albany: SUNY Press, 2010.

Litwack, Leon. *Been in the Storm So Long: The Aftermath of Slavery*. New York: Knopf, 1979.

Lloyd, Arnold, and Herbert G. Wood, eds. *Quaker Social History, 1669–1738*. London: Longmans, Green, 1950.

Locke, John, and Richard Cox, eds. *Second Treatise of Government*. 1690; Arlington Heights, IL: Harlan Davidson, 1982.

Lofton, Williston H. "Northern Labor and the Negro during the Civil War," *Journal of Negro History* 32 (1949): 251–73.

Long, Carolyn Morrow. *A New Orleans Voudou Priestess: The Legend and Reality of Marie Laveau*. Gainesville: University Press of Florida, 2006.

McClintock, Anne. *Imperial Leather: Race, Gender, and Sexuality in the Colonial Contest*. New York: Routledge, 1995.

McGinnis, Frederick A. *History of Wilberforce*. Blanchester, OH: Brown, 1941.

McGraw, Marie Tyler. *At the Falls: Richmond, Virginia, and Its People*. Chapel Hill: University of North Carolina Press, 1994.

MacGregor, Neil. *A History of the World in 100 Objects*. New York: Penguin Books, 2008.

McLaurin, Melton A. *Celia, a Slave: A True Story*. Athens: University of Georgia Press, 1991.

McPherson, James M. *Battle Cry of Freedom: The Civil War Era*. New York: Oxford University Press, 1988.

Manganelli, Kimberly Snyder. *Transatlantic Spectacles of Race: The Tragic Mulatta and the Tragic Muse*. New Brunswick, NJ: Rutgers University Press, 2011.

Manning, Chandra. *What This Cruel War Was Over: Soldiers, Slavery, and the Civil War*. New York: Knopf, 2007.

Mastrogiovanni, Francis J. "Cincinnati's Black Community, 1840–1850." Master's thesis, University of Cincinnati, 1972.

Metaxas, Eric. *Amazing Grace: William Wilberforce and the Heroic Campaign to End Slavery*. New York: HarperOne, 2007.

Miles, Tiya. *Ties That Bind: The Story of an Afro-Cherokee Family in Slavery and Freedom*. Berkeley: University of California Press, 2006.

Mitchell, Mary Niall. *Raising Freedom's Child: Black Children and Visions of Freedom after Slavery*. American History and Culture. New York: New York University Press, 2011.

Mohl, Raymond A. *The New City: Urban America in the Industrial Age, 1860–1920*. Arlington Heights, IL: Harlan Davidson, 1985.

Moller, Herbert. "Sex Composition and Correlated Culture Patterns of Colonial America." *William and Mary Quarterly* 2.2 (April 1945): 113–53.

Monahan, Thomas P. "An Overview of Statistics on Interracial Marriage in the United States with Data on Its Extent from 1963–1970." *Journal of Marriage and the Family* 38.2 (May 1976): 223–31.

Morgan, Edmund. "The Puritans and Sex." *New England Quarterly* 15.4 (December 1942): 591–607.

Morgan, Jennifer L. *Laboring Women: Reproduction and Gender in New World Slavery*. Philadelphia: University of Pennsylvania Press, 2004.

Morgan, Philip D. "Interracial Sex in the Chesapeake and the British Atlantic World." In Jan Ellen Lewis and Peter S. Onuf, eds., *Sally Hemings and Thomas Jefferson: History, Memory and Civic Culture*. Charlottesville: University Press of Virginia, 1999. 52–85.

Monette, John Wesley. *Observations on the Epidemic Yellow Fever of Natchez, and of the South-west*. Louisville, KY: Prentice and Weissinger, 1842.

Morales, R. Isabela. "Letters from a Planter's Daughter: Understanding Freedom and Independence in the Life of Susanna Townsend (1853–1869)." BA thesis, University of Alabama. Repr. *University of Alabama McNair Journal* 12 (March 2012).

———. "The Townsends: Reconstructing the Lives of Seven Enslaved Women, 1830–1856." Unpublished. Available at acumen.lib.ua.edu/content/u0015/ . . . /u0015_0000002_0000006.pdf (accessed August 20, 2013).

Myers, Amrita Chakrabarti. *Forging Freedom: Black Women and the Pursuit of Liberty in Antebellum Charleston*. Chapel Hill: University of North Carolina Press, 2011.

———. "Public Rhetoric, Private Realities: Julia Chinn, Richard Johnson, and Debates over Interracial Sex in Antebellum America." Paper presented at the 6th Biennial Conference of the Association for the Study of the Worldwide African Diaspora (ASWAD), Pittsburgh, PA, November 3–6, 2011.

O'Brien, Patricia. "Michel Foucault's History of Culture." In Lynn Hunt, ed., *The New Cultural History*. Berkeley: University of California Press, 1989. 25–46.

Olmsted, F. L. *Cotton Kingdom: A Traveller's Observations on Cotton and Slavery in the American Slave States*. Vol. 2. New York: Mason Brothers, 1862.

———. *The Cotton Kingdom: A Traveller's Observations on Cotton and Slavery in the American Slave States based upon three former volumes of journeys and investigations by the same author.* Vol. 1. Ed. Arthur M. Schlesinger Sr. New York: Knopf, 1953.

Owen, Thomas W. *History of Alabama and Dictionary of Alabama Biography.* Vol. 2. Chicago: S. J. Clarke, 1921.

Oxford English Dictionary. 2nd ed. New York: Oxford University Press, [1989, 1993] 1997.

Painter, Nell Irvin. *Exodusters: Black Migration to Kansas after Reconstruction.* New York: Alfred A. Knopf, 1977.

———. "Thinking about the Languages of Money and Race: A Response to Michael O'Malley, 'Specie and Species.'" *American Historical Review* 99.2 (April 1994): 438–49.

Passel, Jeffrey S., Wendy Wang, and Paul Taylor. "Marrying Out: One in Seven New U.S. Marriages Is Interracial or Interethnic." PEW Research Center, A Social and Demographic Trends Report, June 15, 2010.

Penningroth, Dylan C. *The Claims of Kinfolk: African American Property and Community in the Nineteenth-Century South.* Chapel Hill: University of North Carolina Press, 2003.

Pleck, Elizabeth H. "The Two-Parent Household: Black Family Structure in Late Nineteenth-Century Boston." *Journal of Social History* 6.1 (Fall 1972): 3–31.

Post, Robert C. *Urban Mass Transit: The Life Story of a Technology.* Baltimore: Johns Hopkins University Press, 2010.

Potter, Eliza. *A Hairdresser's Experience in High Life.* 1859; New York: Oxford University Press, 1991.

Putman, John. "Racism and Temperance: The Politics of Class and Gender in Late 19th Century Seattle." *Pacific Northwest Quarterly* 95.2 (Spring 2004): 70–81.

Rawick, George P., ed. *The American Slave: A Composite Autobiography.* Vol. 1. Westport, CT: Greenwood, 1972.

Redkey, Edwin S. *Black Exodus: Black Nationalist and Back-to-Africa Movements, 1890–1910.* New Haven, CT: Yale University Press, 1969.

Reid, Mayne. *The Quadroon: A Lover's Adventures in Louisiana.* New York: G. W. Dillingham Co., 1897.

Ridion, Florence. *A Black Physician's Struggle for Equal Rights: Edward C. Mazique.* Albuquerque: University of New Mexico Press, 2005.

Roark, James L. *Masters without Slaves: Southern Planters in the Civil War and Reconstruction.* New York: Norton, 1977.

Roberts, Frances Cabaniss. "An Experiment in Emancipation of Slaves by an Alabama Planter." Master's thesis, University of Alabama, 1940.

Roediger, David R. *Wages of Whiteness: Race and the Making of the American Working Class.* New York: Verso, 1991.

Roediger, David R., and Elizabeth D. Esch. *The Production of Difference: Race and the Management of Labor in U.S. History*. New York: Oxford University Press, 2012.

———. *Seizing Freedom: Slave Emancipation for All*. New York: Verso, 2014.

Rose, Al. *Storyville, New Orleans: Being an Authentic, Illustrated Account of the Notorious Red-Light District*. Tuscaloosa: University of Alabama Press, 1974.

Rose, Sarah. *For All the Tea in China: How England Stole the World's Favorite Drink and Changed History*. New York: Penguin, 2011.

Rosewein, Barbara H. *Emotional Communities in the Early Middle Ages*. Ithaca, NY: Cornell University Press, 2006

Ross, Steven J. *Workers on the Edge: Work, Leisure, and Politics in Industrializing Cincinnati, 1788–1890*. New York: Columbia University Press, 1985.

Rothman, Joshua. "James Callender and Social Knowledge of Interracial Sex in Antebellum Virginia." In Jan Ellen Lewis and Peter S. Onuf, eds., *Sally Hemings and Thomas Jefferson: History, Memory and Civic Culture*. Charlottesville: University Press of Virginia, 1999. 87–113.

———. *Flush Times and Fever Dreams: A Story of Capitalism and Slavery in the Age of Jackson*. Athens: University of Georgia Press, 2012.

———. *Notorious in the Neighborhood: Sex and Families across the Color Line in Virginia, 1787–1861*. Chapel Hill: University of North Carolina Press, 2003.

Sandweiss, Martha A. *Passing Strange: A Gilded Age Tale of Love and Deception across the Color Line*. New York: Penguin, 2009.

Saulny, Susan. "Census Data Presents Rise in Multiracial Population of Youths." *New York Times*, March 24, 2011.

Savage, John W. *Black Pioneers: Images of the Black Experience on the Northern Frontier*. Salt Lake City: University of Utah Press, 1997.

Savage, W. Sherman. *Blacks in the West*. Contributions in Afro-American and African Studies. New York: Greenwood Press, 1977.

Scarborough, William Kauffman. *Masters of the Big House: Elite Slaveholders of the Mid-Nineteenth-Century South*. Baton Rouge: Louisiana State University Press, 2006.

Schafer, Judith Kelleher. *Becoming Free, Remaining Free: Manumission and Enslavement in New Orleans, 1846–1862*. Baton Rouge: Louisiana State University Press, 2003.

Schell, William, Jr. *Integral Outsiders: The American Colony in Mexico City, 1876–1911*. Wilmington, DE: Scholarly Resources, 2000.

Schlesinger, Arthur Meier, Sr. *The Rise of the City, 1878–1898*. 1933; Columbus: Ohio State University Press, 1999.

Schuessler, Jennifer. "Some Scholars Reject Dark Portrait of Jefferson." *New York Times*, November 26, 2012, www.nytimes.com/2012/11/27/books/henry-wienceks-master-of-the-mountain-irks-historians.html?pagewanted=all&_r=0 (accessed December 4, 2012).

Schwartz, Marie Jenkins. *Birthing a Slave: Motherhood and Medicine in the Antebellum South*. Cambridge, MA: Harvard University Press, 2006.

Scott, James. *Domination and the Arts of Resistance*. New Haven, CT: Yale University Press, 1990.

Scott, Joan Wallach. *Gender and the Politics of History*. New York: Columbia University Press, 1988, 1999.

Scott, Mark. "Permira to Buy Ancestry.com for $1.6 Billion." *New York Times*, October 22, 2012, http://dealbook.nytimes.com/2012/10/22/permira-said-to-buy-ancestry-com-for-1-6-billion/?_r=0 (accessed July 2, 2013).

Sears, John F. *Sacred Places: American Tourist Attractions in the Nineteenth Century*. Amherst: University of Massachusetts Press, 1999.

Shevitz, Amy Hill. *Jewish Communities on the Ohio River: A History*. Lexington: University Press of Kentucky, 2007

Smith, P. Clay, Jr. *Emancipation: The Making of the Black Lawyer, 1844–1944*. Philadelphia: University of Pennsylvania Press, 1999.

Somerville, Siobhan B. *Queering the Color Line: Race and the Invention of Homosexuality in American Culture*. Durham, NC: Duke University Press, 2000.

Spear, Jennifer M. *Race, Sex, and the Social Order in Early New Orleans*. Baltimore: Johns Hopkins University Press, 2009.

Stampp, Kenneth M. *The Peculiar Institution: Slavery in the Ante-Bellum South*. New York: Vintage, 1956.

Stanley, Amy Dru. *From Bondage to Contract: Wage Labor, Marriage and the Market in the Age of Slave Emancipation*. New York: Cambridge University Press, 1998.

Stephenson, W. H. *Isaac Franklin: Slave Trader and Planter of the Old South; With Plantation Records*. Baton Rouge: Louisiana State University Press, 1938.

Sterne, Ellin. "Prostitution in Birmingham, Alabama, 1890–1925." MA thesis, Samford University, 1977.

Stowe, Steven M. *Doctoring the South: Southern Physicians and Everyday Medicine in the Mid-Nineteenth Century*. Chapel Hill: University of North Carolina Press, 2004.

Sugrue, Thomas J. *Not Even Past: Barack Obama and the Burden of Race*. Princeton, NJ: Princeton University Press, 2010.

Sydnor, Charles S. "The Free Negro in Mississippi before the Civil War." *American Historical Review* 32.4 (July 1927): 777–79.

Tadman, Michael. *Speculators and Slaves: Masters, Traders, and Slaves in the Old South*. Madison: University of Wisconsin Press, 1989.

Taylor, Henry Louis, Jr. "City Building, Public Policy, and the Rise of the Industrial City, and Black Ghetto-Slum Formation in Cincinnati (1850–1860)." In Henry Louis Taylor Jr., ed., *Race and the City: Work, Community, and Protest in Cincinnati, 1820–1970*. Urbana: University of Illinois Press, 1993. 156–91.

———, ed. *Race and the City: Work, Community, and Protest in Cincinnati, 1820–1970*. Urbana: University of Illinois Press, 1993.

Taylor, Nikki M. *America's First Black Socialist: The Radical Life of Peter H. Clark*. Lexington: University Press of Kentucky, 2013.

———. *Frontiers of Freedom: Cincinnati's Black Community, 1802–1868*. Athens: Ohio University Press, 2005.

Terborg-Penn, Rosalyn. "Migration and Trans-Racial/National Identity Re-Formation: Becoming African Diaspora Women." *Black Women, Gender and Families* 15.2 (Fall 2011): 4–24.

Tower, Philo. *Slavery Unmasked*. New York: Negro Universities Press, 1969.

Tractenberg, Alan. *The Incorporation of America: Culture and Society in the Gilded Age*. New York: Hill and Wang, 1982.

Tragen, Irving G. "Statutory Prohibitions against Interracial Marriage." *California Law Review* 32.3 (September 1944): 269–80.

Trollope, Frances. *Domestic Manners of the Americans*. Ed. Donald Smalley. 1832; Gloucester, MA: Peter Smith, 1974.

Trotter, Joe William, Jr. *River Jordan: African American Urban Life in the Ohio Valley*. Lexington: University of Kentucky Press, 1998.

Troutman, Philip, Edward Baptist, and Stephanie Camp. "Correspondences in Black and White: Sentiment and the Slave Market Revolution." In Edward Baptist and Stephanie Camp., eds., *New Studies in the History of American Slavery*. Athens: University of Georgia Press, 2006. 211–42.

Tucker, Neely. *Love in the Driest Season*. New York: Three Rivers, 2004.

von Reizenstein, Ludwig. *The Mysteries of New Orleans*. Trans. and ed. Steven Rowan. Baltimore: Johns Hopkins University Press, 2002.

Ward, David. *Cities and Immigrants: A Geography of Change in Nineteenth-Century America*. New York: Oxford University Press, 1971.

Watson, Harry L. *Liberty and Power: The Politics of Jacksonian America*. New York: Hill and Wang, 1990.

West, Emily. *Chains of Love: Slave Couples in Antebellum South Carolina*. Urbana: University of Illinois Press, 2004.

———. *Family or Freedom: People of Color in the Antebellum South*. Lexington: University Press of Kentucky, 2012.

White, Deborah Gray. *Ar'n't I a Woman? Females Slaves in the Plantation South*. New York: Norton, 1985.

Wilberforce, William, Robert Isaac Wilberforce, and Samuel Wilberforce, eds. *The Life of William Wilberforce, Cambridge Library Collection—Slavery and Abolition (Volume 1)*. Cambridge: Cambridge University Press, 2011.

Wilentz, Sean. *The Rise of American Democracy: Jefferson to Lincoln*. New York: Norton, 2005.

"William Bolden Townsend: Kansas Memory." www.kansasmemory.org/item/213465 (accessed August 15, 2013).

Williams, Yohuru, and Jama Lazerow, eds. *Liberated Territory: Untold Local Perspectives on the Black Panther Party*. Durham, NC: Duke University Press, 2009.

Woodman, Harold D. *King Cotton and His Retainers: Financing and Market-*

ing the Cotton Crop of the South, 1800–1925. Columbia: University of South Carolina Press, 1968.

Woodson, Carter G., ed., *The Mind of the Negro as Reflected in Letters during the Crisis, 1800–1860*. Eastford, CT: Martino Fine Books, 2010.

Woodward, C. Vann. *The Strange Career of Jim Crow*. 2nd ed. New York: Oxford University Press [1955] 1966.

Wooster, Ralph A. "Early Texas Politics: The Henderson Administration." *Southwestern Historical Quarterly* 73 (October 1969): 176–92.

Yarbrough, Fay A. "Power, Perception and Interracial Sex: Former Slaves Recall Multiracial South." *Journal of Southern History* 71.3 (August 2005): 559–88.

Young, Bernice Fearn. "Howard Weeden, A Rose of Yesterday." A. S. Williams III Americana Collection, Gorgas Library, University of Alabama. n.d.

Zaborney, John J. *Slaves for Hire: Renting Enslaved Laborers in Antebellum Virginia*. Baton Rouge: Louisiana State University Press, 2012.

Index

EARLY AMERICAN PLACES

*Cultivating Regionalism: Higher Education and the Making
of the American Midwest*
by Kenneth H. Wheeler

*Race and Rights: Fighting Slavery and Prejudice in the Old Northwest,
1830–1870*
by Dana E. Weiner

*Confronting Slavery: Edward Coles and the Rise of Antislavery Politics
in Nineteenth-Century America*
by Suzanne Cooper Guasco

*Parading Patriotism: Independence Day Celebrations in the Urban
Midwest, 1826–1876*
by Adam Criblez

*Senator Benton and the People: Master Race Democracy
on the Early American Frontiers*
by Ken Mueller